Mr. Popper's
PENGUINS

Mr. Popper's
PENGUINS

BY RICHARD AND FLORENCE ATWATER
ILLUSTRATED BY JIM MADSEN

Mr. Popper's Penguins

Text copyright © 1938 by Katherine Elizabeth Bishop and Alexander Harding Bishop

Text copyright © renewed 1966 by Katherine Elizabeth Bishop and Alexander Harding Bishop

Illustrations copyright © 2018 by Jim Madsen

ISBN 979-11-91343-23-6 14740

Longtail Books

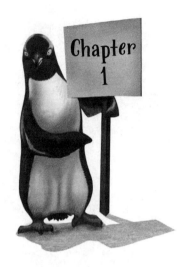

STILLWATER

IT WAS AN afternoon in late September. In the **pleasant** little city of Stillwater, Mr. Popper, the house painter, was going home from work.

He was carrying his **buckets**, his **ladders**, and his **boards** so that he had rather a hard time moving along. He was **spatter**ed here and there with paint and calcimine,[1] and there were bits of **wallpaper cling**ing to his hair and **whiskers**, for he was rather an **untidy** man.

---

1 calcimine 석회를 물에 녹인 도료. 건물의 벽, 울타리, 가구 표면을 하얗게 마무리하는데 사용한다.

The children looked up from their play to smile at him as he passed, and the **housewives**, seeing him, said, "Oh dear, there goes Mr. Popper. I must remember to ask John to have the house painted over in the spring."

No one knew what went on inside of Mr. Popper's head, and no one guessed that he would one day be the most famous person in Stillwater.

He was a dreamer. Even when he was busiest **smooth**ing down the **paste** on the wallpaper, or painting the outside of other people's houses, he would forget what he was doing. Once he had painted three sides of a kitchen green, and the other side yellow. The housewife, instead of being angry and making him do it over, had liked it so well that she had made him leave it that way. And all the other housewives, when they saw it, **admired** it too, so that pretty soon everybody in Stillwater had two-colored kitchens.

The reason Mr. Popper was so **absent-minded** was that he was always dreaming about far-away countries. He had never been out of Stillwater. Not that he was unhappy. He had a nice little house of his own, a wife whom he loved **dearly**, and two children, named Janie and Bill. Still, it would have been nice, he often thought, if he could have seen something of the world before he met Mrs. Popper and **settled down.** He had never hunted tigers in India, or climbed the **peaks** of the Himalayas,[2] or **dived** for pearls in the South Seas.[3] **Above all**, he had never seen the **Poles.**

That was what he **regret**ted most of all. He had never seen those great shining white **expanses** of ice and snow. How he wished that he had been a scientist, instead of a house painter in Stillwater, so that he might have joined

---

2 Himalayas 히말라야 산맥. 아시아 대륙의 남부에 위치하며 최고봉은 에베레스트 산이다.
3 South Seas 남양(南洋). 태평양의 적도를 경계로 하여 그 남북에 걸쳐 있는 지역을 통틀어 이르는 말.

some of the great **Polar expeditions**. Since he could not go, he was always thinking about them.

Whenever he heard that a Polar movie was in town, he was the first person at the ticket-window,[4] and often he sat through three shows. Whenever the town library had a new book about the **Arctic** or the **Antarctic**—the North Pole or the South Pole—Mr. Popper was the first to borrow it. Indeed, he had read so much about Polar **explorer**s that he could name all of them and tell you what each had done. He was quite an **authority** on the **subject**.

His evenings were the best time of all. Then he could sit down in his little house and read about those cold **region**s at the top and bottom of the earth. As he read he could take the little **globe** that Janie and Bill had given him the Christmas before, and search out the exact **spot** he was reading about.

So now, as he **made his way** through the streets, he was happy because the day was over, and because it was the end of September.

When he came to the gate of the **neat** little bungalow[5] at 432 Proudfoot Avenue, he turned in.

---

4   ticket-window 매표소.
5   bungalow 넓은 베란다가 딸린 단층 목조 주택.

"Well, my love," he said, setting down his buckets and ladders and boards, and kissing Mrs. Popper, "the decorating season is over. I have painted all the kitchens in Stillwater; I have **papered** all the rooms in the new apartment building on Elm Street. There is no more work until spring, when people will want their houses painted."

Mrs. Popper **sighed**. "I sometimes wish you had the kind of work that **lasted** all year, instead of just from pring until fall," she said. "It will be very nice to have you at home for a vacation, of course, but it is a little hard to **sweep** with a man sitting around reading all day."

"I could decorate the house for you."

"No, indeed," said Mrs. Popper **firmly**. "Last year you painted the bathroom four different times, because you had nothing else to do, and I think that is enough of that. But what worries me is the money. I have saved a little, and I **daresay** we can **get along** as we have other winters. No more **roast** beef,[6] no more ice cream, not even on Sundays."

"Shall we have beans every day?" asked Janie and Bill, coming in from play.

---

6 **roast beef** 로스트 비프. 쇠고기에 소금, 후추로 간단하게 간을 하고 통째로 오븐에서 구워낸 요리이다.

"I'm afraid so," said Mrs. Popper. "Anyway, go wash your hands, for **supper**. And Papa, put away this **litter** of paints, because you won't be needing them for quite a while."

THE VOICE IN THE AIR

THAT EVENING, when the little Poppers had been put to bed, Mr. and Mrs. Popper settled down for a long, quiet evening. The neat living room at 432 Proudfoot Avenue was much like all the other living rooms in Stillwater, except that the walls were hung with pictures from the *National Geographic Magazine.*[1] Mrs. Popper picked up her mending, while Mr. Popper collected his pipe, his

---

1 National Geographic Magazine 내셔널 지오그래픽 잡지. 내셔널 지오그래픽 협회에서 매달 내는 학회지이자 교양지. 매달 세계 탐험, 문화, 동물, 역사 등의 다양한 주제를 다루며, 이에 대한 단행본도 발간한다.

book, and his **globe**.

From time to time Mrs. Popper **sigh**ed a little as she thought about the long winter ahead. Would there really be enough beans to **last**, she wondered.

Mr. Popper was not worried, however. As he put on his **spectacles**, he was quite **pleased** at the **prospect** of a whole winter of reading travel books, with no work to **interrupt** him. He set his little globe beside him and began to read.

"What are you reading?" asked Mrs. Popper.

"I am reading a book called *Antarctic Adventures*. It is very interesting. It tells all about the different people who have gone to the South **Pole** and what they have found there."

"Don't you ever get tired of reading about the South Pole?"

"No, I don't. Of course I would much rather go there than read about it. But reading is the next best thing."

"I think it must be very boring down there," said Mrs. Popper. "It sounds very **dull** and cold, with all that ice and snow."

"Oh, no," answered Mr. Popper. "You wouldn't think it was dull if you had gone with me to see the movies of the Drake **Expedition** at the Bijou last year."

"Well, I didn't, and I don't think any of us will have

any money for movies now," answered Mrs. Popper, a little **sharply**. She was not at all a **disagreeable** woman, but she sometimes got rather **cross** when she was worried about money.

"If you had gone, my love," **went on** Mr. Popper, "you would have seen how beautiful the Antarctic is. But I think the nicest part of all is the penguins. **No wonder** all the men on that expedition had such a good time playing with them. They are the funniest birds in the world. They don't fly like other birds. They walk **erect** like little men. When they get tired of walking they just lie down on their **stomach**s and **slide**. It would be very nice to have one for a pet."

"Pets!" said Mrs. Popper. "First it's Bill wanting a dog and then Janie **begging** for a **kitten**. Now you and penguins! But I won't have any pets around. They make too much dirt in the house, and I have enough work now, trying to keep this place **tidy**. **To say nothing of** what it costs to **feed** a pet. Anyway, we have the bowl of **goldfish**."

"Penguins are very **intelligent**," continued Mr. Popper. "Listen to this, Mamma. It says here that when they want to catch some **shrimp**s, they all crowd over to the **edge** of an ice **bank**. Only they don't just jump in, because a sea leopard² might be waiting to eat the penguins. So they crowd and push until they manage to **shove** one penguin off, to see if it's safe. I mean if he doesn't get eaten up, the rest of them know it's safe for them all to jump in."

"Dear me!³" said Mrs. Popper in a shocked **tone**. "They sound to me like pretty **heathen** birds."

"It's a **queer** thing," said Mr. Popper, "that all the **polar** bears⁴ live at the North Pole and all the penguins at the South Pole. I should think the penguins would like the North Pole, too, if they only knew how to get there."

At ten o'clock Mrs. Popper **yawn**ed and laid down her mending. "Well, you can go on reading about those heathen birds, but I am going to bed. Tomorrow is Thursday, September thirtieth, and I have to go to the first meeting of the Ladies' Aid and **Missionary** Society.⁵"

"September thirtieth!" said Mr. Popper in an excited tone. "You don't mean that tonight is Wednesday, September twenty-ninth?"

"Why,⁶ yes, I suppose it is. But **what of it?**"

---

2   sea leopard 얼룩무늬물범. 남극에 있는 물범 중 남방코끼리물범에 이어 두 번째로 큰 종으로 남극 해역에서 펭귄 등을 잡아 먹는다.

3   dear me '이것 참', '이런 세상에'라는 뜻의 실망이나 놀라움 등을 나타내는 표현.

4   polar bear 북극곰. 몸의 길이는 2~2.5미터이며, 온몸에 순백색의 털이 촘촘히 나 있고 코, 입술, 발톱은 검은 색이다. 헤엄을 잘 치며 주로 북극 지방에서 산다.

5   Ladies' Aid and Missionary Society 모금 운동이나 사회적 행사를 조직하여 소속 교회의 활동을 지지하는 여성 단체.

6   why 이유를 묻거나 말할 때 쓰는 의문사 또는 관계사가 아닌 '어머', '아니'라는 뜻의 감탄사로 쓰였다.

Mr. Popper put down his book of *Antarctic Adventures* and moved **hastily** to the radio.

"What of it!" he repeated, pushing the **switch**. "Why, this is the night the Drake Antarctic Expedition is going to start **broadcast**ing."

"That's nothing," said Mrs. Popper. "Just a lot of men at the bottom of the world saying 'Hello, Mamma. Hello, Papa.'"

"*Sh!*" **command**ed Mr. Popper, laying his ear close to the radio.

There was a **buzz**, and then suddenly, from the South Pole, a **faint** voice **float**ed out into the Popper living room.

"This is Admiral[7] Drake speaking. Hello, Mamma. Hello, Papa. Hello, Mr. Popper."

"**Gracious** goodness," **exclaim**ed Mrs. Popper. "Did he say 'Papa' or 'Popper'?"

"Hello, Mr. Popper, up there in Stillwater. Thanks for your nice letter about the pictures of our last expedition. **Watch for** an answer. But not by letter, Mr. Popper. Watch for a surprise. **Sign**ing **off**. Signing off."

"*You* wrote to Admiral Drake?"

"Yes, I did," Mr. Popper admitted. "I wrote and told

---

7 Admiral 제독. 해군의 함대사령관 또는 해군장성에 대한 통칭.

him how funny I thought the penguins were."

"Well, I never,[8]" said Mrs. Popper, very much **impress**ed.

Mr. Popper picked up his little globe and found the Antarctic. "And to think he spoke to me all the way from there. And he even mentioned my name. Mamma, what do you suppose he means by a surprise?"

"I haven't any idea," answered Mrs. Popper, "but I'm going to bed. I don't want to be late for the Ladies' Aid and Missionary Society meeting tomorrow."

---

8 Well, I never '그럴 리가!', '맙소사!'라는 뜻의 놀라움을 나타내는 표현.

OUT OF THE ANTARCTIC

WHAT WITH THE excitement of having the great Admiral Drake speak to him over the radio, and his **curiosity** about the Admiral's message to him, Mr. Popper did not sleep very well that night. He did not see how he could possibly wait to find out what the Admiral meant. When morning came, he was almost sorry that he had nowhere to go, no houses to paint, no rooms to **paper**. It would have helped to pass the time.

"Would you like the living room papered over?" he asked Mrs. Popper. "I have quite a lot of Paper Number

88, **left over** from the **Mayor**'s house."

"I would not," said Mrs. Popper **firmly**. "The paper on now is plenty good enough. I am going to the first meeting of the Ladies' Aid and **Missionary** Society today and I don't want any **mess** around to clean up when I get home."

"Very well, my love," said Mr. Popper **meek**ly, and he **settled down** with his pipe, his **globe**, and his book of *Antarctic Adventures*. But somehow, as he read today, he could not **keep his mind on** the printed words. His thoughts kept **stray**ing away to Admiral Drake. What could he have meant by a surprise for Mr. Popper?

Fortunately for his peace of mind, he did not have so very long to wait. That afternoon, while Mrs. Popper was still away at her meeting, and Janie and Bill had not yet come home from school, there was a loud **ring** at the front door.

"I suppose it is just the **postman**. I won't **bother** to answer it," he said to himself.

The bell rang again, a little louder this time. **Grumbling** to himself, Mr. Popper went to the door.

It was not the postman who stood there. It was an expressman[1] with the largest box Mr. Popper had ever

---

1 expressman 급행 운송 회사 직원.

seen.

"**Party** by the name of Popper live here?"

"That's me."

"Well, here's a package that's come Air Express all the way from **Antarctica**. Some journey, I'll say."

Mr. Popper signed the receipt and **examine**d the box. It was covered all over with **markings**. "UNPACK AT ONCE," said one. "KEEP COOL," said another. He **noticed** that the box was **punch**ed here and there with air holes.

You can imagine that once he had the box inside the house, Mr. Popper **lost no time in** getting the screw driver,[2] for by this time, of course, he had guessed that it was the surprise from Admiral Drake.

He had succeeded in removing the outer **board**s and part of the packing, which was a **layer** of dry ice,[3] when from the depths of the packing case he suddenly heard a **faint** "*Ork*." His heart stood still. Surely he had heard that sound before at the Drake Expedition movies. His hands were **trembling** so that he could **scarcely** lift off the last of the **wrapp**ings.

There was not the **slight**est **doubt** about it. It was a penguin.

---

2   screw driver 스크루 드라이버. 각종 나사를 죄고 푸는 데 사용하는 공구.
3   dry ice 드라이아이스. 기체인 이산화탄소를 압축한 고체 이산화탄소로 만든 냉각제. 식료품 등을 냉각하는 데 주로 쓴다.

Mr. Popper was **speechless** with **delight**.

But the penguin was not speechless. *"Ork,"* it said again, and this time it held out its **flippers** and jumped over the packing **debris**.

It was a **stout** little **fellow** about two and a half feet[4] high. Although it was about the size of a small child, it looked much more like a little gentleman, with its **smooth** white waistcoat[5] in front and its long black tailcoat[6] **dragging** a little behind. Its eyes were set in two white circles in its black head. It turned its head from one side to the other, as first with one eye and then with the other, it examined Mr. Popper.

Mr. Popper had read that penguins are extremely curious, and he soon found that this was true, for stepping out, the visitor began to **inspect** the house. Down the hall it went and into the bedrooms, with its strange, **pompous** little **strut**. When it, or he — Mr. Popper had already begun to think of it as he — got to the bathroom, it looked around with a **pleased** expression on its face.

"Perhaps," thought Mr. Popper, "all that white **tiling** reminds him of the ice and snow at the South Pole. Poor thing, maybe he's **thirsty**."

---

4   feet 길이의 단위 피트. 1피트는 약 30.48센티미터이다.
5   waistcoat 웨이스트코트. 흔히 조끼라고 부른다. 셔츠 위, 재킷 아래에 입는 짧은 의복으로 소 매가 없고 앞쪽에 단추가 달려 있으며 깊은 V넥으로 되어 있다.
6   tailcoat 연미복. 남자용 서양식 예복. 상의의 뒷자락이 제비 꼬리처럼 길게 갈라져 있다.

Carefully Mr. Popper began to fill the **bathtub** with cold water. This was a little difficult because the **inquisitive** bird kept reaching over and trying to **bite** the **faucet**s with its sharp red **beak**. Finally, however, he succeeded in getting the **tub** all filled. Since the penguin kept looking over, Mr. Popper picked it up and dropped it in. The penguin seemed not to mind.

"Anyway, you're not shy," said Mr. Popper. "I guess you've got sort of used to playing around with those **explorer**s at the Pole."

When he thought the penguin had had enough of a bath, he drew out the **stopper**. He was just wondering what to do next when Janie and Bill **burst** in from school.

"Papa," they shouted together at the bathroom door. "What is it?"

"It's a South Pole penguin sent to me by Admiral Drake."

"Look!" said Bill. "It's **march**ing."

The delighted penguin was indeed marching. With little pleased **nod**s of his handsome black head he was **parading** up and down the inside of the bathtub. Sometimes he seemed to be counting the steps it took—six steps for the length, two steps for the width, six steps for the length again, and two more for the width.

"For such a big bird he takes **awfull**y small steps," said Bill.

"And look how his little black coat drags behind. It almost looks as if it were too big for him," said Janie.

But the penguin was tired of marching. This time, when it got to the end of the tub, it decided to jump up the **slippery** curve. Then it turned, and with **outstretched** flippers, **tobogan**ed down on its white **stomach**. They could see that those flippers, which were black on the outside, like the **sleeve**s of a tailcoat, were white underneath.

"*Gook! Gook!*" said the penguin, trying its new game again and again.

"What's his name, Papa?" asked Janie.

"*Gook! Gook!*" said the penguin, **sliding** down once more on his **glossy** white stomach.

"It sounds something like 'Cook,'" said Mr. Popper. "Why, that's it, of course. We'll call him Cook—Captain Cook.[7]"

---

7 **Captain Cook** 영국의 탐험가이자 항해가인 제임스 쿡(James Cook)에게서 따온 이름. 그의 탐험으로 현재와 거의 같은 태평양 지도가 만들어졌다.

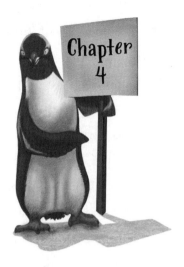

CAPTAIN COOK

"**CALL WHO** Captain Cook?" asked Mrs. Popper, who had come in so quietly that none of them had heard her.

"Why, the penguin," said Mr. Popper. "I was just saying," he **went on**, as Mrs. Popper sat down suddenly on the floor to **recover** from her surprise, "that we'd name him after Captain Cook. He was a famous English explorer who lived about the time of the American Revolution.[1] He **sail**ed all over where no one had ever

---

1 American Revolution 미국 독립 혁명. 영국의 식민지였던 미국의 13개 주(州)가 연합하여 영국에 대한 독립과 동시에 내부의 정치 · 사회적 개혁을 달성한 혁명.

been before. He didn't actually get to the South Pole, of course, but he made a lot of important scientific **discoveries** about the Antarctic **regions**. He was a brave man and a kind leader. So I think Captain Cook would be a very **suitable** name for our penguin here."

"Well, I never!" said Mrs. Popper.

"*Gork!*" said Captain Cook, suddenly getting **lively** again. With a **flap** of his **flippers** he jumped from the **tub** to the **washstand**, and stood there for a minute **survey**ing the floor. Then he jumped down, walked over to Mrs. Popper, and began to **peck** her **ankle**.

"Stop him, Papa!" screamed Mrs. Popper, **retreat**ing into the **hallway** with Captain Cook after her, and Mr. Popper and the children following. In the living room she **paused**. So did Captain Cook, for he was **delight**ed with the room.

Now a penguin may look very strange in a living room, but a living room looks very strange to a penguin. Even Mrs. Popper had to smile as they watched Captain Cook, with the light of **curiosity** in his excited **circular** eyes, and his black tailcoat **drag**ging **pompous**ly behind his little **pinkish** feet, **strut** from one **upholster**ed chair to another, pecking at each to see what it was made of. Then he turned suddenly and **march**ed out to the kitchen.

"Maybe he's hungry," said Janie.

Captain Cook **immediately** marched up to the **refrigerator.**

"*Gork?*" he **inquired**, turning to **slant** his head wisely at Mrs. Popper, and looking at her **pleading**ly with his right eye.

"He certainly is cute," she said. "I guess I'll have to forgive him for **biting** my ankle. He probably only did it out of curiosity. Anyway, he's a nice clean-looking bird."

"*Ork?*" repeated the penguin, **nibbling** at the metal handle of the refrigerator door with his **upstretched beak.**

Mr. Popper opened the door for him, and Captain Cook stood very high and **lean**ed his **sleek** black head back so that he could see inside. Now that Mr. Popper's work was over for the winter, the **icebox** was not quite so full as usual, but the penguin did not know that.

"What do you suppose he likes to eat?" asked Mrs. Popper.

"Let's see," said Mr. Popper, as he removed all the food and set it on the kitchen table. "Now then, Captain Cook, take a look."

The penguin jumped up onto a chair and from there onto the **edge** of the table, flapping his flippers again to recover his balance. Then he walked **solemn**ly around the table, and between the dishes of food, **inspec**ting everything with the greatest interest, though he touched nothing. Finally he stood still, very **erect**, raised his beak to point at the **ceiling**, and make a loud, almost **purri**ng sound. "*O-r-r-r-r-h, o-r-r-r-h,*" he **trilled**.

"That's a penguin's way of saying how pleased it is," said Mr. Popper, who had read about it in his Antarctic books.

Apparently, however, what Captain Cook wanted to show was that he was pleased with their kindness, rather than with their food. For now, to their surprise, he jumped down and walked into the dining room.

"I know," said Mr. Popper. "We ought to have some seafood for him, canned **shrimp**s or something. Or maybe he isn't hungry yet. I've read that penguins can go for a

month without food."

"Mamma! Papa!" called Bill. "Come see what Captain Cook has done."

Captain Cook had done it all right. He had discovered the bowl of **goldfish** on the dining-room **window sill**. By the time Mrs. Popper reached over to lift him away, he had already **swallow**ed the last of the goldfish.

"Bad, bad penguin!" **reprove**d Mrs. Popper, **glaring** down at Captain Cook.

Captain Cook **squat**ted **guiltily** on the carpet and tried to make himself look small.

"He knows he's done wrong," said Mr. Popper. "Isn't he smart?"

"Maybe we can train him," said Mrs. Popper. "Bad, **naughty** Captain," she said to the penguin in a loud voice. "Bad, to eat the goldfish." And she **spank**ed him on his round black head.

Before she could do that again, Captain Cook **hastily waddle**d out to the kitchen.

There the Poppers found him trying to hide in the still opened refrigerator. He was squatting under the ice-cube **coil**s, under which he could **barely squeeze**, sitting down. His round, white-circled eyes looked out at them **mysterious**ly from the **dim**ness of the inside of the box.

"I think that's about the right temperature for him,

30

at that," said Mr. Popper. "We could let him sleep there, at night."

"But where will I put the food?" asked Mrs. Popper.

"Oh, I guess we can get another icebox for the food," said Mr. Popper.

"Look," said Janie. "He's gone to sleep."

Mr. Popper turned the cold control **switch** to its coldest so that Captain Cook could sleep more comfortably. Then he left the door **ajar** so that the penguin would have plenty of fresh air to breathe.

"Tomorrow I will have the icebox service department send a man out to **bore** some holes in the door, for air," he said, "and then he can put a handle on the inside of the door so that Captain Cook can go in and out of his refrigerator, as he pleases."

"Well, dear me, I never thought we would have a penguin for a pet," said Mrs. Popper. "Still, he behaves pretty well, **on the whole**, and he is so nice and clean that perhaps he will be a good example to you and the children. And now, I **declare**, we must get busy. We haven't done anything but watch that bird. Papa, will you just help me to set the beans on the table, please?"

"Just a minute," answered Mr. Popper. "I just happened to think that Captain Cook will not feel right on the floor of that icebox. Penguins make their **nest**s of

pebbles and stones. So I will just take some ice cubes out of the tray and put them under him. That way he will be more comfortable."

TROUBLES WITH A PENGUIN

THE NEXT DAY was quite **eventful** at 432 Proudfoot Avenue. First there was the service man and then the policeman and then the trouble about the **license**.

Captain Cook was in the children's room, watching Janie and Bill put together a jigsaw puzzle[1] on the floor. He was very good about not **disturb**ing the pieces after Bill had **spank**ed him for eating one. He did not hear the **refrigerator** service man come to the back door.

---

1 jigsaw puzzle 그림이 그려져 있는 여러 조각을 맞물리게 맞춰 그림을 완성하는 퍼즐.

Mrs. Popper had gone marketing for canned shrimps for the penguin, so that Mr. Popper was alone in the kitchen to explain to the service man what he wanted done to the refrigerator.

The service man put his tool bag down on the kitchen floor, looked at the refrigerator, and then at Mr. Popper, who, **to tell the truth**, had not shaved yet and was not very **tidy**.

"Mister," he said, "you don't need no **ventilating** holes in that there door."

"It's my **icebox**, and I want some holes **bored** in the door," said Mr. Popper.

They argued about it for quite a while. Mr. Popper knew that to get the service man to do what he wanted, all he had to do was to explain that he was going to keep a live penguin in the icebox, and that he wanted his pet to have plenty of fresh air, even though the door was closed all night. He felt a little **stubborn** about explaining, however. He didn't want to discuss Captain Cook with this **unsympathetic** service man, who was already **staring** at Mr. Popper as if he thought Mr. Popper was not quite right in his head.

"Come on, do what I said," said Mr. Popper. "I'm paying you for it."

"With what?" asked the service man.

Mr. Popper gave him a five-dollar **bill**. It made him a little sad to think how many beans it would have bought for Mrs. Popper and the children.

The service man **examined** the bill carefully as if he didn't trust Mr. Popper too much. But at last he put it in his pocket, took a drill from his tool bag, and made five small holes in a **neat** pattern on the refrigerator door.

"Now," said Mr. Popper, "don't get up. Wait a minute. There is one more thing."

"Now what?" said the service man. "I suppose now you want me to take the door off its **hinges** to let in a little more air. Or do you want me to make a radio set out of your icebox?"

"Don't get funny," said Mr. Popper **indignant**ly. "That is no way to talk. Believe it or not, I know what I'm doing. I mean, having you do. I want you to fix an extra handle on the inside of that box so it can be opened from the inside of the box."

"That," said the service man, "is a fine idea. You want an extra handle on the inside. Sure, sure." He picked up his tool bag.

"Aren't you going to do it for me?" asked Mr. Popper.

"Oh, sure, sure," said the service man, edging toward the back door.

Mr. Popper saw that for all his words of agreement,

the service man had no **intention** of putting on an inside handle.

"I thought you were a service man," he said.

"I am. That's the first **sensible** thing you've said yet."

"You're a fine kind of service man if you don't even know how to put an extra handle on the inside of an icebox door."

"Oh, I don't, don't I? Don't think I don't know how. As far as that goes, I've even got a **spare** handle in my tool bag, and plenty of **screw**s. You needn't think I don't know how to do it, if I wanted to."

Mr. Popper silently reached into his pocket and gave the service man his last five-dollar bill. He was pretty sure that Mrs. Popper would be **annoyed** at him for spending all that money, but it could not be helped.

"Mister," said the service man, "you win. I'll fix your extra handle. And while I am doing it, you sit down on that chair over there facing me, where I can **keep an eye on** you."

"Fair enough," said Mr. Popper, sitting down.

The service man was still on the floor, putting in the final screws that held the new handle in place, when the penguin came out to the kitchen on his silent pink feet.

Surprised at seeing a strange man sitting on the floor, Captain Cook quietly walked over and began to

peck him curiously. But the service man was even more surprised than Captain Cook.

"*Ork,*" said the penguin. Or perhaps it was the service man. Mr. Popper was not sure just what had happened when he picked up himself and his chair a moment later. There had been a **shower** of flying tools, a violent **slam**ming of the door, and the service man was gone.

These sudden noises, of course, brought the children running. Mr. Popper showed them how the refrigerator was now all **remodel**ed for the penguin. He showed Captain Cook, too, by shutting him inside it. The penguin **at once notice**d the shiny new inside handle and bit it with his usual curiosity. The door opened, and Captain Cook jumped out.

Mr. Popper **prompt**ly put Captain Cook back inside and shut the door again, to be sure that the penguin learned his lesson. Before long, Captain Cook became quite **skillful** at getting out and was ready to be taught how to get inside when the door was shut.

By the time the policeman came to the back door, Captain Cook was going in and out the refrigerator as easily as if he had lived in one all his life.

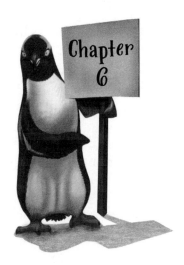

MORE TROUBLES

THE CHILDREN were the first to notice the policeman.

"Look, Papa," said Bill. "There's a policeman at the back door. Is he going to **arrest** you?"

"*Gook,*" said Captain Cook, walking with **dignity** to the door, and trying to **poke** his beak through the **screen**.

"Is this 432 Proudfoot Avenue?"

"It is," answered Mr. Popper.

"Well, I guess this is the place all right," said the policeman, and pointed to Captain Cook. "Is that thing yours?"

"Yes, it is," said Mr. Popper, proudly.

"And what do you do for a living?" asked the policeman sternly.

"Papa is an artist," said Janie.

"He's always getting paint and calcimine all over his clothes," said Bill.

"I'm a house painter, a decorator," said Mr. Popper. "Won't you come in?"

"I won't," said the policeman, "unless I have to."

"Ha, ha!" said Bill. "The policeman is afraid of Captain Cook."

"*Gaw!*" said the penguin, opening his red beak wide, as if he wanted to laugh at the policeman.

"Can it talk?" asked the policeman. "What is it—a giant parrot?"

"It's a penguin," said Janie. "We keep it for a pet."

"Well, if it's only a bird . . ." said the policeman, lifting his cap to scratch his head in a puzzled sort of way. "From the way that fellow with a tool bag yelled at me outside, I thought there was a lion loose in here."

"Mamma says Papa's hair looks like a lion's sometimes," said Bill.

"Keep still, Bill," said Janie. "The policeman doesn't care how Papa's hair looks."

The policeman now scratched his chin. "If it's only a

bird, I suppose it will be O. K. if you keep him in a **cage**."

"We keep him in the icebox," said Bill.

"You can put it in the icebox, **for all I care**," said the policeman. "What kind of a bird did you say it was?"

"A penguin," answered Mr. Popper. "And by the way, I might want to take him walking with me. Would it be all right, if I kept him on a **leash**?"

"**I tell you**," said the policeman, "honestly I don't know what the **municipal ordinance** about penguins is, with or without a leash, on the public streets. I'll ask my sergeant.[1]"

"Maybe I ought to get a **license** for him," suggested Mr. Popper.

"It's certainly big enough for a license," said the policeman. "I tell you what to do. You call up the City Hall and ask them what the **ruling** about penguins is. And good luck to you, Popper. He's kind of a cute little fellow, **at that**. Looks almost human. Good day to you, Popper, and good day to you, Mr. Penguin."

When Mr. Popper telephoned the City Hall to see about a license for Captain Cook, the penguin did his best to **disconnect** the telephone by biting the green **cord**. Perhaps he thought it was some new kind of **eel**. But just

---

1 **sergeant** 미국 경찰 계급인 경사.

then Mrs. Popper came back from market and opened a can of shrimps, so that Mr. Popper was soon left alone at the telephone.

Even so, he found it was not so easy to learn whether or not he must get a license for his strange pet. Every time he would explain what he wanted, he would be told to wait a minute, and much later a new voice would ask him what he wanted. This went on for **considerable** time. At last a new voice seemed to take a little interest in the case. **Pleased** with this **friendly** voice, Mr. Popper began again to tell about Captain Cook.

"Is he an army captain, a police captain, or a navy captain?"

"He is not," said Mr. Popper. "He's a penguin."

"Will you repeat that, please?" said the voice.

Mr. Popper repeated it. The voice suggested that perhaps he had better spell it.

"P-e-n-g-u-i-n," said Mr. Popper. "Penguin."

"Oh!" said the voice. "You mean that Captain Cook's first name is Benjamin?"

"Not Benjamin. Penguin. It's a bird," said Mr. Popper.

"Do you mean," said the phone in his ear, "that Captain Cook wishes a license to shoot birds? I am sorry. The bird-hunting season does not open until November. And please try to speak a little more **distinct**ly, Mr. —

Topper, did you say your name is?"

"My name is Popper, not Topper," shouted Mr. Popper.

"Yes, Mr. Potter. Now I can hear you quite clearly."

"Then listen," **roar**ed Mr. Popper, now completely **outraged**. "If you **folks** at the City Hall don't even know what penguins are, I guess you haven't any rule saying they have to be licensed. I will do without a license for Captain Cook."

"Just a minute, Mr. Popwell. Our own Mr. Treadbottom of the **Bureau** of **Navigation** of Lakes, Rivers, Ponds, and Streams, has just come in. I will let you speak to him **personally**. Perhaps he knows this Benjamin Cook of yours."

In a moment a new voice was speaking to Mr. Popper. "Good morning. This is the **Automobile** License Bureau. Did you have this same car last year, and if so, what was the license number?"

Mr. Popper had been **switch**ed over to the **County** Building.

He decided to **hang up**.

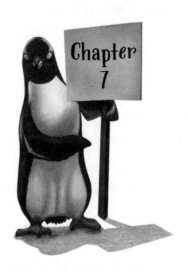

CAPTAIN COOK BUILDS A NEST

VERY RELUCTANTLY, Janie and Bill had to leave Captain Cook and go to school. Mrs. Popper was busy in the kitchen, rather **belated**ly doing the breakfast dishes; and while she **dim**ly realized that the penguin was going in and out the refrigerator pretty frequently, she thought nothing of it at first.

Meanwhile Mr. Popper had **abandon**ed his telephoning and was now busy shaving and making himself neat in **honor** of being the owner of such a **splendid** bird as Captain Cook.

But the penguin, though **thus neglect**ed for the moment, was **by no means idle.**

With the unusual excitement, and having to go to market earlier than usual, Mrs. Popper had not yet got around to **straighten**ing the house. She was an excellent **housekeeper.** Still, with two children like Janie and Bill and a husband with such **untidy** ways, there is no denying the fact that she had to **pick up** the place rather frequently.

Captain Cook was now attending to the picking up.

Into the corners of every room he **prowl**ed and **poked** and pecked with a busy **thorough**ness; into every closet he **stared** with his white-circled eyes; under and behind all the furniture he crowded his **plump figure**, with little **subdued** cries of **curiosity**, surprise, and pleasure.

And each time he found what he seemed to be looking for, he picked it up in the black end of his red **beak**, and carried it, **waddling** proudly on his wide, pink feet, into the kitchen, and into the icebox.

At last it occurred to Mrs. Popper to wonder what **on earth** the busy bird **was up to**. When she looked, she could only scream to Mr. Popper to come quickly and see what Captain Cook had done now.

Mr. Popper, himself looking rather **remarkable**, as Mrs. Popper **noticed** later, joined her in staring with

astonishment into the refrigerator.

Captain Cook came up, too, and helped them look. "*Ork, ork,*" he said with **triumph**.

Mrs. Popper laughed, and Mr. Popper **gasp**ed as they saw the results of Captain Cook's trips through the house.

Two **spool**s of **thread**, one white chess bishop,[1] and six parts of a jigsaw puzzle . . . A teaspoon and a closed box of safety matches . . .[2] A radish,[3] two pennies,[4] a nickel,[5] and a golf ball. Two pencil **stub**s, one **bent** playing card,

---

1   bishop 체스의 비숍. 주교 모자 모양의 말로 사선 방향으로 움직일 수 있다.
2   safety match 발화성 약제인 적린(赤燐)을 성냥개비와 성냥갑에 나누어 붙여서 양쪽을 마찰하여야만 불이 붙는 성냥. 현재 사용하는 성냥 대부분이 이런 형태이다.
3   radish 래디시. 무의 일종으로 뿌리는 적색 또는 자주색이며 샐러드 등의 요리에 사용한다.
4   penny 페니. 미국의 1센트 동전.
5   nickel 니켈. 미국의 5센트 동전.

and a small **ash tray.**

Five hairpins, an olive, two dominoes,[6] and a sock
. . . A nailfile,[7] four buttons of various sizes, a telephone
slug,[8] seven **marble**s, and a tiny doll's chair . . .

Five checker[9] pieces, a bit of graham cracker,[10]
a parcheesi cup,[11] and an eraser . . . A door key, a

---

6 **domino** 도미노 조각. 도미노는 숫자가 적힌 28개의 직사각형의 패를 가지고 노는 게임을 말
   한다. 또한 여러 조각을 줄지어 세우고 그 줄의 한쪽 끝에 서 있는 조각을 밀쳐 다른 조각까지 이
   어 넘어뜨리는 형식의 놀이를 말하기도 한다.
7 **nailfile** 손톱 다듬는 줄. 손톱의 길이와 모양을 조절하거나 표면을 매끄럽게 할 때 사용하는 도
   구.
8 **slug** 자동 판매기 등에 동전 대신 쓰이는 대용 동전.
9 **checker** 체커는 흑백 칸으로 나누어진 보드 위에 빨간색 또는 검정색의 동글납작한 말을 깔아
   놓고, 상대방의 말 뒤의 칸이 비어 있는 경우 그 말 위로 뛰어 넘어서 그것을 잡는 방식으로 이루
   어지는 게임이다. 여기에서는 이 게임의 말을 가리킨다.
10 **graham cracker** 그레이엄 크래커. 통밀로 만든 직사각형의 크래커.
11 **parcheesi cup** 인도 전통 놀이인 파치시(Pachisi)를 응용한 미국 보드 게임 parcheesi에서 사용
   하는 컵. 주로 안에 주사위를 넣어 던질 때 사용한다.

buttonhook,[12] and a **crumple**d piece of **tinfoil** . . . Half of a very old lemon, the head of a china doll,[13] Mr. Popper's pipe, and a ginger-ale[14] **cap** . . . An inkbottle **cork**, two **screw**s, and a belt **buckle** . . .

Six **bead**s from a child's necklace, five building **block**s,[15] a **darn**ing egg,[16] a bone, a small harmonica,[17] and a partly **consume**d lollipop.[18] Two **toothpaste lid**s and a small red notebook.

"I guess this is what you call the **rookery**," said Mr. Popper. "Only he couldn't find any stones to build his nest with."

"Well," said Mrs. Popper, "those penguins may have **heathen** ways at the South **Pole**, but I **declare** I think this one is going to be quite a help around the house."

"*Ork!*" said Captain Cook, and **strut**ting into the living room, he **knock**ed over the best lamp.

"I think, Papa," said Mrs. Popper, "that you had better take Captain Cook outside for a little exercise.

---

12 **buttonhook** 단추 걸이. 구두 등의 단추를 끼울 때 쓰는 갈고리 모양의 기구.

13 **china doll** 도자기 인형. 도자기가 중국에서 유래했기 때문에 'china'라고 부른다.

14 **ginger-ale** 진저에일. 생강 맛이 나는 알코올이 없는 탄산 음료.

15 **building block** 장난감 블록. 플라스틱제의 작은 블록들을 조립하여 건물, 탈 것 등을 만들어 즐기는 완구.

16 **darning egg** 구멍이 난 옷이나 양말을 꿰맬 때 적절한 모양을 잡기 위해 안에 넣는 둥근 달걀 모양의 나무 또는 플라스틱 받침.

17 **harmonica** 하모니카. 입에 대고 입김을 불어넣거나 들이마셔서 리드를 진동시켜 음을 내는 악기.

18 **lollipop** 막대사탕. 손으로 들고 빨아먹을 수 있도록 막대에 꽂혀있는 사탕.

Good **gracious**, but you're all dressed up. Why, you look almost like a penguin yourself."

Mr. Popper had **smooth**ed down his hair and shaved off his **whiskers**. Never again would Mrs. Popper have to **reproach** him for looking as wild as a lion. He had put on a white shirt with a white tie and white flannel[19] **trousers**, and a pair of bright tan,[20] oxblood[21] shoes. He had got out of the cedar chest[22] his old black evening tailcoat, that he had been married in, and brushed it carefully, and put it on, too.

He did indeed look a little like a penguin. He turned and strutted like one now, for Mrs. Popper.

But he did not forget his duty to Captain Cook.

"Can I have a few yards[23] of **clothesline**, please, Mamma?" asked Mr. Popper.

---

19 **flannel** 플란넬. 면이나 양모를 섞어 만든 가벼운 천으로, 털이 보풀보풀 일어나고 촉감이 부드럽다.
20 **tan** 황갈색.
21 **oxblood** 거무스름한 짙은 빨간 색.
22 **cedar chest** 의류나 침구가 좀먹지 않도록 삼나무로 만든 옷장.
23 **yard** 길이의 단위 야드. 1야드는 약 0.9144미터이다.

PENGUIN'S PROMENADE

MR. POPPER soon found that it was not so easy to take a penguin for a **stroll**.

Captain Cook did not care at first for the idea of being put on a **leash**. However, Mr. Popper was **firm**. He tied one end of the **clothesline** to the penguin's fat **throat** and the other to his own **wrist**.

"*Ork!*" said Captain Cook **indignant**ly. Still, he was a very **reasonable** sort of bird, and when he saw that **protest**ing did him no good, he **recover**ed his **customary dignity** and decided to let Mr. Popper lead him.

Mr. Popper put on his best Sunday[1] derby[2] and opened the front door with Captain Cook waddling **gracious**ly beside him.

"*Gaw,*" said the penguin, stopping at the **edge** of the **porch** to look down at the steps.

Mr. Popper gave him plenty of clothesline leash.

"*Gook!*" said Captain Cook, and raising his **flipper**s, he **lean**ed forward bravely and **toboggan**ed down the steps on his **stomach**.

Mr. Popper followed, though not in the same way. Captain Cook quickly got up on his feet again and **strut**ted to the street ahead of Mr. Popper with many quick turns of his head and pleased comments on the new **scene**.

Down Proudfoot Avenue came a neighbor of the Poppers, Mrs. Callahan, with her arms full of **groceries**. She stared in **astonish**ment when she saw Captain Cook and Mr. Popper, looking like a larger penguin himself in his black tailcoat.

"Heavens have **mercy** on us![3]" she **exclaim**ed as the bird began to **investigate** the **striped** stockings under her house dress. "It isn't an **owl** and it isn't a **goose**."

---

1 **Sunday clothes** 나들이 옷. 일요일에 자신이 가진 가장 좋은 옷을 입고 교회에 가는 것에서 유래한 표현이다.

2 **derby** 중산모. 정수리를 높고 둥글게 만들고 테의 양 옆을 약간 말아 올라가게 한 모자.

3 **heavens have mercy on us!** '아이고, 저런!'이라는 뜻의 놀라움을 나타내는 표현.

"It isn't," said Mr. Popper, **tipp**ing his Sunday derby. "It's an **Antarctic** penguin, Mrs. Callahan."

"Get away from me," said Mrs. Callahan to Captain Cook. "An anteater,[4] is it?"

"Not anteater," explained Mr. Popper. "Antarctic. It was sent to me from the South Pole."

"Take your South Pole goose away from me **at once**," said Mrs. Callahan.

Mr. Popper pulled **obedient**ly at the clothesline, while Captain Cook took a **parting peck** at Mrs. Callahan's striped stockings.

"Heaven **preserve us!**[5]" said Mrs. Callahan. "I must **stop in** and see Mrs. Popper at once. I would never have believed it. I will be going now."

"So will I," said Mr. Popper as Captain Cook **dragge**d him off down the street.

Their next stop was at the **drugstore** at the corner of Proudfoot Avenue and Main Street. Here Captain Cook **insist**ed on looking over the window **display**, which consisted of several open packages of shiny white boric **crystals.**[6] These he **evidently mistook for polar** snow, for

---

4 anteater 개미핥기. 혀가 매우 길며, 그 표면에 덮여 있는 끈끈한 타액을 이용하여 개미 등을 혀에 붙여서 끌어내어 잡아 먹는다.

5 heaven preserve us! '아이고, 깜짝이야!'라는 뜻의 놀라움을 나타내는 표현.

6 boric crystal 붕소. 비금속 원소 가운데 하나로 검은빛을 띤 갈색의 금속 광택을 지닌 무정형 고체로, 다이아몬드 다음으로 단단하다.

he began to peck at the window **vigorous**ly.

Suddenly a car **wheel**ed to the near-by **curb** with a **shriek** of its **brake**s, and two young men sprang out, one of them **bear**ing a camera.

"This must be it," said the first young man to the other.

"It's them, all right," said the second young man.

The cameraman set up his **tripod** on the **sidewalk**. By this time a small crowd had **gather**ed around, and two men in white coats had even come out of the drugstore to watch. Captain Cook, however, was still too much interested in the window **exhibit**s to **bother** to turn around.

"You're Mr. Popper of 432 Proudfoot Avenue, aren't you?" asked the second young man, pulling a notebook out of his pocket.

"Yes," said Mr. Popper, realizing that his picture was about to be taken for the newspaper. The two young men had, **as a matter of fact**, heard about the strange bird from the policeman, and had been on their way to the Popper house, to get an interview, when they saw Captain Cook.

"Hey, pelican,[7] turn around and see the pretty

7 pelican 펠리컨. 부리가 길고 목 앞에 커다란 주머니가 달려서 그 주머니 속에 잡은 물고기를
저장했다가 꺼내서 새끼를 먹인다.

54

birdie,[8]" said the photographer.

"That's no pelican," said the other, who was a reporter. "Pelicans have a **pouch** in their **bills**."

"I'd think it was a dodo,[9] only dodos are **extinct**. This will make an **elegant** picture, if I can ever get her to turn around."

"It's a penguin," said Mr. Popper proudly. "Its name

---

is Captain Cook."

"*Gook!*" said the penguin, turning around, now that they were talking about him. Spying the camera tripod, he walked over and examined it.

"Probably thinks it's a three-legged stork," said the photographer.

"This bird of yours—" said the reporter. "Is it a he or a she? The public will want to know."

Mr. Popper hesitated. "Well, I call it Captain Cook."

"That makes it a he," said the reporter, writing rapidly in his notebook.

Still curious, Captain Cook started walking round and round the tripod, till the clothesline, the penguin, Mr. Popper and the tripod were all tangled up. At the advice of one of the bystanders, the tangle was finally straightened out by Mr. Popper's walking around the tripod three times in the opposite direction. At last, Captain Cook, standing still beside Mr. Popper, consented to pose.

Mr. Popper straightened his tie, and the cameraman snapped the picture. Captain Cook shut his eyes, and this is the way his picture appeared later in all the newspapers.

"One last question," said the reporter. "Where did you get your strange pet?"

"From Admiral Drake, the South Pole **explorer**. He sent him to me for a present."

"Yeah," said the reporter. "Anyway, it's a good story."

The two young men jumped into their car. Mr. Popper and Captain Cook continued their walk, with quite a crowd following and asking questions. The crowd was getting so thick that, in order to escape, Mr. Popper led Captain Cook into a **barber**shop.

The man who kept the barbershop had, up to this time, been a very good friend of Mr. Popper's.

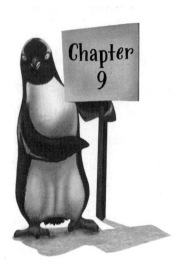

IN THE BARBER SHOP

IT WAS very quiet in the **barber**shop. The barber was shaving an **elderly** gentleman.

Captain Cook found this **spectacle** very interesting, and in order to get a better view, he jumped up on the mirror **ledge**.

"Good night![1]" said the barber.

The gentleman in the barber's chair, his face already white with **lather**, half-lifted his head to see what had happened.

---

1   **good night** 밤에 하는 인사가 아니라 여기에서는 '맙소사', '세상에'라는 뜻의 놀라움이나 짜증, 강조 등을 나타내는 표현으로 쓰였다.

"*Gook!*" said the penguin, **flap**ping his flippers and reaching out his long beak toward the lather on the gentleman's face.

With a **yell** and a **leap**, the gentleman rose from his **reclining** position, left the barber's chair, and **fled** into the street, not even stopping for his coat and hat.

"*Gaw!*" said Captain.

"Hey," said the barber to Mr. Popper. "Take that thing out of my shop. This is no zoo. What's the idea?²"

"Do you mind if I take him out your back door?" asked Mr. Popper.

---

2 what's the idea? '도대체 어쩔 셈이야?' 또는 '어떻게 된 거야?'라는 뜻으로 다른 사람의 행동이 마음에 들지 않을 때 사용하는 표현.

"Any door," said the barber, "as long as it's quick. Now it's **biting** the **teeth** off my **combs**."

Mr. Popper took Captain Cook in his arms, and **amid** cries of "*Quork?*" "*Gawk!*" and "*Ork!*" **made his way** out of the shop and its back room and out a door into an **alley**.

Captain Cook now discovered his first back **stairway**.

Mr. Popper discovered that when a penguin has found steps going up somewhere, it is **absolute**ly impossible to keep him from climbing them.

"All right," said Mr. Popper, **pant**ing up the steps behind Captain Cook. "I suppose, being a bird, and one that can't fly, you have to go up in the air somehow, so you like to climb stairs. Well, it's a good thing this building has only three **stories**. Come on. Let's see what you can do."

Slowly but **unwearying**ly, Captain Cook lifted one pink foot after another from one step to the next, followed by Mr. Popper at the other end of the **clothesline**.

At last they came to the top **landing**.

"Now what?" **inquired** Mr. Popper of Captain Cook.

Finding there were no more steps to climb, Captain Cook turned around and **survey**ed the steps that now went down.

Then he raised his flippers and leaned forward.

Mr. Popper, who was still panting for breath, had not

supposed the **determine**d bird would **plunge** so quickly. He should have remembered that penguins will toboggan whenever they get a chance.

Perhaps he had been unwise in tying one end of the clothesline to his own **wrist**.

At any rate, this time Mr. Popper found himself suddenly **sliding**, on his own white-**clad** stomach, down the three **flight**s of steps. This **delight**ed the penguin, who was enjoying his own slide just ahead of Mr. Popper.

When they reached the bottom, Captain Cook was so eager to go up again that Mr. Popper had to call a taxi, to **distract** him.

"432 Proudfoot Avenue," said Mr. Popper to the driver.

The driver, who was a kind and polite man, did not laugh at his **odd**ly **assort**ed **passenger**s until he had been paid.

"Oh dear!" said Mrs. Popper, when she opened the door to her husband. "You looked so **neat** and handsome when you started for your walk. And now look at the front of you!"

"I am sorry, my love," said Mr. Popper in a **humble tone**, "but you can't always tell what a penguin will do next."

So saying, he went to lie down, for he was quite **exhaust**ed from all the unusual exercise, while Captain Cook had a shower and took a **nap** in the **icebox**.

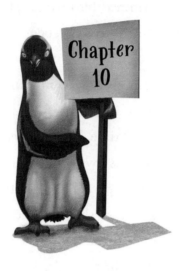

SHADOWS

NEXT DAY the picture of Mr. Popper and Captain Cook appeared in the Stillwater *Morning Chronicle*, with a **paragraph** about the house painter who had received a penguin by air express from Admiral Drake in the **faraway** Antarctic. Then the **Associated** Press[1] picked up the story, and a week later the photograph, in rotogravure,[2] could

---

1 Associated Press 미국의 연합 통신사. 미국을 비롯한 전 세계 언론매체, 통신사 등에 각종 정보와 사진을 제공한다. 영국의 로이터, 프랑스의 AFP와 함께 세계 3대 통신사에 속한다.

2 rotogravure 그라비아 인쇄. 동판의 움푹 들어간 부분에 잉크를 채우고 압력을 주어 찍어내는 오목판 인쇄 방식. 다색 인쇄에 알맞고 고속·대량 인쇄에 적당하다.

be seen in the Sunday edition of the most important newspapers in all the large cities in the country.

Naturally the Poppers all felt very proud and happy.

Captain Cook was not happy, however. He had suddenly **ceased** his **gay**, exploring little walks about the house, and would sit most of the day, **sulk**ing, in the **refrigerator**. Mrs. Popper had removed all the stranger objects, leaving only the **marble**s and checkers, so that Captain Cook now had a nice, **orderly** little **rookery**.

"He won't play with us any more," said Bill. "I tried to get some of my marbles from him, and he tried to bite me."

"**Naughty** Captain Cook," said Janie.

"Better leave him alone, children," said Mrs. Popper. "He feels **mopey**, I guess."

But it was soon clear that it was something worse than mopiness that **ail**ed Captain Cook. All day he would sit with his little white-circled eyes **staring** out sadly from the refrigerator. His coat had lost its lovely, **glossy** look; his round little stomach grew flatter every day.

He would turn away now when Mrs. Popper would offer him some canned **shrimp**s.

One evening she took his temperature. It was one hundred and four degrees.[3]

---

3   one hundred and four degrees 화씨온도 104도는 섭씨온도 40도를 말한다.

x

"Well, Papa," she said, "I think you had better call the **veterinary** doctor. I am afraid Captain Cook is really ill."

But when the veterinary came, he only shook his head. He was a very good animal doctor, and though he had never taken care of a penguin before, he knew enough about birds to see at a **glance** that this one was seriously ill.

"I will leave you some **pills**. Give him one every hour. Then you can try **feed**ing him on sherbet[4] and **wrap**ping him in ice packs. But I cannot give you any **encourage**ment because I am afraid it is a **hopeless** case. This kind of bird was never made for this **climate**, you know. I can see that you have taken good care of him, but an Antarctic penguin can't **thrive** in Stillwater."

That night the Poppers **sat up** all night, **taking turns** changing the ice packs.

It was no use. In the morning Mrs. Popper took Captain Cook's temperature again. It had gone up to one hundred and five.

Everyone was very **sympathetic**. The reporter on the *Morning Chronicle* **stop**ped **in** to **inquire** about the penguin. The neighbors brought in all sorts of broths[5]

---

4   sherbet 셔벗. 과즙에 설탕, 향이 좋은 술, 달걀 흰자, 젤라틴 등을 섞어서 얼려 굳힌 차가운 디저트.
5   broth 물에 육류, 생선, 채소 등을 넣고 약한 불에서 끓인 육수.

and jellies to try to **tempt** the little **fellow**. Even Mrs. Callahan, who had never had a very high opinion of Captain Cook, made a lovely **frozen** custard[6] for him. Nothing did any good. Captain Cook was too **far gone**.

He slept all day now in a heavy **stupor**, and everyone was saying that the end was not far away.

All the Poppers had grown terribly **fond** of the funny, **solemn** little **chap**, and Mr. Popper's heart was frozen with **terror**. It seemed to him that his life would be very empty if Captain Cook went away.

Surely someone would know what to do for a sick

---

6 frozen custard 냉동 커스터드. 우유, 계란에 설탕과 향료 등을 넣어서 가열한 것을 얼린 것으로, 아이스크림과 비슷하다.

penguin. He wished that there were some way of asking advice of Admiral Drake, away down at the South **Pole**, but there was not time.

In his **despair**, Mr. Popper had an idea. A letter had brought him his pet. He sat down and wrote another letter.

It was **address**ed to Dr. Smith, the **Curator** of the great **Aquarium** in Mammoth City, the largest in the world. Surely if anyone anywhere had any idea what could cure a dying penguin, this man would.

Two days later there was an answer from the Curator. "**Unfortunately**," he wrote, "it is not easy to cure a sick penguin. Perhaps you do not know that we too have, in our aquarium at Mammoth City, a penguin from the Antarctic. It is failing **rapid**ly, in spite of everything we have done for it. I have wondered lately whether it is not suffering from loneliness. Perhaps that is what ails your Captain Cook. I am, therefore, **shipp**ing you, **under separate cover**, our penguin. You may keep her. There is just a chance that the birds may get on better together."

And that is how Greta came to live at 432 Proudfoot Avenue.

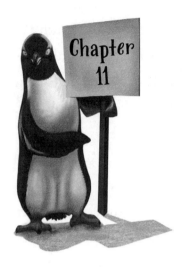

GRETA

SO CAPTAIN COOK did not die, **after all**.

There were two penguins in the **refrigerator**, one standing and one sitting on the **nest** under the ice cubes.

"They're as like as two **pea**s," said Mrs. Popper.

"As two penguins, you mean," answered Mr. Popper.

"Yes, but which is which?"

At this moment the standing penguin jumped out of the **icebox**, reached inside and took one of the checkers from under the sitting penguin, whose eyes were closed in sleep, and laid it at Mr. Popper's feet.

"See, Mamma, he's thanking me," said Mr. Popper, patting the penguin. "At the South Pole that's the way a penguin shows its friendship, only it uses a stone instead of a checker. This one must be Captain Cook, and he's trying to show that he's grateful to us for getting him Greta and saving his life."

"Yes, but how are we going to tell them apart? It's very confusing."

"I will go down in the cellar and get some white paint and paint their names on their black backs."

And he opened the cellar door and started down, nearly tripping when Captain Cook unexpectedly tobogganed down after him. When he came up again, Mr. Popper had a brush and a small paint-can in his hands, while the penguin had a white CAPT. COOK on his back.

"*Gook!*" said Captain Cook, proudly showing his name to the penguin in the icebox.

"*Gaw!*" said the sitting Penguin, and then squirming around in her nest, she turned her back to Mr. Popper.

So Mr. Popper sat down on the floor in front of the icebox, while Captain Cook watched, first with one eye, then with the other.

"What are you going to call her?" asked Mrs. Popper.

"Greta."

"It's a nice name," said Mrs. Popper, "and she seems like a nice bird, too. But the two of them fill the icebox, and pretty soon there will be eggs, and the next thing you know, the icebox won't be big enough for your penguins. Besides, you haven't done a thing about how I'm going to keep the food cold."

"I will, my love," promised Mr. Popper. "It is already pretty cold for the middle of October, and it will soon be cold enough outside for Captain Cook and Greta."

"Yes," said Mrs. Popper, "but if you keep them outside the house, they might run away."

"Mamma," said Mr. Popper, "you put your food back in the icebox tonight, and we will just keep Greta and Captain Cook in the house. Captain Cook can help me move the nest into the other room. Then I will open all the windows and leave them open, and the penguins will be comfortable."

"They will be comfortable, all right," said Mrs. Popper, "but what about us?"

"We can wear our winter **overcoat**s and hats in the house," said Mr. Popper, as he got up to go around and open all the windows.

"It certainly is colder," said Mrs. Popper, **sneezing**.

The next few days were even colder, but the Poppers soon got used to sitting around in their overcoats. Greta and Captain Cook always **occupied** the chairs nearest the open windows.

One night, quite early in November, there was a **blizzard**, and when the Poppers got up in the morning, there were large **drift**s of snow all over the house.

Mrs. Popper wanted to get her **broom** and have Mr. Popper bring his snow **shovel** to clear away the drifts, but the penguins were having so much fun in the snow that Mr. Popper **insisted** it should be left where it was.

In fact, he even **went so far as to** bring an old garden hose up from the **basement** and **sprinkle** all the floors that night until the water was an inch[1] deep. By the next morning all the Popper floors were covered with **smooth** ice, with snowdrifts around the **edge**s near the open windows.

Both Greta and Captain Cook were **tremendously pleased** with all that ice. They would go up on the snowdrift at one end of the living room, and run down, one behind the other, onto the ice, until they were running too fast to keep their balance. Then they would **flop** on their **stomach**s and toboggan across the **slippery** ice.

---

1   inch 길이 단위 인치. 1인치는 약 2.54센티미터이다.

This **amused** Bill and Janie so much that they tried it, too, on the stomachs of their overcoats. This **in turn** pleased the penguins greatly. Then Mr. Popper moved all the furniture in the living room to one side, so that the penguins and the children would have plenty of room for real **sliding**. It was a little hard at first to move the furniture, because the feet of the chairs had **frozen** into the ice.

Toward afternoon the weather got warmer and the ice began to **melt** "Now, Papa," said Mrs. Popper, "you really must do something. We can't **go on** like this."

"But Captain Cook and Greta are both fat and **sleek**, and the children have never been so **rosy**."

"It may be very healthy," said Mrs. Popper, as she **mop**ped up the **flood**, "but it's very **untidy**."

"I will do something about it tomorrow," said Mr. Popper.

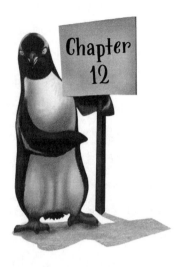

MORE MOUTHS TO FEED

SO THE NEXT DAY Mr. Popper called an engineer and
had a large freezing **plant installed** in the **cellar**, and took
Captain Cook and Greta down there to live. Then he had
the **furnace** taken out and moved upstairs into the living
room. It looked very **odd** there, but, as Mrs. Popper said,
it was a **relief** at least not to have to wear their **overcoats**
all the time.

Mr. Popper was quite worried when he found that
all these changes were going to be very expensive. The
refrigerating engineer was worried, too, when he found

that Mr. Popper had **practically** no money. However, Mr. Popper promised to pay as soon as he could, and the man let him have everything on **credit**.

It was a good thing that Mr. Popper got the penguins moved when he did, because Mrs. Popper had been right about the eggs. The **rookery** had **scarcely** been moved to the **basement** when Greta laid the first egg. Three days later the second one appeared.

Since Mr. Popper knew that penguins lay only two eggs a season, he was **astonish**ed when, a little later, the third egg was found under Greta. Whether the change in **climate** had changed the penguins' **breed**ing habits, Mr. Popper never knew, but every third day a new one would appear until there were ten in all.

Now penguin eggs are so large that the mother can sit on only two at a time, and this created quite a problem. Mr. Popper solved it, however, by **distributing** the extra eggs under hot-water bottles and electric heating-pads,[1] kept just at penguin-body heat.

The penguin **chick**s, when they began to **hatch**, were not so handsomely **mark**ed as their mother and father. They were **fuzzy**, **droll** little creatures who grew at a **tremendous rate**. Captain Cook and Greta were kept

---

1 electric heating-pad 전기 담요.

very busy bringing food to them, though, of course the Poppers all helped, too.

Mr. Popper, who had always been such a great reader, had no difficulty in thinking of names for the penguin children. They were Nelson, Columbus, Louisa, Jenny, Scott, Magellan, Adelina, Isabella, Ferdinand, and Victoria. Still, he was rather **relieve**d that there were no more than ten to name.

Mrs. Popper, too, thought that this was about enough penguins for anybody, though they really did not make much difference to her in her **housework**—as long as Mr. Popper and the children remembered to close the cellar door in the kitchen.

The penguins all loved to climb the stairs that led up to the kitchen, and never knew when to stop unless they found the kitchen door closed. Then, of course, they would turn around and toboggan down the steps again. This made rather a **curious** noise sometimes, when Mrs. Popper was working in the kitchen, but she got used to it, as she had got used to so many other strange things this winter.

The freezing plant that Mr. Popper had got for the penguins downstairs was a large and good one. It made very large **blocks** of ice, instead of small ice cubes, so that soon Mr. Popper had made a sort of ice castle down there for the twelve penguins to live in and climb over.

Mr. Popper also **dug** a large hole in the cellar floor and made a swimming and **diving** pool for the birds. From time to time he would throw live fish into the pool for the penguins to dive for. They found this very **refreshing**, because, **to tell the truth**, they had got a little tired of canned shrimps. The live fish were specially ordered and were brought all the way from the **coast** in tank cars and glass boxes to 432 Proudfoot Avenue. **Unfortunately,** they were quite expensive.

It was nice that there were so many penguins because when two of them (usually Nelson and Columbus) got into a fight, and began to **spar** at each other with their **flippers**, the ten other penguins would all crowd around to watch the fight and make **encouraging remarks**. This made a very interesting little **scene**.

Mr. Popper also **flood**ed a part of the cellar floor for an ice rink, and here the penguins often **drilled** like a sort of small army, in fantastic **march**ing movements and **parades** around the ice. The penguin Louisa seemed especially **fond** of leading these marching drills. It was quite a **sight** to see them, after Mr. Popper had the idea of training Louisa to hold a small American **flag** in her **beak** while she proudly led the solemn parades.

Janie and Bill would often bring their little friends home from school with them, and they would all go down and watch the penguins for hours.

At night, instead of sitting and reading and smoking his pipe in the living room, as he had done before, Mr. Popper would put on his overcoat and take his things downstairs. There he would sit and read, with his **mittens** on, looking up from time to time to see what his pets were doing. He often thought about the cold, **distant** **region**s in which the little creatures really belonged.

Often, too, he thought how different his life had been before the penguins had come to keep him **occupied**. It was January now, and already he **dreaded** to think of the time when spring would come, and he would have to leave them all day and go back to painting houses.

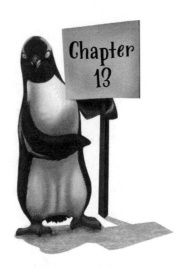

MONEY WORRIES

THERE CAME a night, however, when Mrs. Popper, having put the children to bed, stopped Mr. Popper on his way to the cellar.

"Papa," she said, "I must talk to you. Come and sit down."

"Yes, my love," said Mr. Popper, "what is on your mind?"

"Papa," said Mrs. Popper, "I'm glad to see you having such a nice vacation. And I must say that it's been easier than usual to keep the place tidy, with you down in the basement all the time. But, Papa, what are we to do for money?"

"What is the trouble?" asked Mr. Popper.

"Well, of course, the penguins have to eat, but have you any idea what the **bills** for all those live fish are? I'm sure I don't know how we're ever going to pay for them. And the engineer who put in the basement freezing **plant** keeps ringing the doorbell and asking for his money."

"Is our money all gone?" asked Mr. Popper quietly.

"**Practical**ly all. Of course when it is all gone, maybe we could eat the twelve penguins for a while."

"Oh no, Mamma," said Mr. Popper. "You don't mean that."

"Well, I don't suppose I really could enjoy eating them, especially Greta and Isabella," said Mrs. Popper.

"It would **break** the **children's heart**s, too," said Mr. Popper. He sat there **thoughtful**ly for quite a while.

"I have an idea, Mamma," he said at last.

"Maybe we could sell them to somebody, and then we would have a little money to **live on**," said Mrs. Popper.

"No," said Mr. Popper, "I have a better idea. We will keep the penguins. Mamma, you have heard of trained **seal**s, acting in theaters?"

"Of course I have heard of trained seals," answered Mrs. Popper. "I even saw some once. They balanced balls on the ends of their noses."

"Very well then," said Mr. Popper, "if there can be trained dogs and trained seals, why can't there be trained penguins?"

"Perhaps you are right, Papa."

"Of course I am right. And you can help me train the penguins."

The next day they had the piano moved down into the basement at one end of the ice rink. Mrs. Popper had not played the piano since she had married Mr. Popper, but with a little practice she soon began to remember some of the **pieces** she had forgotten.

"What these penguins like to do most," said Mr. Popper, "is to **drill** like an army, to watch Nelson and Columbus get in a fight with each other, and to climb up steps and toboggan down. And so we will build our act around those **tricks**."

"They don't need **costume**s, anyway," said Mrs. Popper, looking at the **droll** little **figure**s. "They already have a costume."

So Mrs. Popper picked out three different **tunes** to play on the basement piano, one for each different kind of act. Soon the penguins knew, from hearing the music, just what they were to do.

When they were supposed to parade like a lot

of soldiers, Mrs. Popper played Schubert's "**Military** March.[1]"

When Nelson and Columbus were to fight each other with their flippers, Mrs. Popper played the "Merry **Widow** Waltz.[2]"

When the penguins were supposed to climb and toboggan, Janie and Bill would **drag** out into the middle of the ice two **portable stepladder**s and a **board** that Mr. Popper had used when he was decorating houses. Then Mrs. Popper would play a pretty, **descriptive** piece called "By the **Brook**.[3]"

It was cold in the cellar, of course, so that Mrs. Popper had to learn to play the piano with her gloves on.

By the end of January, Mr. Popper was sure the penguins were ready to appear in any theater in the country.

---

1 **Military March** 오스트리아의 작곡가 프란츠 슈베르트(Franz Peter Schubert)가 작곡한 군대 행진곡.

2 **Merry Widow Waltz** 헝가리의 작곡가 프란츠 레하르(Franz Lehár)의 오페레타 'The Merry Widow'에 나오는 노래.

3 **By the Brook** 독일의 작곡가이자 피아니스트 하인리히 호프만(Heinrich Hofmann)의 짧은 피아노곡.

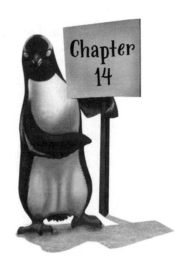

MR. GREENBAUM

"**LOOK HERE**," said Mr. Popper at breakfast one morning. "It says here in the *Morning Chronicle* that Mr. Greenbaum, the owner of the Palace Theater, is in town. He's got a **string** of theaters all over the country; so I guess we had better go down and see him."

That evening—it was Saturday, the twenty-ninth of January—the Popper family and their twelve trained penguins, two of them carrying **flags** in their beaks, left the house to find the Palace Theater.

The penguins were now so well trained that Mr.

Popper decided that it was not necessary to keep them on leashes. Indeed, they walked to the bus line very nicely in the following line of march:—

Mr. Popper

Greta
Captain Cook

Columbus
Victoria

Nelson
Jenny

Mrs. Pop

The bus stopped at the corner, and before the **astonish**ed driver could **protest**, they had all climbed on and the bus was on its way.

Bill Popper
Janie Popper

Ferdinand
Louisa

gellan
delina

Scott
Isabella

"Do I pay half-**fare** for the birds, or do they go free?" asked Mr. Popper.

"Janie goes half-fare, but I'm ten," said Bill.

"**Hush**," said Mrs. Popper as she and the children found their seats. The penguins followed in an **orderly fashion**.

"Say, mister," said the driver, "where do you think you're going with that **exhibit**?"

"Downtown," said Mr. Popper. "Here, let's call it fifty cents, and let it go at that."

"**To tell the truth**, I lost count when they went past me," said the driver.

"It's a trained penguin act," explained Mr. Popper.

"Are they really birds?" asked the driver.

"Oh yes," said Mr. Popper. "I'm just taking them down to the Palace to interview Mr. Greenbaum, the big theater owner."

"Well, if I hear any complaints, off they go at the next corner," said the driver.

"Fair enough," said Mr. Popper, who wanted to ask for **transfers** in that case, but decided to **let well enough alone**.

The penguins were behaving very well. They were sitting quietly two in a seat, while the other **passengers** looked on.

"Sorry," said Mr. Popper, **address**ing everyone in the bus, "but I'll have to open all the windows. These are **Antarctic** penguins and they're used to having it a lot colder than this."

It took Mr. Popper quite a while to open the windows, which were **stuck fast**. When he had succeeded, there were plenty of **remark**s from the other passengers. Many of them began to complain to the driver, who told Mr. Popper to take his birds off the bus. He had to repeat this several times. Finally he refused to take the bus any farther until Mr. Popper got off. By this time, however, the bus had got so far downtown that none of them minded having to get out into the street.

Only a block ahead of them shone the lights of the Palace Theater.

"Hello," said the theater manager, as the Poppers and the penguins **troop**ed past him. "Sure, Mr. Greenbaum's here in my office. You know I've heard about these birds of yours, but I didn't really believe it. Mr. Greenbaum, meet the Popper Penguins. I'll be leaving you. I've got to go **backstage**."

The penguins, now standing politely in two **rows** of six each, looked curiously at Mr. Greenbaum. Their twenty-four white-circled eyes were very **solemn**.

"All you people crowding around the door, go back

where you belong," said Mr. Greenbaum. "This is a private **conference**." Then he got up to shut the door.

The Poppers sat down while Mr. Greenbaum walked up and down the double row of penguins, looking them over.

"It looks like an act," he said.

"Oh, it's an act, all right," said Mr. Popper. "It's Popper's Performing Penguins, First Time on any Stage, Direct from the South **Pole**." He and Mrs. Popper had thought up this name for the act.

"Couldn't we call them Popper's Pink-**toe**d Penguins?" asked Mr. Greenbaum.

Mr. Popper thought for a moment. "No," he said, "I'm afraid we couldn't. That sounds too much like **chorus** girls or ballet dancers, and these birds are pretty serious. I don't think they'd like it."

"All right," said Mr. Greenbaum. "Show me the act."

"There's music to it," said Janie. "Mamma plays the piano."

"Is that true, madam?" asked Mr. Greenbaum.

"Yes, sir," answered Mrs. Popper.

"Well, there's a piano behind you," said Mr. Greenbaum. "You may begin, madam. I want to see this act. If it's any good, you people have come to the right place. I've got theaters from **coast** to coast. But first let's see your penguins perform. Ready, madam?"

"We'd better move the furniture first," said Bill.

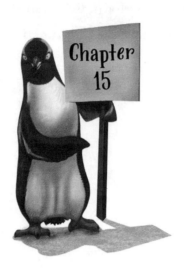

POPPER'S PERFORMING PENGUINS

AT THAT MOMENT they were **interrupt**ed by the manager, who came in with a **groan**.

"What's the matter?" asked Mr. Greenbaum.

"The **Marvelous** Marcos, who close the program, haven't **turn**ed **up**, and the audience are demanding their money back."

"What are you going to do?" asked Mr. Greenbaum.

"Give it to them, I suppose. And here it is Saturday night, the biggest night of the week. I hate to think of losing all that money."

"I have an idea," said Mrs. Popper. "Maybe you won't have to lose it. As long as it's the end of the program, why don't we just have the penguins **rehearse** in there on a real stage? We'd have more room, and I think the audience would enjoy it."

"All right," said the manager. "Let's try it."

So the penguins had their first rehearsal on a real stage.

The manager stepped out on the stage. "Ladies and gentlemen," he said, raising his hand, "with your kind **indulgence** we are going to try out a little **novelty number** tonight. Owing to **unforeseen** circumstances, the Marvelous Marcos are unable to appear. We are going to let you see a rehearsal of the Popper Performing Penguins, instead. I thank you."

In a **dignified** way the Poppers and the penguins walked out on the stage, and Mrs. Popper sat down at the piano.

"Aren't you going to take off your gloves to play?" asked the manager.

"Oh, no," said Mrs. Popper. "I'm so used to playing with them that I'll keep them on, if you don't mind."

Then she started Schubert's "**Military March**." The penguins began to **drill** very nicely, **wheeling** and changing their **formation**s with great **precision**, until

Mrs. Popper stopped playing in the middle of the piece.

The audience clapped vigorously.

"There's more to it," explained Mrs. Popper, half to the manager and half to the audience, "where they form in a hollow square and march in that formation. It's so late we'll skip that tonight and jump to the second part."

"You're sure you don't want to take your gloves off, madam?" asked the manager.

Mrs. Popper smilingly shook her head and began the "Merry Widow Waltz."

Ten of the penguins now formed in a semicircle as Nelson and Columbus in their midst put on a wild sparring contest. Their round black heads leaned far back so that they could watch each other with both round white eyes.

"*Gork,*" said Nelson, punching Columbus in the stomach with his right flipper, and then trying to push him over with his left flipper.

"*Gaw,*" said Columbus, going into a clinch and hanging his head over Nelson's shoulder as he tried to punch him in the back.

"Hey! No fair!" said the manager. Columbus and Nelson broke loose as the other ten penguins, looking on, applauded with their flippers.

Columbus now sparred politely with Nelson until

Nelson hit him on the eye, **whereupon** Columbus **retreat**ed with a loud "*Ork.*" The other penguins began to clap, and the audience joined them. As Mrs. Popper finished the Waltz, both Nelson and Columbus stopped fighting, put down their flippers and stood still, facing each other.

"Which bird won? Who's ahead?" shouted the audience.

"*Gook!*" said all the ten penguins in the semicircle.

This must have meant "Look!" for Nelson turned to look at them, and Columbus **immediate**ly punched him in the stomach with one flipper and **knock**ed him down with the other. Nelson lay there, with his eyes closed.

Columbus then counted ten over the **prostrate** Nelson, and again the ten other penguins applauded.

"That's part of the act," explained Janie. "The other penguins all like Columbus to win, and so they all say '*Gook!*' at the end. That always makes Nelson look away, so Columbus can **sock** him good."

Nelson now rose to his feet, and all the penguins formed in a **row**, and **bow**ed to the manager.

"Thank you," said the manager, bowing back.

"Now comes part three," said Mr. Popper.

"Oh, Papa," said Mrs. Popper. "You forgot to bring the two painting **stepladder**s and the board!"

"That's all right," said the manager. "I'll get the **stagehand**s to bring some."

In no time at all a pair of **ladder**s and a board were brought in and Mr. Popper and the children showed them how the ladders had to be set up with the board resting on top. Then Mrs. Popper began playing the pretty **descriptive** piece "By the **Brook**."

At this point in the act the penguins always forgot their **discipline** and got **dreadful**ly excited. They would all begin **shoving at once** to see which could be the first to climb the ladders. However, the children had always told Mr. Popper that the act was all the funnier for all this pushing and **scrambling**, and Mr. Popper supposed

94

it was.

So now with a great deal of **squawk**ing the penguins fought and climbed the ladders and ran across the board in complete **confusion**, often knocking each other entirely off to the floor below, and then hurrying to **toboggan** down the other ladder and knock off any penguins who were trying to climb up there.

This part of the act was very wild and **noisy** in spite of Mrs. Popper's **delicate** music. The manager and the audience were all **hold**ing **their sides**, laughing.

At last Mrs. Popper got to the end of the music and took off her gloves.

"You'll have to get those ladders off the stage, or I'll never get these birds under control," said Mr. Popper. "The curtain is supposed to fall at this point."

So the manager gave the **signal** for the curtain to go down, and the audience stood up and cheered.

When the ladders had been taken away, the manager had twelve ice-cream cones brought in for the penguins. Then Janie and Bill began to cry, so the manager ordered several more, and everybody had one.

Mr. Greenbaum was the first to **congratulate** the Poppers.

"I don't mind telling you, Mr. Popper, that I think you've got something **absolute**ly **unique** in those birds.

Your act is a **sensation**. And the way you helped out my friend the manager, here, shows that you're real **trouper**s—the kind we need in the show business. I'd like to **predict** that your penguins will soon be packing the biggest theaters from Oregon to Maine.

"And now to come to **term**s, Mr. Popper," he continued. "How about a ten-week **contract** at five thousand dollars a week?"

"Is that all right, Mamma?" asked Mr. Popper.

"Yes, that's very **satisfactory**," answered Mrs. Popper.

"Well, then," said Mr. Greenbaum, "just sign these papers. And be ready to open next Thursday in Seattle."

"And thanks again," said the manager. "Would you mind putting on your gloves again for just a minute, Mrs. Popper? I'd like you to start playing that 'Military March' again and let the penguins **parade** for a minute. I want to get my **usher**s in here to look at those birds. It would be a lesson to them."

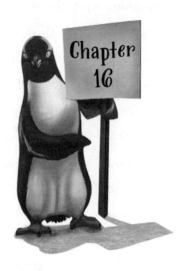

ON THE ROAD

DURING THE NEXT day there was much to be done at 432 Proudfoot Avenue. There were new clothes to buy for all of them, and the old ones to pack away in mothballs.[1] Then Mrs. Popper had to **scrub** and **polish** and **straighten** the whole place, for she was much too good a **housekeeper** to leave everything **at sixes and sevens** while the Poppers were away.

Mr. Greenbaum sent them their first week's pay in

---

1   mothball 작은 공 모양으로 생긴 좀약.

advance. The first thing they did was to pay off the man who had **installed** the **freezing plant** in the **basement**. He had been getting rather **uneasy** about his money; and **after all**, without him they could never have trained the penguins. Next they sent a check to the company who had been **ship**ping the fresh fish all the way from the coast.

At last everything was done, and Mr. Popper turned the key in the door of the little house.

They were a little late in arriving at the **railway** station **on account of** the argument with the **traffic** policeman. The argument was on account of the accident to the two taxicabs.

With four Poppers and twelve penguins, not to mention the eight suitcases and **pail** of water with the live fish for the penguins' lunch, Mr. Popper found that they could not all fit into one cab; so he had to call a second one.

Each of the taxi-drivers was eager to be the first to get to the station and surprise the people there by opening the door of his cab and letting out six penguins. So they **race**d each other all the way, and in the last **block** they tried to pass each other, and one of the fenders² got **torn** off.

---

2 fender 펜더. 자동차의 바퀴 덮개.

The traffic officer naturally got very much **annoyed**.

The train was about to **pull out** of the station when they arrived. Even with both taxi-drivers helping them through the gate and over the **brass** rails onto the **rear observation platform**, they **barely made it**. The penguins were **gasp**ing.

It had been decided that Mr. Popper should ride in the baggage car with the penguins to keep them from getting nervous, while Mrs. Popper and the children should ride in one of the Pullmans.[3] Because of getting on at the observation end of the train, Mr. Popper had to take the birds through the whole length of the train.

It was easy enough to get them through the club car,[4] even with the pail of fish to carry. In the sleeping cars, however, where the **porter** was already making up some of the **berth**s, there was trouble.

The porters' ladders offered too much **temptation** to the penguins.

There were a **dozen** happy *Orks* from a dozen **ecstatic** beaks. Popper's Performing Penguins, completely forgetting their **discipline**, fought to climb the ladders and get into the upper berths.

Poor Mr. Popper! One old lady screamed that she was

---

3 Pullman 침대 설비가 갖춰진 특별 객차.
4 club car 기차에서 휴식이나 식사를 할 수 있는 특별 객차.

going to get off the train, whether it was going ninety miles⁵ an hour or not. A gentleman wearing a **clergyman's collar** suggested opening a window, so that the penguins could jump out. Two porters tried to **shoo** the birds out of the berths. Finally the **conductor** and the **brakeman**, with a lantern, came to the **rescue**.

It was quite a while before Mr. Popper got his pets safely into the baggage car.

Mrs. Popper worried a little, at the start, over the idea of having Janie and Bill miss ten weeks of school while they were on the road, though the children did not seem to mind.

"And you must remember, my love," said Mr. Popper, who had never before been out of Stillwater, in spite of his dreams of **distant** countries, "that travel is very **broaden**ing."

From the start the penguins were a **riotous** success. Even their opening performance in Seattle **went off** without a **hitch**—probably because they had already **rehearsed** on a real stage.

It was here that the penguins added a little **novelty number** of their own to the program. They were the first thing on the **bill**. When they finished their regular act,

---

5   **mile** 거리 단위 마일. 1마일은 약 1,609미터이다. 90마일은 약 144킬로미터이다.

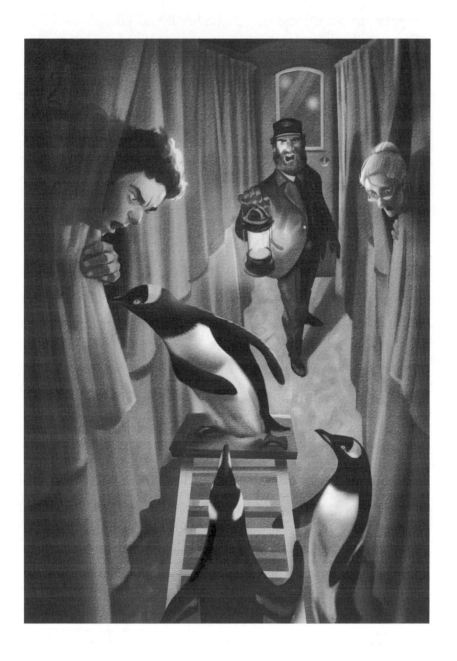

the audience went wild. They **clap**ped and **stamp**ed and **roar**ed for more of Popper's Performing Penguins.

Janie and Bill helped their father **herd** the penguins off the stage, so that the next act could go on.

This next act was a **tightrope** walker, named Monsieur[6] Duval. The trouble was that instead of watching him from the **wings**, as they should have done, the penguins got interested and walked out on the stage again to watch him more closely.

Unfortunately at this moment Monsieur Duval was doing a very difficult dance on the **wire overhead**.

The audience, of course, had thought that the penguins were all through, and were very much **pleased** to see them return and line up with their backs to the audience and look up at Monsieur Duval, dancing so carefully on the wire high above them.

This made everyone laugh so hard that Monsieur Duval lost his balance.

"*Ork!*" said the penguins **waddling** away **hurried**ly, in order not to be under him when he fell.

Cleverly **recover**ing his balance, Monsieur Duval caught the wire by the inside of his **elbow** and saved himself. He was very angry when he saw the Popper

---

6 monsieur '~씨', '~님'이라는 뜻으로 영어의 Mr. 또는 Sir에 해당하는 프랑스어의 경칭.

Performing Penguins opening wide their twelve red beaks, as if they were laughing at him.

"Go away, you stupid things," he said to them in French.

"*Ork?*" said the penguins, pretending not to understand, and making **remark**s to each other in penguin language about Monsieur Duval.

And whenever they appeared, the more they **interfere**d with the other acts on the program the better the audiences liked them.

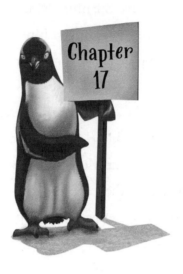

FAME

THE BIRDS SOON became so famous that whenever it was known that the Popper Performing Penguins were to appear at any theater, the crowds would stand in line for half a mile down the street, waiting their turn to buy tickets.

The other actors on the program were not always so **pleased**, however. Once, in Minneapolis,[1] a **celebrated** lady opera singer got very much **annoyed** when she heard

---

1   Minneapolis 미니애폴리스. 미국 미네소타 주(州) 미시시피 강 상류에 있는 도시.

that the Popper Penguins were to appear on the same program. In fact, she refused to go on the stage unless the penguins were put away. So the **stagehands** helped Mr. and Mrs. Popper and the children get the birds off the stage and downstairs to a **basement** under the stage, while the manager **guard**ed the stage **entrance** to make sure that the penguins did not get past.

Down in the basement, the birds soon discovered another little **flight** of steps going up; and in another minute the audience was **shriek**ing with laughter, as the penguins' heads suddenly appeared, one by one, in the orchestra **pit**, where the musicians were playing.

The musicians kept on playing, and the lady on the stage, when she saw the penguins, sang all the louder to show how angry she was. The audience was laughing so hard that nobody could hear the words of her song.

Mr. Popper, who had followed the penguins up the stairs, stopped when he saw that it led to the orchestra pit.

"I don't think I'm supposed to go up there with the musicians," he told Mrs. Popper.

"The penguins did," said Mrs. Popper.

"Papa, you'd better get them off before they start **biting** the **peg**s and **string**s off the **fiddle**s," said Bill.

"Oh dear, I just don't know what to do," said Mr.

Popper, sitting down **helpless**ly on the top step.

"Then *I* will catch the penguins," said Mrs. Popper, climbing up past him, with Janie and Bill following.

When they saw Mrs. Popper coming after them, the penguins felt very **guilty**, because they knew they did not belong there. So they jumped up on the stage, ran over the footlights,[2] and hid under the singing lady's blue skirts.

That stopped the singing entirely except for one high, **shrill note** that had not been written in the music.

The birds loved the bright lights of the theater, and the great, laughing audiences, and all the traveling. There was always something new to see.

From Stillwater out to the Pacific **coast**[3] they traveled. It was a long way now to the little house at 432 Proudfoot Avenue, where the Poppers had had to worry about whether their money would **hold out** until spring.

And every week they got a check for five thousand dollars.

When they were not actually playing in some theater, or traveling on trains between cities, their life was spent

---

2 footlight 각광(脚光). 무대나 진열장 등의 바닥에서 위쪽을 향하여 투사되는 조명.
3 Pacific coast 태평양 연안. 미국에서 태평양에 닿아 있는 지역을 말한다.

in the larger hotels.

Now and then a **startled** hotelkeeper[4] would **object** to having the birds **register** there.

"Why, we don't even allow **lap** dogs in this hotel," he would say.

"Yes, but do you have any rule against penguins?" Mr. Popper would ask.

Then the hotelkeeper would have to admit that there was no rule at all about penguins. And of course, when he saw how **neat** the penguins were, and how other guests came to his hotel in the hope of seeing them, he was very glad to have them. You might think that a large hotel would offer a great many opportunities for **mischief** to a lot of penguins, but they behaved very well, **on the whole**, never doing anything worse than riding up and down too often in the elevators, and **occasional**ly biting the **brass** buttons off some bellboy's[5] uniform.

Five thousand dollars a week may sound like a great deal of money, and yet the Poppers **were far from** rich. It was quite expensive to live in grand hotels and travel about town in taxicabs. Mr. Popper often thought that the penguins could just as well have walked **back and**

---

4   hotelkeeper 호텔 경영자.
5   bellboy 벨보이. 호텔에서 손님들의 짐을 운반하는 사람.

forth between hotels and theaters, but every one of their walks looked so much like a parade that it always **tied up** the **traffic**. So Mr. Popper, who never liked to be a **nuisance** to anyone, always took taxis instead.

It was expensive to have huge **cakes** of ice brought up to their hotel rooms, to cool the penguins. The bills in the fine restaurants where the Poppers often took their meals were often **dreadfully** high. **Fortunately**, however, the penguins' food had stopped being an **expense** to them. **On the road**, they had to **give up** having tank cars of live fish **ship**ped to them, because it was so hard to get deliveries **on time**. So they went back to **feed**ing the birds on canned **shrimp**s.

This cost them **absolutely** nothing, for Mr. Popper had written a **testimonial** saying: "Popper's Performing Penguins **thrive** on Owens' Oceanic Shrimp."

This statement, with a picture of the twelve penguins, was printed in all the **leading** magazines, and the Owens Oceanic Shrimp Company gave Mr. Popper an order that was good for free cans of shrimps at any **grocery** store anywhere in the country.

Several other companies, such as the Great Western **Spinach** Growers' **Association** and the **Energetic** Breakfast **Oats** Company, wanted him to recommend their product, too, and offered him large sums of cash.

But the penguins simply refused to eat spinach or oats, and Mr. Popper was much too honest to say they would, even though he knew the money would come in **handy**.

From the Pacific coast they turned east again, to cross the **continent**. They had time enough, on this brief tour, to touch only the larger cities. After Minneapolis, they played Milwaukee, Chicago, Detroit, Cleveland, and Philadelphia.

Wherever they went, their **reputation** traveled ahead of them. When, early in April, they reached Boston, huge crowds awaited them in the **railway** station.

Up to now, it had not been too difficult to keep the penguins comfortable. But a warm spring wind was blowing across Boston Common,[6] and at the hotel Mr. Popper had to have the ice brought up to his rooms in thousand-pound[7] cakes. He was glad that the ten-week **contract** was almost up, and that the next week, when his birds were to appear in New York, was the last.

Already Mr. Greenbaum was writing about a new contract. Mr. Popper was beginning to think, however, that he had better be getting back to Stillwater, for the penguins were growing **irritable**.

---

6   **Boston Common** 미국 매사추세츠 주(州) 보스턴에 있는, 미국에서 가장 오래된 공원.
7   **pound** 무게 단위 파운드. 1파운드는 약 0.454킬로그램이다.

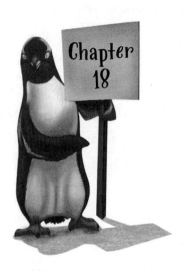

APRIL WINDS

IF IT WAS unseasonably warm in Boston, it was actually hot in New York. In their rooms at the great Tower Hotel, **overlook**ing Central Park,[1] the penguins were feeling the heat badly.

Mr. Popper took them up to the **roof** garden to catch whatever cool **breeze** might be blowing. The penguins were all **charm**ed by the **sparkling** lights and the **confusion** of the city below. The younger birds began

---

1 Central Park 센트럴 파크. 뉴욕 시의 맨해튼에 있는 큰 도시 공원.

crowding over to the **edge** of the roof and looking down at the great **canyon**s beneath them. It made Mr. Popper very nervous to see them **shoving** each other, as if at any moment they might succeed in pushing one over. He remembered how the South **Pole** penguins always did this to find out what danger lay below.

The roof was not a safe place for them. Mr. Popper had never forgotten how badly **frighten**ed he had been when Captain Cook had been so ill, before Greta came. He could not risk the chance of losing one of his penguins now.

Where the penguins were **concern**ed, nothing was ever too much trouble for him. He took them downstairs again and bathed them under the cold showers in the bathroom. This kept him busy a large part of the night.

With all this **lack** of sleep, he was quite **drowsy** the next morning when he had to call the taxis to get to the theater. Besides, Mr. Popper had always been a little **absent-minded**. That is how he made his great mistake when he said to the first taxi-driver: —

"Regal Theater."

"Yes, sir," said the driver, **thread**ing his way in and out the **traffic** of Broadway,[2] which greatly interested

---

2 **Broadway** 브로드웨이. 뉴욕 타임스 광장 주변에 있는 극장가.

both the children and the penguins.

They had almost reached the theater, when the driver suddenly turned. "Say," he said, "you don't mean to say those penguins are going to be on the same bill with Swenson's Seals, do you?"

"I don't know what else is on the bill," said Mr. Popper, paying him. "Anyway, here's the Regal." And they piled out and filed in the stage entrance.

In the wings stood a large, burly, red-faced man. "So these are the Popper Performing Penguins, huh?" he said. "Well, I want to tell you, Mr. Popper, that I'm Swen Swenson, and those are my seals in there on the stage now, and if your birds try any funny business, it'll be too bad for them. My seals are tough, see? They'd think nothing of eating two or three penguins apiece."

From the stage could be heard the hoarse barks of the seals, who were going through their act.

"Papa," said Mrs. Popper, "the penguins are the last act on the bill. You go run back quick and get those taxis and we'll let the penguins ride around a while until it's time for their number."

Mr. Popper hurried out to catch the drivers.

When he returned, it was too late. The Popper Performing Penguins had already discovered the Swenson Seals.

"Papa, I can't look!" cried the children.

There was a sound of **dreadful** confusion on the stage, the audience was in an **uproar**, and **the curtain** was quickly **rung down**.

When the Poppers **rush**ed onto the stage, both penguins and seals had found the **stairway** leading to the Swenson **dressing room** and were on their way upstairs.

"I can't **bear** to think what's happening up there," said Mr. Popper, with a **shudder**.

Mr. Swenson only laughed. "I hope your birds were **insure**d, Popper," he said. "How much were they worth? Well, let's go up and look."

"You go up, Papa," said Mrs. Popper. "Bill, you run out of the theater and call the police to come and try to save some of our penguins."

"I'll go get the fire department," said Janie.

When the firemen, with a great **clang**ing, came and set up their **ladder**s so that they could get in through the window of Mr. Swenson's dressing room, they were a little **vexed** to find that there was no fire at all. However, when they found six black-**mustache**d seals, sitting barking in the middle of the room, with twelve penguins **parading gaily** around them in a square, they felt better.

Then the policemen came in their **patrol**, and climbed up the ladder which the firemen had left against

the building. By the time they too came through the
window, they could **scarcely** believe their eyes. For the
firemen had put firemen's helmets on the penguins,
which made the **delight**ed birds look very **silly** and girlish.

Seeing the firemen so **friendly** with the penguins,
the policemen naturally **took sides** with the seals and
put policemen's caps on them. The seals looked very
fierce, with their long black mustaches and black faces
underneath.

The penguins under their firemen's helmets were

parading in front of the policemen, while the seals, in their policemen's caps, were barking at the firemen, when Mr. Popper and Mr. Swenson finally opened the door.

Mr. Popper sat down. His **relief** was so great that for a moment he could not speak.

"You policemen had better get your hats off my seals now," said Mr. Swenson. "I got to go down on the stage and finish the act now." Then he and his six seals **slip**ped out of the room, with a few **part**ing barks.

"Well, good-bye, ducks," said the firemen, **regretful**ly removing their helmets from the penguins and putting them on their own heads. Then they disappeared down the ladder. The penguins, of course, wanted to follow, but Mr. Popper held them back.

Just then the door flew open, and the theater manager **burst** into the room.

"Hold that man," he shouted to the policemen, pointing at Mr. Popper. "I have a **warrant** for his **arrest**."

"Who, me?" said Mr. Popper, in a **daze**. "What have I done?"

"You've **broken into** my theater and thrown the place into a **panic**, that's what you've done. You're a **disturb**er of the peace."

"But I'm Mr. Popper, and these are my Performing Penguins, famous from coast to coast."

"I don't care who you are, you haven't any business in my theater."

"But Mr. Greenbaum is going to pay us five thousand dollars for a week at the Regal."

"Mr. Greenbaum's theater is the Royal, not the Regal. You've come to the wrong theater. Anyway, out you go, you and your Performing Penguins. The patrol is waiting outside."

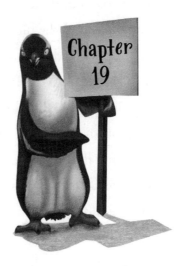

ADMIRAL DRAKE

SO MR. POPPER, with Captain Cook, Greta, Columbus, Louisa, Nelson, Jenny, Magellan, Adelina, Scott, Isabella, Ferdinand, and Victoria, was **bundled** into the **patrol wagon** and **hustled** off to the police station.

None of his **plea**s could move the desk sergeant.[1]

"That theater manager is pretty mad at the way you **bust**ed into his theater, so I'm **hold**ing you. I'm going to give you all a nice quiet **cell**—unless you **furnish bail**.

---

1 **desk sergeant** 경찰서에서 내근을 하고 있는 경사.

I'm putting the bail at five hundred dollars for you and one hundred dollars for each of the birds."

Of course Mr. Popper did not have that much money about him. Neither did Mrs. Popper when they telephoned her at the hotel. The hotel **bill** was paid for several days ahead, but she had no cash. The check for the final week's **salary** was not due until the end of the week. Indeed, it now looked as if the Poppers would never see that check, since they could not get the penguins out of **jail** long enough to put on their act at the Royal Theater.

If only they could have got in touch with Mr. Greenbaum, Mr. Popper knew, that kind man would have got them out. But Mr. Greenbaum was somewhere in Hollywood, out on the Pacific **Coast**, and the Poppers had no idea how to reach him.

It was very **dull** for the birds in jail. Wednesday came and there was still no word from Mr. Greenbaum. Thursday, and the birds began to **droop**. It was soon **apparent** that the **lack** of exercise, combined with the heat, might **prove** too much for them. There were no more **tricks** or **merry** games. Even the younger birds sat all day in **dismal** silence, and Mr. Popper could not cheer them up.

Mr. Popper had a feeling that Mr. Greenbaum would probably **turn up** by the end of the week, to see about

renewing the contract. But Friday passed, without any news of him.

Saturday morning Mr. Popper got up very early and smoothed his hair. Then he dusted off the penguins as well as he could, for he wanted everything to look as presentable as possible, in case Mr. Greenbaum should appear.

About ten o'clock there was a sound of footsteps in the corridor, and a jingling of keys, and the door of the cell was opened.

"You're free, Mr. Popper. There's a friend of yours here."

Mr. Popper stepped out into the light with the penguins.

"You're barely in time, Mr. Greenbaum," he was about to say.

Then, as his eyes became accustomed to the light, he looked again.

It was not Mr. Greenbaum who stood there.

It was a great, bearded man in a splendid uniform. Smiling, he held out his hand to Mr. Popper.

"Mr. Popper," he said, "I am Admiral Drake."

"Admiral Drake!" gasped Mr. Popper. "Not back from the South Pole!"

"Yes," said the Admiral, "the Drake Antarctic

Expedition ship returned yesterday. You should have seen the **reception** New York gave us. You can read about it in today's paper. But I read about the trouble you were having over the penguins, and so here I am. I have a long story to tell you."

"Could we go to the hotel and talk about it?" asked Mr. Popper. "My wife will be **anxious** to see us back."

"Certainly," said the Admiral. And when they were all settled in the Popper rooms at the hotel, with the penguins **cluster**ing round to listen, Admiral Drake began: —

"Naturally, when I knew that I was coming back to America, I often thought about the man to whom I had sent the penguin. It takes us a long time to hear things, down there, and I often wondered how you and the bird were **getting along**. Last night, at the **Mayor**'s dinner for us, I heard about the wonderful trained penguin act you had been putting on all over the country. This morning I picked up the paper, and the first thing I read was that Mr. Popper and his twelve penguins were still being held in jail. But *twelve* penguins, Mr. Popper—how **on earth**—"

Then Mr. Popper told how Greta had arrived to keep Captain Cook from being lonely, and how the little penguins had grown, and how the clever little **band** had saved the day for the Poppers, when things looked bad.

"It's amazing," said Admiral Drake. "I've seen a lot of penguins in my time, but never such educated ones as these. It certainly shows what patience and training can do.

"But now to get to my real point, Mr. Popper. You probably know that I have explored the North Pole as well as the South Pole?"

"Oh yes," said Mr. Popper respectfully, "I have read books about both your Arctic and your Antarctic expeditions."

"Well, then," said the Admiral, "maybe you know why we explorers prefer the South Pole?"

"Could it be on account of the penguins, sir?" asked Janie, who had been listening very hard.

Admiral Drake patted her head. "Yes, my dear. Those long Polar nights get pretty dull when you have no pets to play with. Of course, there are polar bears up there, but you can't play with *them*. Nobody knows why there are no penguins at the North Pole. For a long time the United States Government has been wanting me to lead an expedition up there for the purpose of establishing a breed of penguins. I must come to the point, Mr. Popper. You've had such remarkable success with these birds of yours, why not let me take them to the North Pole and

124

start a **race** of penguins there?"

Just then Mr. Greenbaum and another gentleman were **announced**. They shook hands all around and were introduced to the Admiral.

"Well, Popper," said Mr. Greenbaum, "too bad about that **mix-up** over the theaters. But never mind. Here's Mr. Klein, who owns the **Colossal** Film Company. He's going to make your **fortune**. You'll be a poor man no longer, Mr. Popper."

"Poor!" said Mr. Popper, "I'm not poor. These birds have been earning us five thousand dollars a week."

"Oh, five thousand dollars," said Mr. Klein. "What's that? **Pin money**. I want to put those birds in the movies, Mr. Popper. We've got the story department working on stories for them already. Why, I'll put each of those birds under a contract that will keep you and the missus[2] **on Easy Street** the rest of your lives."

"Papa," **whisper**ed Mrs. Popper, "I don't want to live on Easy Street. I want to go back to Proudfoot Avenue."

"Better consider, Mr. Popper," said the Admiral. "I can't offer you anything like that."

"You say those men at the North Pole get lonely because there are no penguins?" asked Mr. Popper.

---

2 missus 다른 사람의 부인을 부를 때 쓰는 호칭.

"Very lonely," said the Admiral.

"But if there were penguins up there, mightn't the polar bears eat them?"

"Oh, **ordinary** penguins, yes," said the Admiral **judicious**ly; "but not such highly-trained birds as yours, Mr. Popper. They could **outwit** any polar bear, I guess."

It was now Mr. Klein's turn to speak.

"In every moving picture house[3] in America little children would have the pleasure of seeing stories acted by the Popper Performing Penguins," he said.

"Of course if we succeeded in establishing the breed at the North Pole," said the Admiral, "the name might have to be changed a little. I imagine that hundreds of years from now scientists would be calling them the Popper Arctic Penguins."

Mr. Popper was silent for a moment.

"Gentlemen," he said, "I want to thank you both. I'll give you my decision tomorrow."

---

3 **moving picture house** 영화관.

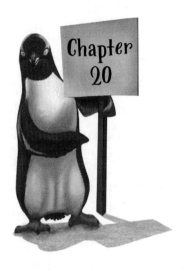

FAREWELL, MR. POPPER

IT WAS A hard decision to make. Long after the visitors had gone, Mr. and Mrs. Popper sat and discussed what was best for everybody. Mrs. Popper could see the **advantage**s of both offers, and she pointed these out, without trying to **influence** him.

"I feel that the penguins are really your **responsibility**," she said, "and you must **make up your mind**."

It was a **pale** and **haggard** Mr. Popper who was ready to **announce** his decision the next day.

"Mr. Klein," he said, "I want you to know how much

I **appreciate** your offer of putting my birds in the movies. But I am afraid I have to refuse. I do not believe the life in Hollywood would be good for the penguins."

Then he turned to Admiral Drake. "Admiral Drake, I am going to give you the birds. In doing this, I am considering the birds **first of all**. I know that they have been comfortable and happy with me. Lately, though, with the excitement and the warm weather, I've been worried about them. The birds have done so much for me that I have to do what is best for them. **After all**, they belong in a cold **climate**. And then I can't help being sorry for those men up at the North **Pole**, without any penguins to help them pass the time."

"Your Government will thank you, Mr. Popper," answered the Admiral.

"**Congratulation**s, Admiral," said Mr. Klein. "Maybe you're right at that, Popper. Hollywood might have been too much for the birds. I wish you'd let me make one short movie of them here in New York, though, before they go. Just some pictures of the sort of thing they do on the stage, you know. We'd show the film everywhere with an announcement that these are the famous Popper Penguins that are being taken to the North Pole by Admiral Drake of the United States **Arctic** Penguin **Foundation Expedition**, or something like that."

"I'd like that very much," said Mr. Popper.

"We'd pay you, of course," continued Mr. Klein. "Not a **fortune**, as we could have if you'd let us give them a **contract**, but, say, twenty-five thousand dollars."

"We could use it," said Mrs. Popper.

"It will be very quiet at 432 Proudfoot Avenue," said Mr. Popper, when everyone had left.

Mrs. Popper did not answer. She knew that nothing she could say could really **comfort** him.

"However," said Mr. Popper, "now that spring is here, a lot of people will be wanting their houses painted, so we'd better be getting back."

"Anyway," said Bill, "we've had ten whole weeks of vacation right in the middle of the year, and not many children in Stillwater can say that."

The next day the cameramen arrived to make the picture of the penguins doing their **tricks**. It was arranged that the Poppers should stay in New York just long enough to see the Expedition off.

Meanwhile, in the **harbor**, the great **sail**ing ship of Admiral Drake was being made ready for its long trip north. Every day huge boxes of **supplies** of all sorts were **hustle**d on **board**. The most comfortable **quarter**s on the ship were turned over to the penguins, who were the cause of the **voyage**.

Captain Cook was already quite familiar with the ship, since it was the same one the Admiral had sailed to the South Pole, where Captain Cook had often seen it. Greta, too, had seen **vessel**s of its kind. The two of them were kept very busy showing and explaining everything to Nelson, Columbus, Louisa, Jenny, Scott, Magellan, Adelina, Isabella, Ferdinand, and Victoria.

The sailors all took the greatest **delight** in watching the **curious** little birds at their **exploration**s.

"It looks as if this will be a pretty **lively** trip," they would say. "These Popper Penguins certainly **live up to** their **reputation**."

But at last everything was ready, and the day came when the Poppers were to go down and say good-by. Bill and Janie ran all over the ship, and did not want to leave when it was time to draw up the gangplank.[1] The Admiral shook hands with them and Mrs. Popper, and thanked them for having helped to train the **extraordinary** penguins that were to be a real **contribution** to science.

Mr. Popper had gone down below to say a private farewell to his birds. All that kept him from **breaking down** completely was the knowledge that what he was doing was best for them, too. First he said good-by to

---

1 **gangplank** 배의 건널판. 배와 부두 사이에 다리처럼 걸쳐 놓은 판자를 말한다.

all the younger penguins. Then to Greta, who had saved Captain Cook. Then, last of all, he **lean**ed over and said a special good-by to Captain Cook, who had come and made life so different for Mr. Popper.

Then he **wiped** his eyes, **straighten**ed his back, and went up on **deck** to say good-by to Admiral Drake.

"Good-by, Admiral Drake," he said.

"Good-by?" repeated the Admiral. "Why, what do you mean? Aren't you coming with us?"

"Me — go with you to the North Pole?"

"Why, of course, Mr. Popper."

"But how could I go with you? I'm not an explorer or a scientist. I'm only a house painter."

"You're the **keeper** of the penguins, aren't you?" **roar**ed the Admiral. "Man alive,[2] aren't those penguins the reason for this whole Expedition? And who's going to see that they're well and happy if you're not along? Go put on one of those **fur suit**s, like the rest of us. We're pulling **anchor** in a minute."

"Mamma," shouted Mr. Popper to Mrs. Popper, who had already gone up the gangplank, "I'm going, too! I'm going, too! Admiral Drake says he needs me. Mamma, do you mind if I don't come home for a year or two?"

---

2 man alive '맙소사', '이런 세상에'라는 뜻의 놀라움이나 당혹스러움을 나타내는 표현.

"Oh, as to that," said Mrs. Popper, "I'll miss you very much, my dear. But we have money to **live on** for a few years. And in winter it will be much easier to keep the house **tidy** without a man sitting around all day. I'll be getting back to Stillwater. Tomorrow is the day for the meeting of the Ladies' Aid and **Missionary** Society, and I'll be just **in time**. So good-by, my love, and good luck."

"Good-by and good luck!" **echo**ed the children.

And the penguins, hearing their voices, **scuttle**d up on deck and stood there beside the Admiral and Mr. Popper. Then they **solemn**ly lifted their **flipper**s and **wave**d, as the great ship moved slowly down the river toward the sea.

Richard Atwater and his wife, Florence Atwater, never intended to collaborate on a book. *Mr. Popper's Penguins* was begun by Mr. Atwater, a newspaper columnist and a onetime classics instructor at the University of Chicago. But when a serious illness forced him to stop writing, Mrs. Atwater completed the story. Together they created one of the most beloved children's books of all time.

Mr. Popper's
PENGUINS

Mr. Popper's Penguins

1판 1쇄	2016년 11월 4일
2판 3쇄	2024년 1월 15일

지은이	Richard Atwater Florence Atwater
책임편집	김보경 정소이
콘텐츠제작및감수	롱테일 교육 연구소
번역	정소이
저작권	명채린
마케팅	두잉글 사업 본부

펴낸이	이수영
펴낸곳	롱테일북스
출판등록	제2015-000191호
주소	04033 서울특별시 마포구 양화로 113, 3층(서교동, 순흥빌딩)
전자메일	help@ltinc.net

ISBN 979-11-91343-23-6 14740

Mr. Popper's
PENGUINS

FLORENCE AND RICHARD ATWATER

Contents

'아동 도서계의 노벨상!' 미국 최고 권위의 아동 문학상

뉴베리 상(Newbery Award)은 미국 도서관 협회에서 해마다 미국 아동 문학 발전에 가장 크게 이바지한 작가에게 수여하는 아동 문학상입니다. 1922년에 시작된 이 상은 미국에서 가장 오랜 역사를 지닌 아동 문학상이자, '아동 도서계의 노벨상'이라 불릴 만큼 높은 권위를 자랑하는 상입니다.

뉴베리 상은 그 역사와 권위만큼이나 심사 기준이 까다롭기로 유명한데, 심사단은 책의 주제 의식은 물론 정보의 깊이와 스토리의 정교함, 캐릭터와 문체의 적정성 등을 꼼꼼히 평가하여 수상작을 결정합니다.

그해 최고의 작품으로 선정된 도서에게는 '뉴베리 메달(Newbery Medal)'이라고 부르는 금색 메달을 수여하며, 최종 후보에 올랐던 주목할 만한 작품들에게는 '뉴베리 아너(Newbery Honor)'라는 이름의 은색 마크를 수여합니다.

뉴베리 상을 받은 도서는 미국의 모든 도서관에 비치되어 더 많은 독자들을 만나게 되며, 대부분 수십에서 수백만 부가 판매되는 베스트셀러가 됩니다. 뉴베리 상을 수상한 작가는 그만큼 필력과 작품성을 인정받게 되어, 수상 작가의 다른 작품들 또한 수상작 못지않게 커다란 주목과 사랑을 받습니다.

왜 뉴베리 수상작인가?
쉬운 어휘로 쓰인 '검증된' 영어원서!

뉴베리 수상작들은 '검증된 원서'로 국내 영어 학습자들에게 큰 사랑을 받고 있습니다. 뉴베리 수상작이 원서 읽기에 좋은 교재인 이유는 무엇일까요?

1. 아동 문학인 만큼 어휘가 어렵지 않습니다.
2. 어렵지 않은 어휘를 사용하면서도 '문학상'을 수상한 만큼 문장의 깊이가 상당합니다.
3. 적당한 난이도의 어휘와 깊이 있는 문장으로 구성되어 있기 때문에 초등 고학년부터 성인까지, 영어 초보자부터 실력자까지 모든 영어 학습자들이 읽기에 좋습니다.

실제로 뉴베리 수상작은 국제중·특목고에서는 입시 필독서로, 대학교에서는 영어 강독 교재로 다양하고 폭넓게 활용되고 있습니다. 이런 이유로 뉴베리 수상작은 한국어 번역서보다 오히려 원서가 훨씬 많이 판매되는 기현상을 보이고 있습니다.

'베스트 오브 베스트'만을 엄선한 「뉴베리 컬렉션」

「뉴베리 컬렉션」은 뉴베리 메달 및 아너 수상작, 그리고 뉴베리 수상 작가의 유명 작품들을 엄선하여 한국 영어 학습자들을 위한 최적의 교재로 재탄생시킨 영어원서 시리즈입니다.

1. 어휘 수준과 문장의 난이도, 분량 등 국내 영어 학습자들에게 적합한 정도를 종합적으로 검토하여 선정하였습니다.
2. 기존 원서 독자층 사이의 인기도까지 감안하여 최적의 작품들을 선별하였습니다.
3. 판형이 좁고 글씨가 작아 읽기 힘들었던 원서 디자인을 대폭 수정하여, 판형을 시원하게 키우고 읽기에 최적화된 영문 서체를 사용하여 가독성을 극대화하였습니다.
4. 함께 제공되는 워크북은 어려운 어휘를 완벽하게 정리하고 이해력을 점검하는 퀴즈를 덧붙여 독자들이 원서를 보다 쉽고 재미있게 읽을 수 있도록 구성하였습니다.
5. 기존에 높은 가격에 판매되어 구입이 부담스러웠던 오디오북을 부록으로 제공하여 리스닝과 소리 내어 읽기에까지 원서를 두루 활용할 수 있도록 했습니다.

리처드 앳워터(Richard Atwater)는 가족과 함께 본 남극 탐험에 대한 다큐멘터리에 감명을 받았고, 남극의 펭귄에 대한 책을 쓰게 되었습니다. 그것이 바로 『Mr. Popper's Penguins』입니다. 하지만 그는 1934년에 뇌졸중으로 쓰러져 이 작품을 끝내지 못하게 되었고, 그의 부인인 **플로렌스 앳워터(Florence Atwater)**가 그를 대신해서 작품을 마무리 짓습니다. 1938년에 출간된 『Mr. Popper's Penguins』는 큰 성공을 거두어 1939년에는 뉴베리 아너를 수상하였습니다. 『Mr. Popper's Penguins』는 전세계에서 여러 언어로 출간되었으며 2011년에는 동명의 영화가 제작될 만큼 지금까지도 많은 아이들의 사랑을 받는 아동 문학 고전입니다.

『Mr. Popper's Penguins』는 작은 도시 스틸워터(Stillwater)에 사는 주택 도장공인 파퍼 씨(Mr. Popper)에게 일어난 마법 같은 이야기를 담고 있습니다. 언제나 남극 탐험가가 되기를 마음속으로 꿈꾸지만, 현실에서는 스틸워터를 벗어난 적이 없는 파퍼 씨에게 어느 날 커다란 소포가 도착합니다. 그것은 바로 남극에서 드레이크 제독(Admiral Drake)이 파퍼 씨의 팬레터에 대해서 보낸 답장이었습니다. 소포를 풀자 그 안에는 진짜 살아있는 펭귄 한 마리가 들어 있었습니다! 펭귄과의 생활에 적응하기 위해서 파퍼 씨네 가족들은 고군분투합니다. 정신을 차려보니 어느새 펭귄은 열두 마리로 늘어납니다. 파퍼 씨와 파퍼 부인은 자신의 아이들뿐만 아니라, 이 열두 마리나 되는 펭귄들을 먹여 살릴 궁리를 하기 시작합니다. 그러면서 파퍼 씨네 가족과 열두 마리의 펭귄에게 새로운 모험이 펼쳐집니다.

이 책의 구성

원서 본문

내용이 담긴 원서 본문입니다.
원어민이 읽는 일반 원서와 같은 텍스트지만, 암기해야 할 중요 어휘들은 볼드체로 표시되어 있습니다. 이 어휘들은 지금 들고 계신 워크북에 챕터별로 정리되어 있습니다.

학습 심리학 연구 결과에 따르면, 한 단어씩 따로 외우는 단어 암기는 거의 효과가 없다고 합니다. 단어를 제대로 외우기 위해서는 문맥 (Context) 속에서 단어를 암기해야 하며, 한 단어당 문맥 속에서 15번 이상 마주칠 때 완벽하게 암기할 수 있다고 합니다.

이 책의 본문에서는 중요 어휘를 볼드체로 강조하여, 문맥 속의 단어들을 더 확실히 인지(Word Cognition in Context)하도록 돕고 있습니다. 또한 대부분의 중요 단어들은 다른 챕터에서도 반복해서 등장하기 때문에 이 책을 읽는 것만으로도 자연스럽게 어휘력을 향상시킬 수 있습니다.

또한 본문 하단에는 내용 이해를 돕기 위한 '각주'가 첨가되어 있습니다. 각주는 굳이 암기할 필요는 없지만, 알아 두면 도움이 될 만한 정보를 설명하고 있습니다. 각주를 참고하면 스토리를 더 깊이 있게 이해할 수 있어 원서를 읽는 재미가 배가됩니다.

워크북(Workbook)

Check Your Reading Speed
해당 챕터의 단어 수가 기록되어 있어, 리딩 속도를 측정할 수 있습니다. 특히 리딩 속도를 중시하는 독자들이 유용하게 사용할 수 있습니다.

Build Your Vocabulary
본문에 볼드 표시되어 있던 단어들이 정리되어 있습니다. 리딩 전 · 후에 반복해서 보면 원서를 더욱 쉽게 읽을 수 있고, 어휘력도 빠르게 향상될 것입니다.

단어는 〈스펠링 – 빈도 – 발음기호 – 품사 – 한글 뜻 – 영문 뜻〉 순서로 표기되어 있으며 빈도 표시(★)가 많을수록 필수 어휘입니다. 반복해서 등장하는 단어는 빈도 대신 '복습'으로 표기되어 있습니다. 품사는 아래와 같이 표기했습니다.

n. 명사 | a. 형용사 | ad. 부사 | v. 동사
conj. 접속사 | prep. 전치사 | int. 감탄사 | idiom 숙어 및 관용구

Comprehension Quiz
간단한 퀴즈를 통해 읽은 내용에 대한 이해력을 점검해 볼 수 있습니다.

한국어 번역
영문과 비교할 수 있도록 최대한 직역에 가까운 번역을 담았습니다.

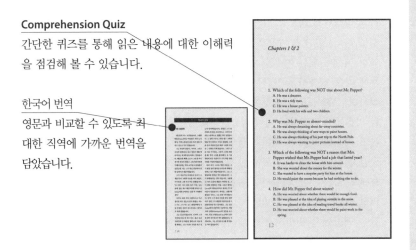

「뉴베리 컬렉션」 이렇게 읽어 보세요!

아래와 같이 프리뷰(Preview) → 리딩(Reading) → 리뷰(Review) 세 단계를 거치면서 읽으면, 더욱 효과적으로 영어 실력을 향상할 수 있습니다.

1. 프리뷰(Preview) : 오늘 읽을 내용을 먼저 점검하자!

• 워크북을 통해 오늘 읽을 챕터에 나와 있는 단어들을 쭉 훑어봅니다. 어떤 단어들이 나오는지, 내가 아는 단어와 모르는 단어는 어떤 것들이 있는지 가벼운 마음으로 살펴봅니다.

• 평소처럼 하나하나 쓰면서 암기하려고 하지는 마세요! 익숙하지 않은 단어들을 주의 깊게 보되, 어차피 리딩을 하면서 점차 익숙해질 단어라는 것을 기억하며 빠르게 훑어봅니다.

• 뒤 챕터로 갈수록 '복습'이라고 표시된 단어들이 늘어나는 것을 알 수 있습니다. '복습' 단어인데도 여전히 익숙하지 않다면 더욱 신경을 써서 봐야겠죠? 매일매일 꾸준히 읽는다면, 익숙한 단어들이 점점 많아진다는 것을 몸으로 느낄 수 있습니다.

2. 리딩(Reading) : 내용에 집중하며 빠르게 읽어 나가자!

• 프리뷰를 마친 후 바로 리딩을 시작합니다. 방금 살펴봤던 어휘들을 문장 속에서 다시 만나게 되는데, 이 과정에서 단어의 쓰임새와 어감을 자연스럽게 익히게 됩니다.

• 모르는 단어나 이해되지 않는 문장이 나오더라도 멈추지 말고 전체적인 맥락을 파악하면서 속도감 있게 읽어 나가세요. 이해되지 않는 문장들은 따로 표시를 하되, 일단 넘어가고 계속 읽는 것이 좋습니다. 뒷부분을 읽다 보면 자연히 이해가 되는 경우도 있고, 정 이해가 되지 않는 부분은 리딩을 마친 이후에 따로 리뷰하는 시간을 가지면 됩니다. 문제집을 풀듯이 모든 문장을 분석하면서 원서를 읽는 것이 아니라, 리딩을 할 때는 리딩에만, 리뷰를 할 때는 리뷰에만 집중하는 것이 필요합니다.

• 볼드 처리된 단어의 의미가 궁금하더라도 워크북을 바로 펼치지 마세요. 정 궁금하다면 한 번씩 참고하는 것도 나쁘진 않지만, 워크북과 원서를 번갈아 보면서 읽는 것은 리딩의 흐름을 끊고 단어 하나하나에 집착하는 좋지 않은 리딩 습관을 심어 줄 수 있습니다.

• 같은 맥락에서 번역서를 구해 원서와 동시에 번갈아 보는 것도 좋은 방법이 아닙니다. 한글 번역을 가지고 있다고 해도 일단 영어로 읽을 때는 영어에만 집중하고 어느 정도 분량을 읽은 후에 번역서와 비교하도록 하세요.

10

모든 문장을 일일이 번역해서 완벽하게 이해하려는 것은 오히려 좋지 않은 리딩 습관을 심어 주어 장기적으로는 바람직하지 않은 결과를 얻을 수 있습니다. 처음부터 완벽하게 이해하려고 하는 것보다는 빠른 속도로 2-3회 반복해서 읽는 방식이 실력 향상에 더 도움이 됩니다. 만일 반복해서 읽어도 내용이 전혀 이해되지 않아 곤란하다면 책 선정에 문제가 있다고 할 수 있습니다. 그럴 때는 좀 더 쉬운 책을 골라 실력을 다진 뒤 다시 도전하는 것이 좋습니다.

• 초보자라면 분당 150단어의 리딩 속도를 목표로 잡고 리딩을 합니다. 분당 150단어는 원어민이 말하는 속도로, 영어 학습자들이 리스닝과 스피킹으로 넘어가기 위해 가장 기초적으로 달성해야 하는 단계입니다. 분당 50-80단어 정도의 낮은 리딩 속도를 가지고 있는 경우는 대부분 영어 실력이 부족해서라기보다 '잘못된 리딩 습관'을 가지고 있어서 그렇습니다. 이해력이 조금 떨어진다고 하더라도 분당 150단어까지는 속도에 대한 긴장감을 놓치지 말고 속도감 있게 읽어 나가도록 하세요.

3. 리뷰(Review) : 이해력을 점검하고 꼼꼼하게 다시 살펴보자!

• 해당 챕터의 Comprehension Quiz를 통해 이해력을 점검해 봅니다.

• 오늘 만난 어휘들을 다시 한번 복습합니다. 이때는 읽으면서 중요하다고 생각했던 단어를 연습장에 써 보면서 꼼꼼하게 외우는 것도 좋습니다.

• 이해가 되지 않는다고 표시해 두었던 부분도 주의 깊게 분석해 봅니다. 다시 한번 문장을 꼼꼼히 읽고, 어떤 이유에서 이해가 되지 않았는지 생각해 봅니다. 따로 메모를 남기거나 노트를 작성하는 것도 좋은 방법입니다.

• 사실 꼼꼼히 리뷰하는 것은 매우 고된 과정입니다. 원서를 읽고 리뷰하는 시간을 가지는 것이 영어 실력 향상에 많은 도움이 되기는 하지만, 이 과정을 철저히 지키려다가 원서 읽기의 재미를 반감시키는 것은 바람직하지 않습니다. 그럴 때는 차라리 리뷰를 가볍게 하는 것이 좋을 수 있습니다. '내용에 빠져서 재미있게', 문제집에서는 상상도 못할 '많은 양'을 읽으면서, 매일매일 조금씩 꾸준히 실력을 키워 가는 것이 원서를 활용하는 기본적인 방법이며, 영어 공부의 왕도입니다. 문제집 풀듯이 원서 읽기를 시도하고 접근해서는 실패할 수밖에 없습니다.

• 이런 방식으로 원서를 끝까지 다 읽었다면, 다시 반복해서 읽거나 오디오북을 활용하는 등 다양한 방식으로 원서 읽기를 확장해 나갈 수 있습니다. 이에 대한 자세한 안내가 워크북 말미에 실려 있습니다.

Chapters 1 & 2

1. Which of the following was NOT true about Mr. Popper?
   A. He was a dreamer.
   B. He was a tidy man.
   C. He was a house painter.
   D. He lived with his wife and two children.

2. Why was Mr. Popper so absent-minded?
   A. He was always dreaming about far-away countries.
   B. He was always thinking of new ways to paint houses.
   C. He was always thinking of his past trip to the North Pole.
   D. He was always wanting to paint pictures instead of houses.

3. Which of the following was NOT a reason that Mrs. Popper wished that Mr. Popper had a job that lasted year?
   A. It was harder to clean the house with him around.
   B. She was worried about the money for the winter.
   C. She wanted to have a surprise party for him at the house.
   D. He would paint the rooms because he had nothing else to do.

4. How did Mr. Popper feel about winter?
   A. He was worried about whether there would be enough food.
   B. He was pleased at the idea of playing outside in the snow.
   C. He was pleased at the idea of reading travel books all winter.
   D. He was worried about whether there would be paint work in the spring.

5. Why did Mrs. Popper respond a little sharply to Mr. Popper mentioning the movies of the Drake Expedition?
   A. She was a very disagreeable woman.
   B. She was worried about money.
   C. She was never invited to movies.
   D. She thought that movies were boring.

6. How did Mr. Popper say that penguins knew if water was safe to jump into?
   A. They would push rocks into the water.
   B. They would all enter the water at once.
   C. They would check to see where ice was broken.
   D. They would crowd and push a penguin into the water.

7. Why was Mr. Popper surprised when listening to the radio broadcast?
   A. Admiral Drake told Mr. Popper that he was sending him a penguin.
   B. Admiral Drake spoke to him and told him to watch for a surprise.
   C. Admiral Drake was quitting his expedition and going to Stillwater.
   D. Admiral Drake had made a new and important discovery at the South Pole.

Check Your Reading Speed

1분에 몇 단어를 읽는지 리딩 속도를 측정해보세요.

$$\frac{822 \text{ words}}{\text{reading time ( ) sec}} \times 60 = (\quad) \text{ WPM}$$

Build Your Vocabulary

pleasant**
[plézənt]

a. 쾌적한, 즐거운; 상냥한, 예의 바른
Something that is pleasant is nice, enjoyable, or attractive.

bucket*
[bʌ́kit]

n. 양동이, 들통
A bucket is a round metal or plastic container with a handle attached to its sides.

ladder*
[lǽdər]

n. 사다리
A ladder is a piece of equipment used for climbing up something or down from something.

board***
[bɔːrd]

n. 판자; 이사회; v. 승선하다, 탑승하다
A board is a flat, thin, rectangular piece of wood or plastic which is used for a particular purpose.

spatter
[spǽtər]

v. (액체 방울 등이) 튀기다; 후두두 떨어지다; n. (액체 등이) 튀는 것
If a thick wet substance splatters on something or is splattered on it, it drops or is thrown over it.

wallpaper
[wɔ́ːlpeipər]

n. 벽지
Wallpaper is thick colored or patterned paper that is used for covering and decorating the walls of rooms.

cling*
[kliŋ]

v. 들러붙다; 매달리다, 꼭 붙잡다; 애착을 갖다
If you cling to someone or something, you hold onto them tightly.

whisker*
[wískər]

n. (pl.) 구레나룻; (고양이·쥐 등의) 수염
You can refer to the hair on a man's face, especially on the sides of his face, as his whiskers.

untidy*
[ʌntáidi]

a. 깔끔하지 못한; 단정치 못한, 어수선한
If you describe a person as untidy, you mean that they do not care about whether things are neat and well arranged, for example in their house.

housewife*
[háuswàif]

n. (pl. housewives) (전업)주부
A housewife is a woman whose main occupation is caring for her family, managing household affairs, and doing housework, while her husband or partner goes out to work.

smooth**
[smuːð]

v. 고루 펴 바르다; 매끈하게 하다; a. 매끈한; 순조로운
If you smooth something, you move your hands over its surface to make it smooth and flat.

paste
[peist]

n. 풀; (밀가루 등의) 반죽; v. 풀로 붙이다
Paste is a soft, wet, sticky mixture of a substance and a liquid, which can be used to stick things together.

admire
[ædmáiər]

v. 감탄하다; 존경하다, 칭찬하다
If you admire someone or something, you look at them with pleasure.

absent-minded
[æbsənt-máindid]

a. 멍하니 있는, 넋놓은, 방심 상태의
Someone who is absent-minded forgets things or does not pay attention to what they are doing.

dearly
[díərli]

ad. 대단히, 몹시; 비싼 대가를 치르고
If you love someone dearly, you love them very much.

settle down

idiom (조용히 한 곳에 자리 잡고) 정착하다; 편안히 앉다
To settle down means to start to have a calmer or quieter way of life, without many changes, especially living in one place.

peak
[pi:k]

n. (산의) 봉우리; 뾰족한 끝; 절정, 정점; v. 최고조에 달하다
A peak is a mountain or the top of a mountain.

dive
[daiv]

v. 잠수하다; (물 속으로 거꾸로) 뛰어들다; n. (물 속으로) 뛰어들기
If you dive, you go under the surface of the sea or a lake, using special breathing equipment.

above all

idiom 무엇보다도; 특히
You say above all to indicate that the thing you are mentioning is the most important point.

pole
[poul]

n. (지구의) 극; 기둥, 장대
The earth's poles are the two opposite ends of its axis, its most northern and southern points.

regret
[rigrét]

v. 후회하다; 안타깝게 생각하다; n. 유감, 애석; 후회
If you regret something that you have done, you wish that you had not done it.

expanse
[ikspǽns]

n. 넓게 퍼진 지역; 팽창, 확장
An expanse of something, usually sea, sky, or land, is a very large amount of it.

polar
[póulər]

a. 북극의, 남극의, 극지의; 정반대되는
Polar means near the North and South Poles.

expedition
[èkspədíʃən]

n. 탐험, 원정; 원정대
An expedition is an organized journey that is made for a particular purpose such as exploration.

Arctic
[á:rktik]

n. 북극; a. 북극의, 북극 지방의
The Arctic is the area of the world around the North Pole.

Antarctic
[æntá:rktik]

n. 남극; a. 남극의, 남극 지방의
The Antarctic is the area around the South Pole.

explore
[iksplɔ́:r]

v. 탐험하다, 탐사하다; 분석하다 (explorer n. 탐험가)
An explorer is someone who travels to places about which very little is known, in order to discover what is there.

authority**
[əθɔ́:rəti]

n. 권위자; 지휘권; 권한
Someone who is an authority on a particular subject knows a lot about it.

subject**
[sʌ́bdʒikt]

n. (논의 등의) 주제, 대상; 학과, 과목; a. ~의 권한 아래 있는
The subject of something such as a conversation, letter, or book is the thing that is being discussed or written about.

region**
[rí:dʒən]

n. 지방, 지역, 영역
A region is a large area of land that is different from other areas of land.

globe**
[gloub]

n. 지구본; 지구; 세계; 구체
A globe is a ball-shaped object with a map of the world on it.

spot**
[spat]

n. (특정한) 곳, 장소; (작은) 점; v. 발견하다, 찾다, 알아채다
You can refer to a particular place as a spot.

make one's way

idiom 나아가다, 가다
When you make your way somewhere, you walk or travel there.

neat**
[ni:t]

a. 아기자기한; 정돈된, 단정한; 깔끔한
If you describe someone or something as neat, you mean that they are small and pleasing in appearance.

paper***
[péipər]

v. 도배하다; n. 신문; 벽지
If you paper a wall, you put wallpaper on it.

sigh*
[sai]

v. 한숨을 쉬다, 한숨짓다; 탄식하듯 말하다; n. 한숨
When you sigh, you let out a deep breath, as a way of expressing feelings such as disappointment, tiredness, or pleasure.

last**
[læst]

v. (특정한 시간 동안) 계속되다; 오래가다; 충분하다; ad. 맨 끝에, 마지막에
If an event, situation, or problem lasts for a particular length of time, it continues to exist or happen for that length of time.

sweep**
[swi:p]

v. (빗자루·손 등으로) 쓸다; (거칠게) 휩쓸고 가다; n. 쓸기, 비질하기
If you sweep an area of floor or ground, you push dirt or rubbish off it using a brush with a long handle.

firm***
[fə:rm]

a. 단호한, 확고한; 단단한 (firmly ad. 단호하게)
If you describe someone as firm, you mean they behave in a way that shows that they are not going to change their mind, or that they are the person who is in control.

daresay

idiom 아마도 ~일 것이다
You can use 'I daresay' before or after a statement to indicate that you believe it is probably true.

get along

idiom 해나가다, 살아가다; 사이 좋게 지내다
To get along means to manage to continue doing something or make progress in a situation.

roast*
[roust]

a. 구운; v. 굽다; ~을 데우다; (남을) 혹평하다; n. 구이 요리
Roast meat has been cooked by dry heat in an oven or over a fire.

16

supper*
[sʌ́pər]

n. 저녁 (식사)
Some people refer to the main meal eaten in the early part of the evening as supper.

litter*
[lítər]

n. 어질러져 있는 것들; 쓰레기; v. 흐트러져 어지럽히다; (쓰레기 등을) 버리다
A litter of things is a quantity of them that are lying around in a disorganized way.

Check Your Reading Speed

1분에 몇 단어를 읽는지 리딩 속도를 측정해 보세요.

$$\frac{942 \text{ words}}{\text{reading time ( ) sec}} \times 60 = (\quad) \text{ WPM}$$

Build Your Vocabulary

settle down^{복습}
idiom 편안히 앉다; (조용히 한 곳에 자리 잡고) 정착하다
To settle down means to get yourself into a comfortable position when you are sitting or lying.

neat^{복습}
[ni:t]
a. 정돈된, 단정한; 깔끔한; 아기자기한
A neat place, thing, or person is tidy and smart, and has everything in the correct place.

geography**
[dʒiágrəfi]
n. 지리학 (geographic a. 지리학의, 지리적인)
Geographical or geographic means concerned with or relating to the study of the Earth's physical features and the people, plants, and animals that live in different regions of the world.

mend***
[mend]
v. (옷 등을) 꿰매다, 수선하다; (문제·불화 등을) 해결하다 (mending n. 수선할 것)
Mending is the sewing and repairing of clothes that have got holes in them.

globe^{복습}
[gloub]
n. 지구본; 지구; 세계; 구체
A globe is a ball-shaped object with a map of the world on it.

sigh^{복습}
[sai]
v. 한숨을 쉬다, 한숨짓다; 탄식하듯 말하다; n. 한숨
When you sigh, you let out a deep breath, as a way of expressing feelings such as disappointment, tiredness, or pleasure.

last^{복습}
[læst]
v. 충분하다; (특정한 시간 동안) 계속되다; 오래가다; ad. 맨 끝에, 마지막에
If something lasts for a particular length of time, it continues to be able to be used for that time.

spectacle*
[spéktəkl]
n. (pl.) 안경; 광경, 장관
Glasses are sometimes referred to as spectacles.

pleased*
[pli:zd]
a. 기뻐하는, 만족해하는
If you are pleased, you are happy about something or satisfied with something.

prospect**
[práspekt]
n. (어떤 일이 있을) 기대, 가망; 전망
If there is some prospect of something happening, there is a possibility that it will happen.

interrupt**
[intərápt]
v. (말·행동을) 방해하다; 중단시키다
If you interrupt someone who is speaking, you say or do something that causes them to stop.

Antarctic^{복습}
[æntá:rktik]
a. 남극의, 남극 지방의; n. 남극
The Antarctic is the area around the South Pole.

18

pole ^{복습}
[poul]

n. (지구의) 극; 기둥, 장대
The earth's poles are the two opposite ends of its axis, its most northern and southern points.

dull**
[dʌl]

a. 따분한, 지루한
If you describe someone or something as dull, you mean they are not interesting or exciting.

expedition ^{복습}
[èkspədíʃən]

n. 원정대; 탐험, 원정
An expedition is an organized journey that is made for a particular purpose such as exploration.

sharply*
[ʃáːrpli]

ad. (비판 등을) 날카롭게, 신랄하게
If someone says something sharply, they say it suddenly and rather firmly or angrily.

disagreeable*
[dìsəgríːəbl]

a. 무례한, 무뚝뚝한; 유쾌하지 못한
Someone who is disagreeable is unfriendly or unhelpful.

cross***
[krɔːs]

a. 짜증난, 약간 화가 난; v. (가로질러) 건너다; 서로 겹치게 놓다; 반대하다
Someone who is cross is rather angry or irritated.

go on

idiom 말을 계속하다; (어떤 상황이) 계속되다
To go on means to continue speaking after a short pause.

no wonder

idiom ~하는 것도 당연하다; ~은 (별로) 놀랄 일이 아니다
If you say 'no wonder,' 'little wonder,' or 'small wonder,' you mean that something is not surprising.

erect*
[irékt]

a. 똑바로 선, 직립의; v. 직립시키다, 곤두 세우다
People or things that are erect are straight and upright.

stomach**
[stʌ́mək]

n. 복부, 배
You can refer to the front part of your body below your waist as your stomach.

slide*
[slaid]

v. 미끄러지다; 슬며시 움직이다; n. 떨어짐; 미끄러짐
When something slides somewhere or when you slide it there, it moves there smoothly over or against something.

beg*
[beg]

v. 간청하다, 애원하다; 구걸하다
If you beg someone to do something, you ask them very anxiously or eagerly to do it.

kitten*
[kitn]

n. 새끼 고양이
A kitten is a very young cat.

tidy**
[táidi]

a. 깔끔한, 잘 정돈된, 단정한; v. 치우다, 정돈하다
Something that is tidy is neat and is arranged in an organized way.

to say nothing of

idiom (게다가) ~은 말할 것도 없고
You use to say nothing of when you mention an additional thing which gives even more strength to the point you are making.

feed**
[fiːd]

v. 먹이를 주다; 공급하다; n. (동물의) 먹이
If you feed a person or animal, you give them food to eat and sometimes actually put it in their mouths.

goldfish
[góuldfiʃ]

n. 금붕어
Goldfish are small gold or orange fish which are often kept as pets.

intelligent**
[intélədʒənt]

a. 총명한, 똑똑한; 지능이 있는
A person or animal that is intelligent has the ability to think, understand, and learn things quickly and well.

shrimp
[ʃrimp]

n. 새우
Shrimps are small shellfish with long tails and many legs.

edge**
[edʒ]

n. 끝, 가장자리, 모서리; 우위; v. 조금씩 움직이다
The edge of something is the place or line where it stops, or the part of it that is furthest from the middle.

bank**
[bæŋk]

n. 둑, 제방; 은행
A bank is a raised area of land along the side of a river.

shove*
[ʃʌv]

v. (거칠게) 밀치다; 아무렇게나 놓다; n. 힘껏 떠밂
If you shove someone or something, you push them with a quick, violent movement.

tone*
[toun]

n. 어조, 말투; (글 등의) 분위기; 음색
Someone's tone is a quality in their voice which shows what they are feeling or thinking.

heathen
[híːðən]

a. 야만적인; 이교도의; n. 교양 없는 사람, 야만인
If you describe someone as heathen, you mean that they behave as if they are not educated.

queer*
[kwiər]

a. 별난, 기묘한, 이상한
Something that is queer is strange.

polar복습
[póulər]

a. 북극의, 남극의, 극지의; 정반대되는
Polar means near the North and South Poles.

yawn*
[jɔːn]

v. 하품하다; n. 하품
If you yawn, you open your mouth very wide and breathe in more air than usual, often when you are tired or when you are not interested in something.

missionary*
[míʃənèri]

a. 전도의, 선교(사)의; n. 선교사
Missionary is relating to or characteristic of a missionary or a religious mission.

what of it

idiom 그래서 뭐?
You say 'what of it?' or 'so what?' to indicate that the previous remark seems unimportant, uninteresting, or irrelevant to you.

hasty*
[héisti]

a. 서두른, 성급한; 경솔한 (hastily ad. 급히, 서둘러서)
A hasty movement, action, or statement is sudden, and often done in reaction to something that has just happened.

switch*
[swiʧ]

n. 스위치; 전환; v. 전환하다, 바꾸다; 엇바꾸다
A switch is a small control for an electrical device which you use to turn the device on or off.

20

broadcast^{**}
[brɔ́:dkæst]

v. 방송하다; 널리 알리다, 광고하다; n. 방송
To broadcast a program means to send it out by radio waves, so that it can be heard on the radio or seen on television.

command^{**}
[kəmǽnd]

v. 지시하다, 명령하다; ~을 장악하다; n. 명령; 지휘
If someone in authority commands you to do something, they tell you that you must do it.

buzz[*]
[bʌz]

n. 윙윙거리는 소리; 웅성거림; v. 윙윙거리다; 부산스럽다, 활기가 넘치다
You can use buzz to refer to a long continuous sound, usually caused by lots of people talking at once.

faint[*]
[feint]

a. 희미한, 약한; v. 실신하다, 기절하다; n. 실신, 기절
A faint sound, color, mark, feeling, or quality has very little strength or intensity.

float^{**}
[flout]

v. (물 위나 공중에서) 떠가다; (물에) 뜨다
Something that floats in or through the air hangs in it or moves slowly and gently through it.

gracious[*]
[gréiʃəs]

int. 세상에, 맙소사; a. 우아한; 자애로운, 품위 있는
Some people say 'good gracious' or 'goodness gracious' in order to express surprise or annoyance.

exclaim[*]
[ikskléim]

v. 소리치다, 외치다
If you exclaim, you cry out suddenly in surprise, strong emotion, or pain.

watch for

idiom (~이 나타나기를) 기다리다
If you watch for someone or something, you pay attention so that you will see them when they arrive or something happens.

sign off

idiom 방송을 마치다; 편지를 끝맺다
To sign off means to end a broadcast by saying goodbye or playing a piece of music.

impress[*]
[imprés]

v. 깊은 인상을 주다, 감동을 주다 (impressed a. 감명을 받은)
If something impresses you, you feel great admiration for it.

Chapters 3 & 4

1. How did Mr. Popper know the box contained a penguin?
    A. There was a picture of a penguin on the box.
    B. He could see the penguin through the holes.
    C. The postman told him it was from Antarctica.
    D. He had heard the penguin sound before at the movies.

2. How did the penguin react to Mr. Popper's house?
    A. He was very scared and hid in the bathroom.
    B. He was very curious and begin to inspect the house.
    C. He was very tired and went to sleep in the bedroom.
    D. He was very hungry and went to eat in the kitchen.

3. Why did Mr. Popper think the penguin liked the bathroom?
    A. He thought that the penguin liked to swim in the bathtub.
    B. He thought that the bathroom was the coldest room in the house.
    C. He thought that all the white tiling reminded him of ice and snow.
    D. He thought that the penguin wanted to play with the faucets.

4. Why did Mr. Popper name the penguin Cook?
    A. The penguin liked to cook food.
    B. The penguin was going to sleep in the kitchen.
    C. The explorer Captain Cook had discovered Antarctica.
    D. It sounded like he was saying something like 'Cook.'

5. How did Mrs. Popper feel about Captain Cook pecking her ankle when they went into the living room?

   A. She wanted to get rid of the penguin immediately.

   B. She thought that penguins were just naturally mean.

   C. She forgave him and thought he only did it out of curiosity.

   D. She worried that he would peck holes in all of their furniture.

6. Why was Mrs. Popper upset with Captain Cook in the dining room?

   A. Captain Cook had spilled water all over the floor.

   B. Captain Cook ate all of the goldfish in the bowl.

   C. Captain Cook broke her favorite dishes on the table.

   D. Captain Cook pecked at all of the food but wouldn't eat any of it.

7. How did Mr. Popper want to make Captain Cook more comfortable while sleeping?

   A. He put some ice cubes under him.

   B. He wanted to wrap him in a blanket.

   C. He wanted to leave the light on for him.

   D. He moved the refrigerator into the living room.

Check Your Reading Speed

1분에 몇 단어를 읽는지 리딩 속도를 측정해 보세요.

$$\frac{1,050 \text{ words}}{\text{reading time ( ) sec}} \times 60 = (\quad) \text{ WPM}$$

Build Your Vocabulary

curious**
[kjúəriəs]
a. 궁금한; 호기심이 많은; 별난, 특이한 (curiosity n. 호기심)
Curiosity is a desire to know about something.

paper복습
[péipər]
v. 도배하다; n. 신문; 벽지
If you paper a wall, you put wallpaper on it.

be left over
idiom (필요한 것을 쓰고 난 뒤) 남다
If food or money is left over, it remains when the rest has been eaten or used up.

mayor*
[meiər]
n. (시·군 등의) 시장
The mayor of a town or city is the person who has been elected to represent it for a fixed period of time or to run its government.

firm복습
[fə:rm]
a. 단호한, 확고한; 단단한 (firmly ad. 단호하게)
If you describe someone as firm, you mean they behave in a way that shows that they are not going to change their mind, or that they are the person who is in control.

missionary복습
[míʃənèri]
a. 전도의, 선교(사)의; n. 선교사
Missionary is relating to or characteristic of a missionary or a religious mission.

mess*
[mes]
n. (지저분하고) 엉망인 상태; (많은 문제로) 엉망인 상황; v. 엉망으로 만들다
If you say that something is a mess or in a mess, you think that it is in an untidy state.

meek*
[mi:k]
a. 유순한, 순한, 온순한 (meekly ad. 유순하게)
If you describe a person as meek, you think that they are gentle and quiet, and likely to do what other people say.

settle down복습
idiom 편안히 앉다; (조용히 한 곳에 자리 잡고) 정착하다
To settle down means to get yourself into a comfortable position when you are sitting or lying.

globe복습
[gloub]
n. 지구본; 지구; 세계; 구체
A globe is a ball-shaped object with a map of the world on it.

keep one's mind on
idiom ~에 주의를 기울이다; 전념하다
If you keep your mind on someone or something, you concentrate on them.

stray^{★★}
[strei]

v. (생각 등이) 옆길로 새다; 제 위치를 벗어나다; a. 길 잃은; 빗나간
If your mind or your eyes stray, you do not concentrate on or look at one particular subject, but start thinking about or looking at other things.

fortunately[★]
[fɔ́ːrtʃənətli]

ad. 다행스럽게도, 운 좋게도
Fortunately is used to introduce or indicate a statement about an event or situation that is good.

ring^{★★}
[riŋ]

n. 종소리; 벨을 누르기; v. (종이) 울리다; (어떤 특질이) 그득하다
A ring is the sound a bell makes.

postman
[póustmæn]

n. 우편집배원, 우체부
A postman is a man whose job is to collect and deliver letters and packages that are sent by post.

bother[★]
[báðər]

v. 신경 쓰다, 애를 쓰다; 괴롭히다; 귀찮게 하다; n. 성가심
If you do not bother to do something or if you do not bother with it, you do not do it, consider it, or use it because you think it is unnecessary or because you are too lazy.

grumble[★]
[grʌmbl]

v. 투덜거리다, 불평하다; n. 투덜댐; 불평
If someone grumbles, they complain about something in a bad-tempered way.

party^{★★★}
[páːrti]

n. 특정인, 사람; 일행; 모임, 파티; 당, 당파
A party can be referred to a person, especially one with specified characteristics.

Antarctica
[æntáːrktikə]

n. 남극 대륙
The Antarctica is a continent around the South Pole.

examine^{★★★}
[igzǽmin]

v. 조사하다; 검사하다; 시험을 실시하다
If you examine something, you look at it carefully.

marking
[máːrkiŋ]

n. (도로·차량 등에 그려진) 표시; 무늬
Markings are colored lines, shapes, or patterns on the surface of something, which help to identify it.

unpack
[ʌnpǽk]

v. 꺼내다, (짐을) 풀다
When you unpack a suitcase, box, or similar container, or you unpack the things inside it, you take the things out of the container.

at once

idiom 즉시, 당장; 동시에, 한꺼번에
If you do something at once, you do it immediately.

notice^{★★★}
[nóutis]

v. 알아채다, 인지하다; 주목하다; n. 신경씀, 주목, 알아챔
If you notice something or someone, you become aware of them.

punch[★]
[pʌntʃ]

v. 구멍을 뚫다; 주먹으로 치다; n. 주먹으로 침
If you punch holes in something, you make holes in it by pushing or pressing it with something sharp.

lose no time in

idiom 곧 ~하다
If you lose no time in doing something, you do it quickly and without delay.

board^{복습}
[bɔːrd]

n. 판자; 이사회; v. 승선하다, 탑승하다
A board is a flat, thin, rectangular piece of wood or plastic which is used for a particular purpose.

layer*
[leiər]

n. 층, 막; v. 층층이 놓다
A layer of a material or substance is a quantity or piece of it that covers a surface or that is between two other things.

faint^{복습}
[feint]

a. 희미한, 약한; v. 실신하다, 기절하다; n. 실신, 기절
A faint sound, color, mark, feeling, or quality has very little strength or intensity.

tremble*
[trembl]

v. (몸을) 떨다; (가볍게) 흔들리다; (걱정·두려움으로) 떨리다; n. 떨림, 전율
If you tremble, you shake slightly because you are frightened or cold.

scarcely*
[skéərsli]

ad. 겨우, 간신히; 거의 ~않다; ~하자마자
You use scarcely to emphasize that something is only just true or only just the case.

wrap**
[ræp]

v. 싸다, 포장하다; 둘러싸다; n. 포장지 (wrapping n. 포장 재료, 포장지)
Wrapping is something such as paper or plastic which is used to cover and protect something.

slight**
[slait]

a. 약간의, 조금의; 작고 여윈, 가냘픈
Something that is slight is very small in degree or quantity.

doubt***
[daut]

n. 의심, 의혹; v. 확신하지 못하다, 의심하다
If you say you have no doubt about it, you mean that you are certain it is true.

speechless
[spíːʃlis]

a. 말을 못 하는
If you are speechless, you are temporarily unable to speak, usually because something has shocked you.

delight*
[diláit]

n. 기쁨, 즐거움; v. 많은 기쁨을 주다, 아주 즐겁게 하다
Delight is a feeling of very great pleasure.

flipper
[flípər]

n. (바다표범·거북 등의) 지느러미발; (잠수·수영 때 신는) 오리발
The flippers of an animal that lives in water, for example a seal or a penguin, are the two or four flat limbs which it uses for swimming.

debris
[dəbríː]

n. 파편, 잔해; 쓰레기
Debris is pieces from something that has been destroyed or pieces of rubbish or unwanted material that are spread around.

stout*
[staut]

a. 통통한; 용감한, 굳센
A stout person is rather fat.

fellow**
[félou]

n. 녀석, 친구; 동료, 동년배; a. 동료의
A fellow is a man or boy.

smooth^{복습}
[smuːð]

a. 매끈한; 순조로운; v. 매끈하게 하다; 고루 펴 바르다
A smooth surface has no roughness, lumps, or holes.

drag*
[dræg]

v. 질질 끌리다; 끌고 가다; 힘들게 움직이다; n. 끌기; 장애물
If you drag something, you pull it along the ground, often with difficulty.

26

inspect*
[inspékt]

v. 면밀하게 살피다, 점검하다; 시찰하다
If you inspect something, you look at every part of it carefully in order to find out about it or check that it is all right.

pompous
[pámpəs]

a. 점잔 빼는, 거드름 피우는
If you describe someone as pompous, you mean that they behave or speak in a very serious way because they think they are more important than they really are.

strut
[strʌt]

n. 거만한 걸음걸이; 지주, 버팀대; v. 점잔 빼며 걷다
A strut is a proud and confident way of walking.

pleased복습
[pli:zd]

a. 기뻐하는, 만족해하는
If you are pleased, you are happy about something or satisfied with something.

tiling
[táiliŋ]

n. 타일을 붙인 면
You can refer to a surface that is covered by tiles as tiling.

thirsty*
[θə́:rsti]

a. 목이 마른, 갈증이 나는; (~을) 갈망하는
If you are thirsty, you feel a need to drink something.

bathtub
[bǽθtʌ̀b]

n. (서양식) 욕조
A bathtub is a long container which is filled with water so that a person can sit or lie in it to wash their whole body.

inquisitive
[inkwízətiv]

a. 호기심이 많은, 듣고 싶어 하는, 알고 싶어 하는
An inquisitive person likes finding out about things, especially secret things.

bite**
[bait]

v. (이빨로) 물다; n. 물기; 한 입
If an animal or person bites you, they use their teeth to hurt or injure you.

faucet*
[fɔ́:sit]

n. 수도꼭지
A faucet is a device that controls the flow of a liquid or gas from a pipe or container.

beak*
[bi:k]

n. (새의) 부리
A bird's beak is the hard curved or pointed part of its mouth.

tub*
[tʌb]

n. 목욕통, 욕조; 통
A tub is the same as a bathtub which is a long, usually rectangular container that you fill with water and sit in to wash your body.

explore복습
[iksplɔ́:r]

v. 탐험하다, 탐사하다; 분석하다 (explorer n. 탐험가)
An explorer is someone who travels to places about which very little is known, in order to discover what is there.

stopper
[stápər]

n. (병의) 마개
A stopper is a piece of glass, plastic, or cork that fits into the top of a bottle or jar to close it.

burst**
[bə:rst]

v. (burst-burst) 불쑥 움직이다; 터지다, 파열하다; n. 파열
To burst into or out of a place means to enter or leave it suddenly with a lot of energy or force.

march***
[ma:rʧ]

v. 행진하다; (단호한 태도로 급히) 걸어가다; n. 행진, 행군; 행진곡
When soldiers march somewhere, or when a commanding officer marches them somewhere, they walk there with very regular steps, as a group.

nod**
[nad]

n. (고개를) 끄덕임, 까딱거림; v. (고개를) 끄덕이다, 까딱하다
A nod is a movement up and down with the head.

parade*
[pəréid]

v. (과시하듯) 걸어 다니다; 행진하다; n. 퍼레이드, 가두 행진
If someone parades, they walk about somewhere in order to be seen and admired.

awful**
[ɔ́:fəl]

a. 엄청; 끔찍한, 지독한 (awfully ad. 정말, 몹시)
You can use awfully before an adjective or adverb to mean very or extremely.

slippery*
[slípəri]

a. 미끄러운
Something that is slippery is smooth, wet, or oily and is therefore difficult to walk on or to hold.

outstretched
[àutstréʧt]

a. 쭉 뻗은
If a part of the body of a person or animal is outstretched, it is stretched out as far as possible.

toboggan
[təbágən]

v. 썰매를 타다; n. 터보건 (썰매)
If you toboggan, you move along on a light wooden board with a curved front, to travel down hills on snow or ice.

stomach^{복습}
[stʌ́mək]

n. 복부, 배
You can refer to the front part of your body below your waist as your stomach.

sleeve*
[sli:v]

n. 소매
The sleeves of a coat, shirt, or other item of clothing are the parts that cover your arms.

slide^{복습}
[slaid]

v. 미끄러지다; 슬며시 움직이다; n. 떨어짐; 미끄러짐
When something slides somewhere or when you slide it there, it moves there smoothly over or against something.

glossy
[glási]

a. 광택이 나는, 번질번질한
Glossy means smooth and shiny.

Check Your Reading Speed

1분에 몇 단어를 읽는지 리딩 속도를 측정해 보세요.

$$\frac{1{,}082 \text{ words}}{\text{reading time ( ) sec}} \times 60 = (\quad) \text{ WPM}$$

Build Your Vocabulary

go on 복습
idiom 말을 계속하다; (어떤 상황이) 계속되다
To go on means to continue speaking after a short pause.

recover**
[rikʌ́vər]
v. (의식 등을) 되찾다; 회복되다; (손실 등을) 되찾다
If you recover from an unhappy or unpleasant experience, you stop being upset by it.

revolution*
[rèvəlúːʃən]
n. 혁명; 개혁
A revolution is a successful attempt by a large group of people to change the political system of their country by force.

sail**
[seil]
v. 항해하다; 미끄러지듯 나아가다; n. 돛; 항해
You say a ship sails when it moves over the sea.

discovery**
[diskʌ́vəri]
n. 발견
If someone makes a discovery, they become aware of something that they did not know about before.

region 복습
[ríːdʒən]
n. 지방, 지역, 영역
A region is a large area of land that is different from other areas of land.

suitable**
[súːtəbl]
a. 적합한, 적절한, 알맞은
Someone or something that is suitable for a particular purpose or occasion is right or acceptable for it.

lively*
[láivli]
a. 활기 넘치는; 적극적인, 의욕적인; 선명한
You can describe someone as lively when they behave in an enthusiastic and cheerful way.

flap*
[flæp]
n. 펄럭거림; 덮개; v. (새가 날개를) 퍼덕거리다; 펄럭거리다
A flap is the action of a bird waving its wings when flying, or of something else moving in this way.

flipper 복습
[flípər]
n. (바다표범·거북 등의) 지느러미발; (잠수·수영 때 신는) 오리발
The flippers of an animal that lives in water, for example a seal or a penguin, are the two or four flat limbs which it uses for swimming.

tub 복습
[tʌb]
n. 목욕통, 욕조; 통
A tub is the same as a bathtub which is a long, usually rectangular container that you fill with water and sit in to wash your body.

washstand
[wáʃstænd]
n. 세면대
A washstand is a piece of furniture designed to hold a bowl for washing your hands and face in, which was used in the past.

survey[*]
[sərvéi]

v. 둘러보다, 바라보다; 조사하다; n. 조사
If you survey something, you look at or consider the whole of it carefully.

peck[*]
[pek]

v. (새가) 쪼다, 쪼아 먹다; n. 쪼기, 쪼아 먹기
If a bird pecks at something or pecks something, it moves its beak forward quickly and bites at it.

ankle[*]
[æŋkl]

n. 발목
Your ankle is the joint where your foot joins your leg.

retreat[*]
[ritríːt]

v. 물러가다, 멀어져 가다; 후퇴하다; n. 후퇴, 철수; 물러섬
If you retreat, you move away from something or someone.

hallway
[hɔ́ːlwèi]

n. 복도; 통로; 현관
A hallway in a building is a long passage with doors into rooms on both sides of it.

pause^{**}
[pɔːz]

v. (말·일을 하다가) 잠시 멈추다; 정지시키다; n. (말·행동 등의) 멈춤
If you pause while you are doing something, you stop for a short period and then continue.

delight^{복습}
[diláit]

v. 많은 기쁨을 주다, 아주 즐겁게 하다; n. 기쁨, 즐거움 (delighted a. 아주 즐거워하는)
If you are delighted, you are extremely pleased and excited about something.

curious^{복습}
[kjúəriəs]

a. 궁금한; 호기심이 많은; 별난, 특이한 (curiosity n. 호기심)
Curiosity is a desire to know about something.

circular[*]
[sɔ́ːrkjulər]

a. 원형의, 둥근; 순회하는
Something that is circular is shaped like a circle.

drag^{복습}
[dræg]

v. 질질 끌리다; 끌고 가다; 힘들게 움직이다; n. 끌기; 장애물
If you drag something, you pull it along the ground, often with difficulty.

pompous^{복습}
[pámpəs]

a. 점잔 빼는, 거드름 피우는 (pompously ad. 화려하게, 과장되게)
If you describe someone as pompous, you mean that they behave or speak in a very serious way because they think they are more important than they really are.

pinkish
[píŋkiʃ]

a. 분홍색을 띤
Pinkish means slightly pink in color.

strut^{복습}
[strʌt]

v. 점잔 빼며 걷다; n. 거만한 걸음걸이; 지주, 버팀대
Someone who struts walks in a proud way, with their head held high and their chest out, as if they are very important.

upholster
[ʌphóulstər]

v. (의자 등에) 천을 씌우다 (upholstered a. (의자 등에) 천을 씌운)
Upholstered chairs and seats have a soft covering that makes them comfortable to sit on.

march^{복습}
[maːrtʃ]

v. (단호한 태도로 급히) 걸어가다; 행진하다; n. 행진, 행군; 행진곡
If you say that someone marches somewhere, you mean that they walk there quickly and in a determined way, for example because they are angry.

immediate**
[imíːdiət]

a. 즉각적인; 당면한; 아주 가까이에 있는 (immediately ad. 즉시, 즉각)
If something happens immediately, it happens without any delay.

refrigerator*
[rifrídʒərèitər]

n. 냉장고
A refrigerator is a large container which is kept cool inside, usually by electricity, so that the food and drink in it stays fresh.

inquire*
[inkwáiər]

v. 묻다, 알아보다
If you inquire about something, you ask for information about it.

slant*
[slænt]

v. 기울어지다, 비스듬해지다; n. 비스듬함
Something that slants is sloping, rather than horizontal or vertical.

pleading
[plíːdiŋ]

a. 탄원하는, 간청하는; n. 변론, 변명, 항변 (pleadingly ad. 애원하듯)
A pleading expression or gesture shows someone that you want something very much.

bite^{복습}
[bait]

v. (이빨로) 물다; n. 물기; 한 입
If an animal or person bites you, they use their teeth to hurt or injure you.

nibble
[nibl]

v. 조금씩 물어뜯다, 갉아 먹다; n. 조금씩 물어뜯기, 한 입 분량
If you nibble something, you bite it very gently.

upstretched
[ʌpstréʧt]

a. (팔 등을) 위쪽으로 뻗은, 펼친
Upstretched arms are stretched upward or raised up.

beak^{복습}
[biːk]

n. (새의) 부리
A bird's beak is the hard curved or pointed part of its mouth.

lean**
[liːn]

v. 기울이다, (몸을) 숙이다; ~에 기대다; a. 군살이 없는, 호리호리한
When you lean in a particular direction, you bend your body in that direction.

sleek
[sliːk]

a. 윤이 나는; (모양이) 매끈한; 부티 나는; v. 윤이 나게 하다
Sleek hair or fur is smooth and shiny and looks healthy.

icebox
[áisbàks]

n. 냉장고; 아이스박스
An icebox is the same as a refrigerator which is a large metal container kept cool, usually by electricity, so that food that is put in it stays fresh.

edge^{복습}
[edʒ]

n. 끝, 가장자리, 모서리; 우위; v. 조금씩 움직이다
The edge of something is the place or line where it stops, or the part of it that is furthest from the middle.

solemn*
[sáləm]

a. 엄숙한; 근엄한; 침통한 (solemnly ad. 엄숙하게, 진지하게)
Someone or something that is solemn is very serious rather than cheerful or humorous.

inspect^{복습}
[inspékt]

v. 면밀하게 살피다, 점검하다; 시찰하다
If you inspect something, you look at every part of it carefully in order to find out about it or check that it is all right.

erect^{복습}
[irékt]

a. 똑바로 선, 직립의; v. 직립시키다, 곤두 세우다
People or things that are erect are straight and upright.

ceiling**
[síːliŋ]

n. 천장
A ceiling is the horizontal surface that forms the top part or roof inside a room.

purr
[pəːr]

v. (기분 좋은 듯이) 그르렁거리다; 부르릉 하는 소리를 내다; n. 그르렁거리는 소리
When a cat purrs, it makes a low vibrating sound with its throat because it is contented.

trill
[tril]

v. (새가) 지저귀다; 떨리는 소리를 내다; n. (새가) 지저귀는 소리; 떨리는 목소리
If a bird trills, it sings with short, high-pitched, repeated notes.

apparent*
[əpǽrənt]

a. 분명한, 누가 봐도 알 수 있는 (apparently ad. 보아 하니, 듣자 하니)
You use apparently to say something based only on what you have read or heard, not on what you are certain is true.

shrimp^{복습}
[ʃrimp]

n. 새우
Shrimps are small shellfish with long tails and many legs.

goldfish^{복습}
[góuldfiʃ]

n. 금붕어
Goldfish are small gold or orange fish which are often kept as pets.

window sill
[wíndou sìl]

n. 창턱
A window sill is a shelf along the bottom of a window, either inside or outside a building.

swallow**
[swálou]

v. (음식 등을) 삼키다; 집어삼키다; 마른침을 삼키다; n. [동물] 제비
If you swallow something, you cause it to go from your mouth down into your stomach.

reprove*
[riprúːv]

v. 꾸짖다, 책망하다, 나무라다
If you reprove someone, you speak angrily or seriously to them because they have behaved in a wrong or foolish way.

glare*
[glɛər]

v. 노려보다; 환하다, 눈부시다; n. 노려봄; 환한 빛, 눈부심
If you glare at someone, you look at them with an angry expression on your face.

squat*
[skwat]

v. 웅크리다, 쪼그리고 앉다; a. 땅딸막한; 쪼그리고 앉은
If you squat, you lower yourself toward the ground, balancing on your feet with your legs bent.

guilty**
[gílti]

a. 죄책감이 드는, 가책을 느끼는; 유죄의 (guiltily ad. 죄진 것처럼)
If you feel guilty, you feel unhappy because you think that you have done something wrong or have failed to do something which you should have done.

naughty*
[nɔ́ːti]

a. 버릇없는, 말을 안 듣는; 약간 무례한
If you say that a child is naughty, you mean that they behave badly or do not do what they are told.

spank
[spæŋk]

v. 찰싹 때리다; n. 찰싹 때리기
If someone spanks a child, they punish them by hitting them on the bottom several times with their hand.

hasty^{복습}
[héisti]

a. 서두른, 성급한; 경솔한 (hastily ad. 급히, 서둘러서)
A hasty movement, action, or statement is sudden, and often done in reaction to something that has just happened.

32

waddle
[wadl]

v. 뒤뚱뒤뚱 걷다; n. 뒤뚱거리는 걸음걸이
To waddle somewhere means to walk there with short, quick steps, swinging slightly from side to side.

coil*
[kɔil]

n. 전선; 고리; v. (고리 모양으로) 감다, 휘감다
A coil is a thick spiral of wire through which an electrical current passes.

barely*
[béərli]

ad. 간신히, 가까스로; 거의 ~아니게
You use barely to say that something is only just true or only just the case.

squeeze*
[skwi:z]

v. (좁은 곳에) 밀어 넣다; 짓누르다; (꼭) 짜다; n. (꼭) 짜기
If you squeeze a person or thing somewhere or if they squeeze there, they manage to get through or into a small space.

mysterious**
[mistíəriəs]

a. 이해하기 힘든, 기이한; 신비한 (mysteriously ad. 신비롭게)
Someone or something that is mysterious is strange and is not known about or understood.

dim*
[dim]

a. 어둑한; (기억이) 흐릿한; v. 어둑해지다; (감정·특성이) 약해지다
(dimness n. 어둑함)
A dim place is rather dark because there is not much light in it.

at that

idiom 게다가, 더구나
At that is used after adding a remark that makes what you had said before even more extreme.

switch복습
[swiʧ]

n. 스위치; 전환; v. 전환하다, 바꾸다; 엇바꾸다
A switch is a small control for an electrical device which you use to turn the device on or off.

ajar
[ədʒá:r]

ad. (문 등이) 조금 열린
If a door is ajar, it is slightly open.

bore*
[bɔ:r]

v. (깊은 구멍을) 뚫다; 지루하게 하다
If you bore a hole in something, you make a deep round hole in it using a special tool.

on the whole

idiom 전반적으로 보아, 대체로
You use on the whole to indicate that what you are saying is true in general but may not be true in every case.

declare***
[dikléər]

v. 언명하다, 분명히 말하다; 선언하다
If you declare something, you state officially and formally that it exists or is the case.

nest*
[nest]

n. 둥지; 보금자리; v. 둥지를 틀다
A bird's nest is the home that it makes to lay its eggs in.

pebble*
[pebl]

n. 조약돌, 자갈
A pebble is a small, smooth, round stone which is found on beaches and at the bottom of rivers.

Chapters 5 & 6

1. Why did Mr. Popper call a service man for the refrigerator?
   A. He had broken the cold control switch.
   B. He had broken the door and needed a new handle on the outside.
   C. He wanted to bore holes in the door and install an inside handle.
   D. He wanted to buy a bigger refrigerator to replace the current one.

2. How did Mr. Popper convince the service man to do what he wanted?
   A. He paid him five dollars.
   B. He told him it was for a penguin.
   C. He showed him Captain Cook.
   D. He told him that he didn't even know how to drill.

3. Why did the service man want Mr. Popper to sit on a chair facing him while he worked?
   A. He wanted Mr. Popper to inspect his work.
   B. He wanted to keep an eye on Mr. Popper while he worked.
   C. He wanted Mr. Popper around to help him out if needed.
   D. He wanted to teach Mr. Popper how to fix his refrigerator.

4. Why had the policeman come to the Popper house?
   A. The policeman was a good friend of Mr. Popper.
   B. The policeman came to check Mr. Popper's driver's license.
   C. The policeman wanted to see the penguin for himself.
   D. The policeman thought there was a dangerous animal.

5. Why did the policeman want Mr. Popper to call the City Hall?
   A. He wanted him to give the penguin to the city zoo.
   B. He wanted him to find a better place for the penguin.
   C. He wanted him to ask about the ruling for penguins.
   D. He wanted him to see if other people owned penguins in the City Hall.

6. How did Mr. Popper feel about talking with the people at the City Hall over the phone?
   A. He felt that they were very clear and helpful.
   B. He felt that they should speak more distinctly.
   C. He felt that they should spell out their words.
   D. He felt that they didn't know about penguins.

7. Why did Mr. Popper decide to hang up the phone?
   A. He had been put on hold for a long time listening to music.
   B. He had been switched to the County Building for a hunting license.
   C. He had been switched to the County Building for a military license.
   D. He had been switched to the County Building for an automobile license.

Check Your Reading Speed

1분에 몇 단어를 읽는지 리딩 속도를 측정해 보세요.

$$\frac{966 \text{ words}}{\text{reading time ( ) sec}} \times 60 = (\quad) \text{ WPM}$$

Build Your Vocabulary

eventful
[ivéntfəl]

a. 다사다난한, 파란만장한
If you describe an event or a period of time as eventful, you mean that a lot of interesting, exciting, or important things have happened during it.

license*
[láisəns]

n. 면허증, 자격증; 자유, 방종; v. (공적으로) 허가하다
A license is an official document which gives you permission to do, use, or own something.

disturb**
[distə́:rb]

v. 건드리다; (작업·수면 등을) 방해하다; 불안하게 하다
If something is disturbed, its position or shape is changed.

spank복습
[spæŋk]

v. 찰싹 때리다; n. 찰싹 때리기
If someone spanks a child, they punish them by hitting them on the bottom several times with their hand.

refrigerator복습
[rifrídʒərèitər]

n. 냉장고
A refrigerator is a large container which is kept cool inside, usually by electricity, so that the food and drink in it stays fresh.

to tell the truth

idiom 사실은
You say to tell you the truth or truth to tell in order to indicate that you are telling someone something in an open and honest way, without trying to hide anything.

tidy복습
[táidi]

a. 깔끔한, 잘 정돈된, 단정한; v. 치우다, 정돈하다
Someone who is tidy likes everything to be neat and arranged in an organized way.

ventilate
[véntəlèit]

v. 환기하다 (ventilating hole n. 환기 구멍)
If you ventilate a room or building, you allow fresh air to get into it.

icebox복습
[áisbàks]

n. 냉장고; 아이스박스
An icebox is the same as a refrigerator which is a large metal container kept cool, usually by electricity, so that food that is put in it stays fresh.

bore복습
[bɔ:r]

v. (깊은 구멍을) 뚫다; 지루하게 하다
If you bore a hole in something, you make a deep round hole in it using a special tool.

stubborn*
[stʌ́bərn]

a. 완고한, 고집 센
Someone who is stubborn or who behaves in a stubborn way is determined to do what they want and is very unwilling to change their mind.

unsympathetic
[ʌnsimpəθétik]

a. 인정 없는, 매정한; 동조하지 않는
If someone is unsympathetic, they are not kind or helpful to a person in difficulties.

stare*
[stɛər]

v. 빤히 쳐다보다, 응시하다; n. 빤히 쳐다보기, 응시
If you stare at someone or something, you look at them for a long time.

bill**
[bil]

n. 지폐; (새의) 부리; 고지서, 청구서; (극장 등의) 프로그램
A bill is a piece of paper money.

examine^{복습}
[igzǽmin]

v. 조사하다; 검사하다; 시험을 실시하다
If you examine something, you look at it carefully.

neat^{복습}
[niːt]

a. 깔끔한; 정돈된, 단정한; 아기자기한
A neat object, part of the body, or shape is quite small and has a smooth outline.

hinge*
[hindʒ]

n. (문·뚜껑 등의) 경첩
A hinge is a piece of metal, wood, or plastic that is used to join a door to its frame or to join two things together so that one of them can swing freely.

indignant*
[indígnənt]

a. 분개한, 분해하는 (indignantly ad. 분개하여)
If you are indignant, you are shocked and angry, because you think that something is unjust or unfair.

intention**
[inténʃən]

n. 의사, 의도; 목적
If you say that you have no intention of doing something, you are emphasizing that you are not going to do it.

sensible**
[sénsəbl]

a. 분별 있는, 합리적인; 실용적인
Sensible actions or decisions are good because they are based on reasons rather than emotions.

spare*
[spɛər]

a. 여분의, 예비용의; 남는; v. (시간·돈 등을) 할애하다; 모면하게 하다
You use spare to describe something that is the same as things that you are already using, but that you do not need yet and are keeping ready in case another one is needed.

screw**
[skruː]

n. 나사; v. 나사로 죄다; 비틀다; 쥐어짜다
A screw is a metal object similar to a nail, with a raised spiral line around it.

annoyed*
[ənɔ́id]

a. 짜증이 난, 약이 오른
If you are annoyed, you are fairly angry about something.

keep an eye on

idiom ~을 계속 지켜보다
If you keep an eye on something or someone, you watch them carefully, for example to make sure that they are satisfactory or safe, or not causing trouble.

peck^{복습}
[pek]

v. (새가) 쪼다, 쪼아 먹다; n. 쪼기, 쪼아 먹기
If a bird pecks at something or pecks something, it moves its beak forward quickly and bites at it.

shower*
[ʃáuər]

n. 세례, 빗발침; 소나기; 샤워; v. 샤워를 하다; (많은 것을) 주다
You can refer to a lot of things that are falling as a shower of them.

slam*
[slæm]

v. 쾅 닫다; 세게 놓다; n. 쾅 하고 닫기 (slamming n. 쾅 하는 소리)
If you slam a door or window or if it slams, it shuts noisily and with
great force.

remodel
[ri:mádl]

v. 개조하다, 리모델링하다
To remodel something such as a building or a room means to give it
a different form or shape.

at once복습

idiom 즉시, 당장; 동시에, 한꺼번에
If you do something at once, you do it immediately.

notice복습
[nóutis]

v. 알아채다, 인지하다; 주목하다; n. 신경씀, 주목, 알아챔
If you notice something or someone, you become aware of them.

prompt*
[prampt]

a. 즉각적인, 지체 없는 (promptly ad. 즉시)
If you do something promptly, you do it immediately.

skillful*
[skílfəl]

a. 능숙한, 솜씨 좋은
Someone who is skillful at something does it very well.

38

Check Your Reading Speed

1분에 몇 단어를 읽는지 리딩 속도를 측정해 보세요.

$$\frac{865 \text{ words}}{\text{reading time (} \quad \text{) sec}} \times 60 = (\quad) \text{ WPM}$$

Build Your Vocabulary

arrest**
[ərést]

v. 체포하다; 막다; (시선·관심을) 끌다; n. 체포; 저지, 정지
If the police arrest you, they take charge of you and take you to a police station, because they believe you may have committed a crime.

dignity*
[dígnəti]

n. 위엄, 품위; 존엄성
If someone behaves or moves with dignity, they are calm, controlled, and admirable.

poke*
[pouk]

v. 쑥 내밀다; (손가락 등으로) 쿡 찌르다; n. (손가락 등으로) 찌르기
If you poke one thing into another, you push the first thing into the second thing.

screen**
[skri:n]

n. 방충망; 칸막이; 스크린; v. (방·창 등에) 망을 달다; 가리다
A screen is a protective covering consisting of netting which can be mounted in a frame.

stern*
[stə:rn]

a. 엄중한, 근엄한; 심각한 (sternly ad. 엄격하게, 준엄하게)
Someone who is stern is very serious and strict.

parrot*
[pǽrət]

n. [동물] 앵무새
A parrot is a tropical bird with a curved beak and brightly-colored or gray feathers.

scratch*
[skræʧ]

v. (가려운 데를) 긁다; 긁다, 할퀴다; n. 긁힌 상처; 긁는 소리
If you scratch yourself, you rub your fingernails against your skin because it is itching.

puzzle*
[pʌzl]

v. 어리둥절하게 하다; n. 퍼즐; 수수께끼 (puzzled a. 어리둥절해하는, 얼떨떨한)
Someone who is puzzled is confused because they do not understand something.

fellow^{복습}
[félou]

n. 녀석, 친구; 동료, 동년배; a. 동료의
A fellow is a man or boy.

yell*
[jel]

v. 소리 지르다, 외치다; n. 고함, 외침
If you yell, you shout loudly, usually because you are excited, angry, or in pain.

chin**
[ʧin]

n. 턱
Your chin is the part of your face that is below your mouth and above your neck.

cage*
[keidʒ]

n. 우리; 새장; v. 우리에 가두다
A cage is a structure of wire or metal bars in which birds or animals are kept.

for all one cares	idiom 조금도 알 바는 아니지만 You can use 'for all I care' to emphasize that it does not matter at all to you what someone does.
leash [li:ʃ]	n. 가죽끈, 사슬; 속박, 통제; v. (개를) 줄에 매어 두다 A dog's leash is a long thin piece of leather or a chain, which you attach to the dog's collar so that you can keep the dog under control.
I tell you	idiom 정말이다 You can say 'I tell you,' 'I can tell you,' or 'I can't tell you' to add emphasis to what you are saying.
municipal* [mju:nísəpəl]	a. 지방 자치제의, 시의 Municipal means associated with or belonging to a city or town that has its own local government.
ordinance [ɔ́:rdənəns]	n. 법령, 조례 An ordinance is an official rule or order.
license^{복습} [láisəns]	n. 면허증, 자격증; 자유, 방종; v. (공적으로) 허가하다 A license is an official document which gives you permission to do, use, or own something.
ruling* [rú:liŋ]	n. 결정, 판결; a. 지배하는 A ruling is an official decision made by a judge or court.
at that^{복습}	idiom 게다가, 더구나 At that is used after adding a remark that makes what you had said before even more extreme.
disconnect [diskənékt]	v. 연결을 끊다; 분리하다; n. 연락을 끊는 일; 통화 불능 To disconnect a piece of equipment means to separate it from its source of power or to break a connection that it needs in order to work.
cord* [kɔ:rd]	n. 전선; 끈, 줄 Cord is wire covered in rubber or plastic which connects electrical equipment to an electricity supply.
eel [i:l]	n. [동물] 장어 An eel is a long, thin fish that looks like a snake.
considerable** [kənsídərəbl]	a. 상당한, 많은 Considerable means great in amount or degree.
pleased^{복습} [pli:zd]	a. 기뻐하는, 만족해하는 If you are pleased, you are happy about something or satisfied with something.
friendly** [fréndli]	a. (행동이) 친절한, 우호적인; 상냥한, 다정한 If someone is friendly, they behave in a pleasant, kind way, and like to be with other people.
distinct*** [distíŋkt]	a. 뚜렷한, 분명한; 확실한 (distinctly ad. 분명하게, 뚜렷하게) If something is distinct, you can hear, see, or taste it clearly.

40

roar* [rɔːr]

v. 고함치다; 함성을 지르다; 으르렁거리다; n. 으르렁거림, 포효
If someone roars, they shout something in a very loud voice.

outrage* [áutreidʒ]

v. 격분하게 하다; n. 격분, 격노
If you are outraged by something, it makes you extremely shocked and angry.

folk** [fouk]

n. (일반적인) 사람들; 부모; a. 민속의, 전통적인; 민중의
You can refer to people as folk or folks.

bureau* [bjúərou]

n. (정부의) 국, 부서; 사무실
A bureau is an office, organization, or government department that collects and distributes information.

navigate* [nǽvəgèit]

v. (바다·강 등을) 항해하다; 길을 찾다 (navigation n. 항해; 운항)
You can refer to the movement of ships as navigation.

personally* [pə́ːrsənəli]

ad. 직접, 개인적으로; 개인적인 의견을 말하면
If you do something personally, you do it yourself rather than letting someone else do it.

automobile* [ɔ̀ːtəməbíːl]

n. 자동차
An automobile is a car.

switch복습 [swiʧ]

v. 엇바꾸다; 전환하다, 바꾸다; n. 스위치; 전환
If you switch to something different, for example to a different system, task, or subject of conversation, you change to it from what you were doing or saying before.

county* [káunti]

n. 자치주, 자치군
A county is a region of Britain, Ireland, or the USA which has its own local government.

hang up

idiom 전화를 끊다
If you hang up the phone or hang up on someone, you end a telephone conversation, often very suddenly.

Chapters 7 & 8

1. Why was Mr. Popper making himself look neat?
   A. He was going to start a new job.
   B. He was going out to see a movie.
   C. He was going to surprise his wife.
   D. He was honored to be Captain Cook's owner.

2. Why was Captain Cook making trips through the house?
   A. He was exercising and exploring new rooms.
   B. He was playing a game with the children.
   C. He was picking things up and bringing them into the icebox.
   D. He was following Mrs. Popper as she cleaned the house.

3. Why did Mr. Popper think that Captain Cook collected all the items around the house?
   A. He thought that Captain Cook was building a nest.
   B. He thought that Captain Cook was hungry and looking for food.
   C. He thought that Captain Cook was bored and looking for toys.
   D. He thought that Captain Cook was trying to help clean up the house.

4. Why did Mr. Popper ask for a few yards of clothesline?
   A. He was going to use it to do the laundry.
   B. He was going to use it as a leash to walk Captain Cook.
   C. He was going to give it to Captain Cook to use for his nest.
   D. He was going to tie the icebox door open to help Captain Cook.

5. How did Captain Cook go down the steps?
   A. He slid down the steps.
   B. He took the steps one at a time.
   C. He jumped down the steps.
   D. He marched down the steps.

6. How had the reporters heard about Captain Cook?
   A. They had heard about him from the postman.
   B. They had heard about him from the service man.
   C. They had heard about him from the policeman.
   D. They had heard about him from the radio broadcast.

7. How did Mr. Popper free himself from the tangled clothesline and tripod?
   A. He made Captain Cook follow him slowly.
   B. He walked around the tripod in the opposite direction.
   C. He told the reporter to pick up the tripod and move it.
   D. He cut the clothesline and let Captain Cook walk unleashed.

Check Your Reading Speed
1분에 몇 단어를 읽는지 리딩 속도를 측정해 보세요.

$$\frac{\text{746 words}}{\text{reading time ( ) sec}} \times 60 = (\quad) \text{ WPM}$$

Build Your Vocabulary

nest^{복습}
[nest]

n. 둥지; 보금자리; v. 둥지를 틀다
A bird's nest is the home that it makes to lay its eggs in.

reluctant*
[rilʌ́ktənt]

a. 마지못한, 꺼리는, 주저하는 (reluctantly ad. 마지못해, 꺼려하여)
If you are reluctant to do something, you are unwilling to do it and hesitate before doing it, or do it slowly and without enthusiasm.

belated
[biléitid]

a. 뒤늦은 (belatedly ad. 뒤늦게)
A belated action happens later than it should have done.

dim^{복습}
[dim]

a. (기억이) 흐릿한; 어둑한; v. 어둑해지다; (감정·특성이) 약해지다
(dimly ad. 희미하게)
If you have a dim memory or understanding of something, it is difficult to remember or is unclear in your mind.

meanwhile*
[míːnwàil]

ad. 그 동안에; 그 사이에
Meanwhile means while a particular thing is happening.

abandon*
[əbǽndən]

v. 포기하다; 버리고 떠나다; 버리다, 떠나다
If you abandon an activity or piece of work, you stop doing it before it is finished.

honor***
[ánər]

n. 영광; 명예; 존경, 공경; v. ~에게 영광을 베풀다; 수여하다
(in honor of idiom ~을 기념하여; ~을 축하하여)
If something is arranged in honor of a particular event, it is arranged in order to celebrate that event.

splendid*
[spléndid]

a. 멋진, 훌륭한
If you say that something is splendid, you mean that it is very good.

thus*
[ðʌs]

ad. 이렇게 하여; 이와 같이; 따라서, 그러므로
If you say that something is thus or happens thus you mean that it is, or happens, as you have just described or as you are just about to describe.

neglect**
[niglékt]

v. (돌보지 않고) 방치하다; 무시하다, 등한시하다; n. 방치; 소홀
If you neglect someone or something, you fail to give them the amount of attention that they deserve.

by no means

idiom 결코 ~이 아닌
You use expressions such as 'by no means,' 'not by any means,' and 'by no manner of means' to emphasize that something is not true.

idle**
[aidl]

a. 나태한; 한가하게 보내는; 쓸데없는, 무의미한; v. 빈둥거리다
If you say that someone is idle, you disapprove of them because they are not doing anything and you think they should be.

straighten*
[streitn]

v. 정리하다, 정돈하다; 똑바르게 하다; (자세를) 바로 하다
If you straighten something, you make it tidy or put it in its proper position.

housekeeper*
[háuski:pər]

n. 주부; 가정부
A housekeeper is a married woman who does not have a paid job, but instead looks after her home and children.

untidy^{복습}
[ʌntáidi]

a. 깔끔하지 못한; 단정치 못한, 어수선한
If you describe a person as untidy, you mean that they do not care about whether things are neat and well arranged, for example in their house.

pick up

idiom 치우다, 정리하다
If you pick up a place or things, you make a place clean and tidy.

prowl
[praul]

v. 돌아다니다; 배회하다; 서성거리다
If an animal or a person prowls around, they move around quietly, for example when they are hunting.

poke^{복습}
[pouk]

v. (손가락 등으로) 쿡 찌르다; 쑥 내밀다; n. (손가락 등으로) 찌르기
If you poke someone or something, you quickly push them with your finger or with a sharp object.

thorough*
[θɔ́:rou]

a. 빈틈없는, 철두철미한 (thoroughness n. 철저함)
A thorough action or activity is one that is done very carefully and in a detailed way so that nothing is forgotten.

stare^{복습}
[stɛər]

v. 빤히 쳐다보다, 응시하다; n. 빤히 쳐다보기, 응시
If you stare at someone or something, you look at them for a long time.

plump*
[plʌmp]

a. 포동포동한, 둥그스름한; 속이 가득 찬
You can describe someone or something as plump to indicate that they are rather fat or rounded.

figure***
[fígjər]

n. 모습, 몸매; 수치; v. 생각하다; 판단하다
Your figure is the shape of your body.

subdued
[səbdjú:d]

a. 은은한, 조용조용한; (기분이) 가라앉은
Subdued sounds are not very loud.

curious^{복습}
[kjúəriəs]

a. 궁금한; 호기심이 많은; 별난, 특이한 (curiosity n. 호기심)
Curiosity is a desire to know about something.

beak^{복습}
[bi:k]

n. (새의) 부리
A bird's beak is the hard curved or pointed part of its mouth.

waddle^{복습}
[wadl]

v. 뒤뚱뒤뚱 걷다; n. 뒤뚱거리는 걸음걸이
To waddle somewhere means to walk there with short, quick steps, swinging slightly from side to side.

on earth

idiom 도대체 어떻게
On earth is used for emphasis in questions that begin with words such as 'how,' 'why,' 'what,' or 'where.' It is often used to suggest that there is no obvious or easy answer to the question being asked.

be up to

idiom (특히 나쁜 짓을) 하고 있다
To be up to something means to be secretly doing something that you should not be doing.

remarkable*
[rimáːrkəbl]

a. 놀랄 만한, 놀라운, 주목할 만한
Someone or something that is remarkable is unusual or special in a way that makes people notice them and be surprised or impressed.

notice^{복습}
[nóutis]

v. 알아채다, 인지하다; 주목하다; n. 신경씀, 주목, 알아챔
If you notice something or someone, you become aware of them.

astonish*
[əstániʃ]

v. 깜짝 놀라게 하다 (astonishment n. 깜짝 놀람)
Astonishment is a feeling of great surprise.

triumph*
[tráiəmf]

n. 승리감, 환희; (큰) 업적, 대성공; v. 승리를 거두다, 이기다
Triumph is a feeling of great satisfaction and pride resulting from a success or victory.

gasp*
[gæsp]

v. 헉 하고 숨을 쉬다, 숨이 턱 막히다; 숨을 제대로 못 쉬다; n. 헉 하는 소리를 냄
When you gasp, you take a short quick breath through your mouth, especially when you are surprised, shocked, or in pain.

spool
[spuːl]

n. 실패, 실감개
A spool is a round object onto which thread, tape, or film can be wound, especially before it is put into a machine.

thread**
[θred]

n. 실; (이야기 등의) 맥락; v. 요리조리 빠져나가다; (실 등을) 꿰다
Thread or a thread is a long very thin piece of material such as cotton, nylon, or silk, especially one that is used in sewing.

stub
[stʌb]

n. (쓰다 남은 물건의) 토막; v. ~에 발가락이 차이다
The stub of a cigarette or a pencil is the last short piece of it which remains when the rest has been used.

bend**
[bend]

v. 구부리다; (몸이나 머리를) 굽히다, 숙이다; n. (도로·강의) 굽이
(bent a. 구부러진, 휜)
If an object is bent, it is damaged and no longer has its correct shape.

ash tray
[ǽʃ trei]

n. 재떨이
An ash tray is a small dish in which smokers can put the ash from their cigarettes and cigars.

marble*
[maːrbl]

n. (아이들이 가지고 노는) 구슬; 대리석
A marble is a small ball, usually made of colored or transparent glass, which is used in children's games.

crumple
[krʌmpl]

v. 구기다; 구겨지다; (얼굴이) 일그러지다; 쓰러지다
If you crumple something such as paper or cloth, or if it crumples, it is squashed and becomes full of untidy creases and folds.

tinfoil
[tínfɔil]

n. 은박지
Tinfoil consists of shiny metal in the form of a thin sheet which is used for wrapping food.

cap**
[kæp]

n. 뚜껑; 모자; v. (꼭대기나 끝을) (~으로) 덮다
The cap of a bottle is its lid.

cork*
[kɔ:rk]

n. 코르크 마개
A cork is a piece of cork or plastic that is pushed into the opening of a bottle to close it.

screw^{복습}
[skru:]

n. 나사; v. 나사로 죄다; 비틀다; 쥐어짜다
A screw is a metal object similar to a nail, with a raised spiral line around it.

buckle*
[bʌkl]

n. 버클, 잠금장치; v. 찌그러지다, 휘어지다; 버클로 잠그다
A buckle is a piece of metal or plastic attached to one end of a belt or strap, which is used to fasten it.

bead*
[bi:d]

n. 구슬; (구슬 같은) 방울
Beads are small pieces of colored glass, wood, or plastic with a hole through the middle. Beads are often wire to make jewelery.

block***
[blak]

n. (단단한) 사각형 덩어리; (도로로 나뉘는) 구역, 블록; v. 막다, 차단하다
A block of a substance is a large rectangular piece of it.

darn
[da:rn]

v. (옷의 구멍 난 곳을) 꿰매다; n. (옷의) 꿰맨 자리 (darning n. 짜깁기)
If you darn something knitted or made of cloth, you mend a hole in it by sewing stitches across the hole and then weaving stitches in and out of them.

consume*
[kənsú:m]

v. 먹다; 마시다; (에너지·시간 등을) 소모하다
If you consume something, you eat or drink it.

toothpaste*
[tú:θpeist]

n. 치약
Toothpaste is a thick substance which you put on your toothbrush and use to clean your teeth.

lid*
[lid]

n. 뚜껑
A lid is the top of a box or other container which can be removed or raised when you want to open the container.

rookery
[rúkəri]

n. (바다표범·펭귄 등의) 서식지, 번식지
Rookery is a group of nests made by rooks or other birds that live together.

heathen^{복습}
[hí:ðən]

a. 야만적인; 이교도의; n. 교양 없는 사람, 야만인
If you describe someone as heathen, you mean that they behave as if they are not educated.

pole^{복습}
[poul]

n. (지구의) 극; 기둥, 장대
The earth's poles are the two opposite ends of its axis, its most northern and southern points.

declare^{복습}
[dikléər]

v. 언명하다, 분명히 말하다; 선언하다
If you declare something, you state officially and formally that it exists or is the case.

strut^{복습}
[strʌt]

v. 점잔 빼며 걷다; n. 거만한 걸음걸이; 지주, 버팀대
Someone who struts walks in a proud way, with their head held high and their chest out, as if they are very important.

knock**
[nak]

v. 치다, 부딪치다; (문 등을) 두드리다; n. (문 등을) 두드리는 소리; 부딪침
If you knock something, you touch or hit it roughly, especially so that it falls or moves.

gracious^{복습}
[gréiʃəs]

int. 세상에, 맙소사; a. 우아한; 자애로운, 품위 있는
Some people say 'good gracious' or 'goodness gracious' in order to express surprise or annoyance.

smooth^{복습}
[smuːð]

v. 매끈하게 하다; 고루 펴 바르다; a. 매끈한; 순조로운
(smooth down idiom 매만지다)
If you smooth down something such as your hair or your clothes, you make it smooth and flat with your hands.

whisker^{복습}
[wískər]

n. (pl.) 구레나룻; (고양이·쥐 등의) 수염
You can refer to the hair on a man's face, especially on the sides of his face, as his whiskers.

reproach*
[ripróuʧ]

v. 비난하다, 책망하다; n. 비난, 책망, 나무람
If you reproach someone, you say or show that you are disappointed, upset, or angry because they have done something wrong.

trousers*
[tráuzərz]

n. 바지
Trousers are a piece of clothing that you wear over your body from the waist downward, and that cover each leg separately.

clothesline
[klóuðzlàin]

n. 빨랫줄
A clothesline is a thin rope on which you hang washing so that it can dry.

Check Your Reading Speed

1분에 몇 단어를 읽는지 리딩 속도를 측정해 보세요.

$$\frac{943 \text{ words}}{\text{reading time ( ) sec}} \times 60 = (\quad) \text{ WPM}$$

Build Your Vocabulary

promenade
[pramənéid]

n. 거닐기, 산책; 산책로; v. 거닐다
A promenade is a leisurely walk or ride especially in a public place for pleasure or display.

stroll*
[stroul]

n. 산책, (한가로이) 거닐기; v. 거닐다, 산책하다
A stroll is a slow walk for pleasure.

leash복습
[liːʃ]

n. 가죽끈, 사슬; 속박, 통제; v. (개를) 줄에 매어 두다
A dog's leash is a long thin piece of leather or a chain, which you attach to the dog's collar so that you can keep the dog under control.

firm복습
[fəːrm]

a. 단호한, 확고한; 단단한
If you describe someone as firm, you mean they behave in a way that shows that they are not going to change their mind, or that they are the person who is in control.

clothesline복습
[klóuðzlàin]

n. 빨랫줄
A clothesline is a thin rope on which you hang washing so that it can dry.

throat**
[θrout]

n. 목; 목구멍
Your throat is the front part of your neck.

wrist*
[rist]

n. 손목
Your wrist is the part of your body between your hand and your arm which bends when you move your hand.

indignant복습
[indígnənt]

a. 분개한, 분해하는 (indignantly ad. 분개하여)
If you are indignant, you are shocked and angry, because you think that something is unjust or unfair.

reasonable
[ríːzənəbl]

a. 사리를 아는, 합리적인; 합당한
If you think that someone is fair and sensible you can say that they are reasonable.

protest**
[próutest]

v. 항의하다, 이의를 제기하다; n. 항의
If you protest against something or about something, you say or show publicly that you object to it.

recover복습
[rikʌ́vər]

v. (의식 등을) 되찾다; 회복되다; (손실 등을) 되찾다
If you recover a mental or physical state, it comes back again.

customary*
[kʌ́stəmèri]

a. 습관적인; 관례적인, 관습상의
Customary is used to describe something that a particular person usually does or has.

dignity^{복습}
[dígnəti]

n. 위엄, 품위; 존엄성
If someone behaves or moves with dignity, they are calm, controlled, and admirable.

gracious^{복습}
[gréiʃəs]

a. 우아한; 자애로운, 품위 있는; int. 세상에, 맙소사 (graciously ad. 우아하게)
If you describe someone as gracious, you mean that they are very well-mannered and pleasant.

edge^{복습}
[edʒ]

n. 끝, 가장자리, 모서리; 우위; v. 조금씩 움직이다
The edge of something is the place or line where it stops, or the part of it that is furthest from the middle.

porch*
[pɔːrtʃ]

n. (지붕이 있는) 현관, 포치
A porch is a sheltered area at the entrance to a building, which has a roof and sometimes has walls.

flipper^{복습}
[flípər]

n. (바다표범·거북 등의) 지느러미발; (잠수·수영 때 신는) 오리발
The flippers of an animal that lives in water, for example a seal or a penguin, are the two or four flat limbs which it uses for swimming.

lean^{복습}
[liːn]

v. 기울이다, (몸을) 숙이다; ~에 기대다; a. 군살이 없는, 호리호리한
When you lean in a particular direction, you bend your body in that direction.

toboggan^{복습}
[təbágən]

v. 썰매를 타다; n. 터보건 (썰매)
If you toboggan, you move along on a light wooden board with a curved front, to travel down hills on snow or ice.

stomach^{복습}
[stʌ́mək]

n. 복부, 배
You can refer to the front part of your body below your waist as your stomach.

strut^{복습}
[strʌt]

v. 점잔 빼며 걷다; n. 거만한 걸음걸이; 지주, 버팀대
Someone who struts walks in a proud way, with their head held high and their chest out, as if they are very important.

scene^{★★}
[siːn]

n. 장면, 광경; 현장; 풍경
You refer to a place as a scene when you are describing its appearance and indicating what impression it makes on you.

grocery*
[gróusəri]

n. (pl.) 식료품; 식료 잡화점
Groceries are foods you buy at a grocer's or at a supermarket such as flour, sugar, and tinned foods.

astonish^{복습}
[əstániʃ]

v. 깜짝 놀라게 하다 (astonishment n. 깜짝 놀람)
Astonishment is a feeling of great surprise.

mercy*
[mə́ːrsi]

n. 자비; 고마운 일
If someone in authority shows mercy, they choose not to harm someone they have power over, or they forgive someone they have the right to punish.

50

exclaim^{복습}
[ikskléim]
v. 소리치다, 외치다
If you exclaim, you cry out suddenly in surprise, strong emotion, or pain.

investigate*
[invéstəgèit]
v. 조사하다, 살피다; 연구하다
If someone, especially an official, investigates an event, situation, or claim, they try to find out what happened or what is the truth.

stripe*
[straip]
n. 줄무늬 (striped a. 줄무늬가 있는)
Something that is striped has stripes on it.

owl*
[aul]
n. [동물] 올빼미, 부엉이
An owl is a bird with a flat face, large eyes, and a small sharp beak. Most owls obtain their food by hunting small animals at night.

goose*
[gu:s]
n. [동물] 거위
A goose is a large bird that has a long neck and webbed feet.

tip*
[tip]
v. 기울이다, 젖히다; 살짝 건드리다; n. (뾰족한) 끝
If you tip an object or part of your body or if it tips, it moves into a sloping position with one end or side higher than the other.

Antarctic^{복습}
[æntá:rktik]
a. 남극의, 남극 지방의; n. 남극
The Antarctic is the area around the South Pole.

at once^{복습}
idiom 즉시, 당장; 동시에, 한꺼번에
If you do something at once, you do it immediately.

obedient*
[oubí:diənt]
a. 순종하는, 고분고분한 (obediently ad. 고분고분하게)
A person or animal who is obedient does what they are told to do.

part***
[pa:rt]
v. 헤어지다; (사물이) 갈라지다, 나뉘다 (parting a. 이별의, 작별의)
Your parting words or actions are the things that you say or do as you are leaving a place or person.

peck^{복습}
[pek]
n. 쪼기, 쪼아 먹기; v. (새가) 쪼다, 쪼아 먹다
A peck is a quick, sharp strike with the beak by a bird.

preserve*
[prizə́:rv]
v. 지키다, 보호하다; 보존하다; n. 전유물
If you preserve something, you take action to save it or protect it from damage or decay.

stop in
idiom ~에 잠시 들르다
To stop in means to visit a person or place for a short time, usually when you are going somewhere else.

drag^{복습}
[dræg]
v. 끌고 가다; 질질 끌리다; 힘들게 움직이다; n. 끌기; 장애물
If someone drags you somewhere, they pull you there, or force you to go there by physically threatening you.

drugstore*
[drʌ́gstò:r]
n. 드러그스토어, 약국
In the United States, a drugstore is a shop where drugs and medicines are sold or given out, and where you can buy cosmetics, some household goods, and also drinks and snacks.

insist***
[insíst]
v. 고집하다, 주장하다, 우기다
If you insist on something, you say firmly that it must be done or provided.

display[*]
[displéi]

n. 전시, 진열; v. 전시하다, 진열하다; 드러내다
A display is an arrangement of things that have been put in a particular place, so that people can see them easily.

crystal[*]
[krístl]

n. 결정체; 수정
A crystal is a small piece of a substance that has formed naturally into a regular symmetrical shape.

evident[*]
[évədənt]

a. 분명한, 눈에 띄는 (evidently ad. 분명히, 눈에 띄게)
You use evidently to say that something is obviously true, for example because you have seen evidence of it yourself.

mistake for

idiom ~으로 오해하다
If you mistake one person or thing for another, you wrongly think that they are the other person or thing.

polar^{복습}
[póulər]

a. 북극의, 남극의, 극지의; 정반대되는
Polar means near the North and South Poles.

vigorous[*]
[vígərəs]

a. 격렬한; 활발한; 활기찬, 건강한 (vigorously ad. 맹렬히, 힘차게)
Vigorous physical activities involve using a lot of energy, usually to do short and repeated actions.

wheel^{**}
[hwi:l]

v. (반대 방향으로) 홱 돌다; 선회하다; (바퀴 달린 것을) 밀다;
n. 바퀴; (자동차 등의) 핸들
If you wheel around, you turn around suddenly where you are standing, often because you are surprised, shocked, or angry.

curb[*]
[kə:rb]

n. (보도의) 연석(緣石); 억제; v 억제하다, 제한하다
The curb is the raised edge of a pavement or sidewalk which separates it from the road.

shriek[*]
[ʃri:k]

n. 날카로운 소리; 비명; v. (날카롭게) 비명을 지르다; 악을 쓰며 말하다
A shriek is a loud high sound made by a bird or animal, or by a machine.

brake[*]
[breik]

n. 브레이크, 제동 장치; 제동; v. 브레이크를 밟다; 속도를 줄이다
Brakes are devices in a vehicle that make it go slower or stop.

bear^{**}
[bɛər]

v. 가지고 가다; 참다, 견디다; (아이를) 낳다
If you bear something somewhere, you carry it there or take it there.

tripod
[tráipad]

n. 삼각대
A tripod is a stand with three legs that is used to support something such as a camera or a telescope.

sidewalk[*]
[sáidwɔːk]

n. 보도, 인도
A sidewalk is a path with a hard surface by the side of a road.

gather^{**}
[gǽðər]

v. (사람들이) 모이다; (여기저기 있는 것을) 모으다
If people gather somewhere or if someone gathers people somewhere, they come together in a group.

exhibit^{**}
[igzíbit]

n. 전시품; v. 전시하다; 보이다, 드러내다
An exhibit is a painting, sculpture, or object of interest that is displayed to the public in a museum or art gallery.

bother^{복습}
[báðər]

v. 신경 쓰다, 애를 쓰다; 괴롭히다; 귀찮게 하다; n. 성가심
If you do not bother to do something or if you do not bother with it, you do not do it, consider it, or use it because you think it is unnecessary or because you are too lazy.

as a matter of fact

idiom 사실은, 실제로
You use as a matter of fact to introduce a statement that gives more details about what has just been said, or an explanation of it, or something that contrasts with it.

pouch
[pautʃ]

n. (동물의) 볼주머니; 주머니
A pouch is a bag formed from skin in the mouths of some animals, used for carrying and storing food.

bill^{복습}
[bil]

n. (새의) 부리; 지폐; 고지서, 청구서; (극장 등의) 프로그램
A bird's bill is its beak.

extinct[*]
[ikstíŋkt]

a. 멸종된; 더 이상 존재하지 않는, 사라진
A species of animal or plant that is extinct no longer has any living members, either in the world or in a particular place.

elegant[*]
[éligənt]

a. 멋들어진; 품위 있는, 우아한
If you describe a person or thing as elegant, you mean that they are pleasing and graceful in appearance or style.

spy[*]
[spai]

v. (갑자기) 보다, 알아채다; n. 스파이, 정보원
If you spy someone or something, you notice them.

examine^{복습}
[igzǽmin]

v. 조사하다; 검사하다; 시험을 실시하다
If you examine something, you look at it carefully.

stork
[stɔ:rk]

n. [동물] 황새
A stork is a large bird with a long beak and long legs, which lives near water.

hesitate^{***}
[hézətèit]

v. 망설이다, 주저하다; 거리끼다
If you hesitate, you do not speak or act for a short time, usually because you are uncertain, embarrassed, or worried about what you are going to say or do.

rapid^{**}
[rǽpid]

a. 빠른, 급한; (행동이) 민첩한 (rapidly ad. 빨리, 급속히)
A rapid movement is one that is very fast.

tangle[*]
[tǽŋgl]

v. 헝클어지다, 얽히다; n. (실·머리카락 등이) 엉킨 것; (혼란스럽게) 꼬인 상태
If something is tangled or tangles, it becomes twisted together in an untidy way.

bystander
[báistændər]

n. 구경꾼, 행인
A bystander is a person who is present when something happens and who sees it but does not take part in it.

straighten^{복습}
[streitn]

v. 똑바르게 하다; 정리하다, 정돈하다; (자세를) 바로 하다
If you straighten something, or it straightens, it becomes straight.

consent[*]
[kənsént]

v. 동의하다, 승낙하다; n. 동의, 승낙
If you consent to something, you agree to do it or to allow it to be done.

snap[*]
[snæp]

v. 사진을 찍다; 딱 하고 움직이다; n. 탁 하는 소리
If you snap someone or something, you take a photograph of them.

explore^{복습}
[ikspló:r]

v. 탐험하다, 탐사하다; 분석하다 (explorer n. 탐험가)
An explorer is someone who travels to places about which very little is known, in order to discover what is there.

barber[*]
[bá:rbər]

n. 이발사 (barbershop n. 이발소)
A barbershop is a shop where a barber works.

Chapters 9 & 10

1. How did the barber react to the penguin?
   A. He mistook him for a customer.
   B. He told Mr. Popper to take it out.
   C. He told Mr. Popper that penguins had no hair.
   D. He told Mr. Popper that the barbershop was a zoo.

2. Why did Mr. Popper think that penguins liked to climb stairs?
   A. They were birds and needed to go up in the air.
   B. They were used to high places in Antarctica.
   C. They liked to climb mountains made of ice.
   D. They liked to climb stairs just to slide down them.

3. Why did Mr. Popper call a taxi for him and Captain Cook?
   A. He was too tired to walk home.
   B. He needed to return home quickly.
   C. He wanted Captain Cook to ride in a car.
   D. He called a taxi to distract him from climbing the stairs.

4. Why were the Poppers feeling proud and happy?
   A. They were in the newspapers.
   B. They were making more money.
   C. They were traveling to new places.
   D. They were staring in movies.

5. How did the veterinarian feel about Captain Cook's condition?
   A. He felt that Captain Cook needed more exercise outside.
   B. He felt that Captain Cook was gain healthy weight if he ate ice cream.
   C. He felt that the pills should be enough to make Captain Cook healthy again.
   D. He felt that it was hopeless because penguins were not made for warmer climates.

6. Why did Mr. Popper write a letter to the curator of an aquarium?
   A. He thought that he could have the aquarium send a veterinarian.
   B. He thought that he could have Captain Cook live at the aquarium.
   C. He thought that he could have an idea of how to cure a dying penguin.
   D. He thought that he could have the curator send another penguin to him.

7. How did the aquarium curator try to help Mr. Popper?
   A. He sent him medicine for sick penguins.
   B. He sent him an expert on penguins from the aquarium.
   C. He helped him send Captain Cook back to Antarctica.
   D. He sent him a penguin that he thought was suffering from loneliness.

Check Your Reading Speed

1분에 몇 단어를 읽는지 리딩 속도를 측정해 보세요.

$$\frac{586 \text{ words}}{\text{reading time ( ) sec}} \times 60 = (\quad) \text{ WPM}$$

Build Your Vocabulary

barber^{복습}
[bá:rbər]

n. 이발사 (barbershop n. 이발소)
A barbershop is a shop where a barber works.

elderly*
[éldərli]

a. 나이가 지긋한
You use elderly as a polite way of saying that someone is old.

spectacle^{복습}
[spéktəkl]

n. 광경, 장관; (pl.) 안경
A spectacle is a strange or interesting sight.

ledge*
[ledʒ]

n. (벽에서 튀어나온) 선반; 절벽에서 튀어나온 바위
A ledge is a narrow shelf along the bottom edge of a window.

lather
[lǽðər]

n. 비누거품; v. 비누거품을 칠하다
A lather is a white mass of bubbles which is produced by mixing a substance such as soap or washing powder with water.

flap^{복습}
[flæp]

v. (새가 날개를) 퍼덕거리다; 펄럭거리다; n. 펄럭거림; 덮개
If a bird or insect flaps its wings or if its wings flap, the wings move quickly up and down.

yell^{복습}
[jel]

n. 고함, 외침; v. 소리 지르다, 외치다
A yell is a loud shout given by someone who is afraid or in pain.

leap*
[li:p]

n. 높이 뛰기, 도약; 급증; v. 뛰다, 뛰어오르다; (서둘러) ~하다
A leap is a large jump or sudden movement.

recline*
[rikláin]

v. (편안하게) 비스듬히 기대다; (의자 등받이가) 뒤로 넘어가다
If you recline on something, you sit or lie on it with the upper part of your body supported at an angle.

flee*
[fli:]

v. (fled-fled) 달아나다, 도망치다
If you flee from something or someone, or flee a person or thing, you escape from them.

bite^{복습}
[bait]

v. (이빨로) 물다; n. 물기; 한 입
If an animal or person bites you, they use their teeth to hurt or injure you.

tooth**
[tu:θ]

n. (pl. teeth) (톱·빗 등의) 이, 살; 치아
The teeth of something such as a comb, saw, cog, or zip are the parts that stick out in a row on its edge.

comb*
[koum]

n. 빗; 빗다, 빗질하다
A comb is a flat piece of plastic or metal with narrow pointed teeth along one side, which you use to tidy your hair.

amid
[əmíd]

prep. (흥분·공포심이 느껴지는) 중에; ~으로 에워싸인
If something happens amid noises or events of some kind, it happens while the other things are happening.

make one's way^{복습}

idiom 나아가다, 가다
When you make your way somewhere, you walk or travel there.

alley*
[ǽli]

n. 통로; 골목, 샛길
An alley is a narrow passage or street with buildings or walls on both sides.

stairway
[stéərwèi]

n. (통로로서의) 계단
A stairway is a staircase or a flight of steps, inside or outside a building.

absolute*
[ǽbsəlùːt]

a. 완전한, 완벽한 (absolutely ad. 전적으로, 틀림없이)
Absolutely means totally and completely.

pant*
[pænt]

v. (숨을) 헐떡이다; n. 헐떡거림
If you pant, you breathe quickly and loudly with your mouth open, because you have been doing something energetic.

story**
[stɔ́ːri]

① n. (= storey) (건물의) 층 ② n. 이야기, 소설; 설명
A story of a building is one of its different levels, which is situated above or below other levels.

unwearying
[ʌnwíəriiŋ]

a. 지치지 않는; 물리지 않는; 지속적인 (unwearyingly ad. 지치지 않고)
If you do something unwearyingly, you do it without growing weary or tirelessly.

clothesline^{복습}
[klóuðzlàin]

n. 빨랫줄
A clothesline is a thin rope on which you hang washing so that it can dry.

landing*
[lǽndiŋ]

n. 층계참; 착륙
In a house or other building, the landing is the area at the top of the staircase which has rooms leading off it.

inquire^{복습}
[inkwáiər]

v. 묻다, 알아보다
If you inquire about something, you ask for information about it.

survey^{복습}
[sərvéi]

v. 둘러보다, 바라보다; 조사하다; n. 조사
If you survey something, you look at or consider the whole of it carefully.

determine*
[ditə́ːrmin]

v. ~을 하기로 결정하다; 알아내다, 밝히다 (determined a. 단단히 결심한; 단호한)
If you are determined to do something, you have made a firm decision to do it and will not let anything stop you.

plunge*
[plʌndʒ]

v. (갑자기) 거꾸러지다; 급락하다; n. (갑자기) 떨어져 내림; 급락
If something or someone plunges in a particular direction, especially into water, they fall, rush, or throw themselves in that direction.

wrist^{복습}
[rist]

n. 손목
Your wrist is the part of your body between your hand and your arm which bends when you move your hand.

at any rate	idiom 어쨌든 You use at any rate to indicate that the important thing is what you are saying now, and not what was said before.
slide^{복습} [slaid]	v. 미끄러지다; 슬며시 움직이다; n. 떨어짐; 미끄러짐 When something slides somewhere or when you slide it there, it moves there smoothly over or against something.
clad [klæd]	a. 입은; 덮인 If you are clad in particular clothes, you are wearing them.
flight** [flait]	n. 계단, 층계; 비행; 항공기 A flight of steps or stairs is a set of steps or stairs that lead from one level to another without changing direction.
delight^{복습} [diláit]	v. 많은 기쁨을 주다, 아주 즐겁게 하다; n. 기쁨, 즐거움 (delighted a. 아주 즐거워하는) If you are delighted, you are extremely pleased and excited about something.
distract* [distrǽkt]	v. (주의를) 딴 데로 돌리다; (정신이) 산만하게 하다 If something distracts you or your attention from something, it takes your attention away from it.
odd** [ad]	a. 이상한, 특이한; 홀수의 (oddly ad. 이상하게) Oddly means in an unusual way that attracts your interest or attention.
assort [əsɔ́:rt]	v. 어울리다; 구분하다 (assorted a. 어울리는; 여러 가지의, 갖은) If you describe a group of people or things as oddly assorted, you mean that they do not seem to belong together.
passenger** [pǽsəndʒər]	n. 승객 A passenger in a vehicle such as a bus, boat, or plane is a person who is traveling in it, but who is not driving it or working on it.
neat^{복습} [ni:t]	a. 정돈된, 단정한; 깔끔한; 아기자기한 A neat place, thing, or person is tidy and smart, and has everything in the correct place.
humble* [hʌmbl]	a. 겸손한; 변변치 않은; 보잘것없는; v. 겸손하게 하다 A humble person is not proud and does not believe that they are better than other people.
tone^{복습} [toun]	n. 어조, 말투; (글 등의) 분위기; 음색 Someone's tone is a quality in their voice which shows what they are feeling or thinking.
exhaust* [igzɔ́:st]	v. 기진맥진하게 하다; 다 써 버리다; n. (자동차 등의) 배기가스 (exhausted a. 기진맥진한) If something exhausts you, it makes you so tired, either physically or mentally, that you have no energy left.
nap* [næp]	n. 낮잠; v. 낮잠을 자다 If you have a nap, you have a short sleep, usually during the day.

icebox ^{복습}
[áisbàks]

n. 냉장고; 아이스박스

An icebox is the same as a refrigerator which is a large metal container kept cool, usually by electricity, so that food that is put in it stays fresh.

Check Your Reading Speed

1분에 몇 단어를 읽는지 리딩 속도를 측정해 보세요.

$$\frac{757 \text{ words}}{\text{reading time (\quad) sec}} \times 60 = (\quad) \text{ WPM}$$

Build Your Vocabulary

chronicle
[kránikl]

n. 신문; 연대기; v. 연대순으로 기록하다
Chronicle is sometimes used as part of the name of a newspaper.

paragraph*
[pǽrəgræf]

n. (신문·잡지의) 짧은 기사; 짤막한 논설, 단평; 단락, 절
A paragraph is a short article in a newspaper.

faraway*
[fáːrəwèi]

a. 멀리 떨어진, 먼
A faraway place is a long distance from you or from a particular place.

associated
[əsóuʃièitid]

a. 연합의; 관련된
Associated is used in the name of a company that is made up of a number of smaller companies which have joined together.

cease*
[siːs]

v. 그만두다, 중지하다
If you cease something, you stop it happening or working.

gay*
[gei]

a. 명랑한, 쾌활한
A gay person is fun to be with because they are lively and cheerful.

sulk
[sʌlk]

v. 샐쭉해지다, 부루퉁해지다; n. 샐쭉함, 부루퉁함
If you sulk, you are silent and bad-tempered for a while because you are annoyed about something.

refrigerator^{복습}
[rifrídʒərèitər]

n. 냉장고
A refrigerator is a large container which is kept cool inside, usually by electricity, so that the food and drink in it stays fresh.

marble^{복습}
[maːrbl]

n. (아이들이 가지고 노는) 구슬; 대리석
A marble is a small ball, usually made of colored or transparent glass, which is used in children's games.

orderly*
[ɔ́ːrdərli]

a. 정돈된, 정연한; (행동이) 질서 있는
Something that is orderly is neat or arranged in a neat way.

rookery^{복습}
[rúkəri]

n. (바다표범·펭귄 등의) 서식지, 번식지
A rookery is a breeding ground for gregarious birds such as rooks.

naughty^{복습}
[nɔ́ːti]

a. 버릇없는, 말을 안 듣는; 약간 무례한
If you say that a child is naughty, you mean that they behave badly or do not do what they are told.

mope
[moup]

v. 침울해하다; 맥이 빠져 지내다 (mopey a. 울적해하는, 무척 침울한)
If you mope, you feel miserable and do not feel interested in doing anything.

ail
[eil]

v. (남을) 괴롭히다, 고통을 주다; 앓다, 병들다
If something ails someone, it troubles or afflicts them in mind or body.

stare^{복습}
[stɛər]

v. 빤히 쳐다보다, 응시하다; n. 빤히 쳐다보기, 응시
If you stare at someone or something, you look at them for a long time.

glossy^{복습}
[glási]

a. 광택이 나는, 번질번질한
Glossy means smooth and shiny.

shrimp^{복습}
[ʃrimp]

n. 새우
Shrimps are small shellfish with long tails and many legs.

veterinary
[vétərənèri]

a. 수의(학)의; n. 수의사
Veterinary is used to describe the work of a person whose job is to treat sick or injured animals, or to describe the medical treatment of animals.

glance*
[glæns]

n. 흘낏 봄; v. 흘낏 보다; 대충 훑어보다 (at a glance idiom 한눈에)
If you see something at a glance, you see or recognize it immediately, and without having to think or look carefully.

pill*
[pil]

n. 알약
Pills are small solid round masses of medicine or vitamins that you swallow without chewing.

feed^{복습}
[fi:d]

v. 먹이를 주다; 공급하다; n. (동물의) 먹이
If you feed a person or animal, you give them food to eat and sometimes actually put it in their mouths.

wrap^{복습}
[ræp]

v. 둘러싸다; 싸다, 포장하다; n. 포장지
When you wrap something such as a piece of paper or cloth round another thing, you put it around it.

encourage**
[inkɔ́:ridʒ]

v. 격려하다, 용기를 북돋우다; 부추기다 (encouragement n. 격려(가 되는 것))
Encouragement is words or behavior that give someone confidence to do something.

hopeless*
[hóuplis]

a. 가망 없는, 절망적인
Someone or something thing that is hopeless is certain to fail or be unsuccessful.

climate*
[kláimit]

n. 기후; 분위기, 풍조
The climate of a place is the general weather conditions that are typical of it.

thrive*
[θraiv]

v. 잘 자라다; 번창하다
If someone or something thrives, they do well and are successful, healthy, or strong.

sit up

idiom (평소보다 늦은 시각까지) 안 자다
To sit up means to stay awake and not go to bed although it is late.

take turns

idiom ~을 교대로 하다
If two or more people take turns to do something, they do it one after the other several times, rather than doing it together.

sympathetic*
[simpəθétik]

a. 동정심 있는, 인정 있는; 마음에 드는
If you are sympathetic to someone who is in a bad situation, you are kind to them and show that you understand their feelings.

stop in^{복습}

idiom ~에 잠시 들르다
To stop in means to visit a person or place for a short time, usually when you are going somewhere else.

inquire^{복습}
[inkwáiər]

v. 묻다, 알아보다
If you inquire about something, you ask for information about it.

tempt*
[tempt]

v. 유혹하다; 유도하다, 설득하다
If you tempt someone, you offer them something they want in order to encourage them to do what you want them to do.

fellow^{복습}
[félou]

n. 녀석, 친구; 동료, 동년배; a. 동료의
A fellow is a man or boy.

freeze**
[fri:z]

v. 얼다; 얼리다; (두려움 등으로 몸이) 얼어붙다; n. 동결; 한파
(frozen a. 냉동된; (몸이) 얼어붙은)
If you freeze something such as food, you preserve it by storing it at a temperature below freezing point.

far gone
[fa:r gɔ́:n]

a. (병세 등이) 꽤 진전된, 악화된; 몹시 취한
If you say someone is far gone, you mean that they are very drunk, ill, or in some other advanced and bad state.

stupor
[stjú:pər]

n. 인사불성
Someone who is in a stupor is almost unconscious and is unable to act or think normally, especially as a result of drink or drugs.

fond***
[fand]

a. 애정을 느끼는, 좋아하는
If you are fond of someone, you feel affection for them.

solemn^{복습}
[sáləm]

a. 엄숙한; 침통한; 근엄한
Someone or something that is solemn is very serious rather than cheerful or humorous.

chap*
[ʧæp]

n. 놈, 녀석
A chap is a man or boy.

terror*
[térər]

n. (극심한) 두려움, 공포; 공포의 대상; 테러 (행위)
Terror is very great fear.

pole^{복습}
[poul]

n. (지구의) 극; 기둥, 장대
The earth's poles are the two opposite ends of its axis, its most northern and southern points.

despair*
[dispέər]

n. 절망; v. 절망하다, 체념하다
Despair is the feeling that everything is wrong and that nothing will improve.

address***
[ədrés]

v. (~ 앞으로 우편물을) 보내다; 말을 하다; 연설하다; n. 주소; 연설
If a letter, envelope, or parcel is addressed to you, your name and address have been written on it.

64

curator
[kjuəréitər]

n. (도서관·박물관 등의) 책임자
A curator is someone who is in charge of the objects or works of art in a museum or art gallery.

aquarium
[əkwéəriəm]

n. 수족관
An aquarium is a building, often in a zoo, where fish and underwater animals are kept.

unfortunately**
[ʌnfɔ́:rʧənətli]

ad. 불행하게도, 유감스럽게도
You can use unfortunately to introduce or refer to a statement when you consider that it is sad or disappointing, or when you want to express regret.

rapid^{복습}
[rǽpid]

a. 빠른, 급한; (행동이) 민첩한 (rapidly ad. 급속히, 빨리)
A rapid change is one that happens very quickly.

ship***
[ʃip]

v. 실어 나르다, 운송하다; n. (큰) 배, 선박, 함선
If people or things are shipped somewhere, they are sent there on a ship or by some other means of transport.

under separate cover

idiom 별도의 봉투에
'Under separate cover' is used in a letter for saying that something will be sent separately.

Chapters 11 & 12

1. How did the Poppers tell the penguins apart?
   A. He could tell by their voices.
   B. He put a leash on Captain Cook.
   C. He painted a dress on Greta.
   D. He painted their names on their backs.

2. Why did Mr. Popper tell Mrs. Popper to put the food back into the ice box?
   A. He told her that the food was going to spoil if left out.
   B. He told her they could just keep the penguins in the house with all the windows open.
   C. He told her they could let the penguins live outside in the winter.
   D. He told her that he was going to buy another bigger ice box for the penguins.

3. How did Mr. Popper react to the blizzard that brought snow into the house?
   A. He shoveled the snow into the cellar for the penguins.
   B. He thought that the snow would make it too uncomfortable to live in.
   C. He thought that his children might get sick in such a cold house.
   D. He saw that the penguins were having fun and left the snow there for them.

4. How did Mr. Popper make the cellar a place for Captain Cook and Greta to live?

    A. He moved the ice box down into the cellar.

    B. He brought snow from outside down into the basement.

    C. He put a freezing plant in the cellar and moved the furnace up to the living room.

    D. He opened up all of the windows to the cellar and threw away the furnace.

5. Why was Mr. Popper astonished about the eggs?

    A. Penguins usually only laid eggs in the spring.

    B. Penguins only laid two eggs a season, but Greta laid ten in all.

    C. Penguins usually laid two eggs a season, but Greta only laid one.

    D. Penguins usually made a bigger nest than Greta had made for her eggs.

6. Why did Mr. Popper dig a hole in the cellar floor?

    A. He wanted to dig a space for a nest.

    B. He made a swimming and diving pool for the penguins.

    C. He wanted to make more space for the new baby penguins.

    D. He made stairs and a slide for the penguins to climb and slide down.

7. How did Mr. Popper feel about the coming spring?

    A. He dreaded having to leave the penguins all day and go to work.

    B. He was worried that the weather might be too warm for penguins.

    C. He was thinking about teaching the penguins to help him paint houses.

    D. He was excited about bringing the penguins to the houses that he would paint.

Check Your Reading Speed

1분에 몇 단어를 읽는지 리딩 속도를 측정해 보세요.

$$\frac{863\ words}{reading\ time\ (\quad)\ sec} \times 60 = (\quad)\ WPM$$

Build Your Vocabulary

after all
idiom (예상과는 달리) 결국에는: 어쨌든
You use after all when you are saying that something that you thought might not be the case is in fact the case.

refrigerator^{복습}
[rifrídʒərèitər]
n. 냉장고
A refrigerator is a large container which is kept cool inside, usually by electricity, so that the food and drink in it stays fresh.

nest^{복습}
[nest]
n. 둥지; 보금자리; v. 둥지를 틀다
A bird's nest is the home that it makes to lay its eggs in.

pea*
[pi:]
n. 완두콩 (as like as two peas idiom 똑같이 닮은)
You use 'as like as two peas in a pod' to say that two people or things are very similar to each other.

icebox^{복습}
[áisbàks]
n. 냉장고; 아이스박스
An icebox is the same as a refrigerator which is a large metal container kept cool, usually by electricity, so that food that is put in it stays fresh.

pat*
[pæt]
v. 쓰다듬다; 가볍게 두드리다; n. 쓰다듬기, 토닥거리기
If you pat something or someone, you tap them lightly, usually with your hand held flat.

friendship*
[fréndʃip]
n. 우정; 친선; 교우 관계
You use friendship to refer in a general way to the state of being friends, or the feelings that friends have for each other.

grateful**
[gréitfəl]
a. 고마워하는, 감사하는
If you are grateful for something that someone has given you or done for you, you have warm, friendly feelings toward them and wish to thank them.

tell apart
idiom 구별하다, 분간하다
If you tell someone or something apart, you recognize the difference between two people or things that are very similar.

confuse**
[kənfjú:z]
v. (사람을) 혼란시키다; 혼동하다 (confusing a. 혼란스러운)
Something that is confusing makes it difficult for people to know exactly what is happening or what to do.

cellar*
[sélər]
n. 지하 저장실
A cellar is a room underneath a building, which is often used for storing things in.

trip***
[trip]

v. ~에 걸려 넘어지다; n. 여행; 발을 헛디딤
If you trip when you are walking, you knock your foot against something and fall or nearly fall.

toboggan^{복습}
[təbágən]

v. 썰매를 타다; n. 터보건 (썰매)
If you toboggan, you move along on a light wooden board with a curved front, to travel down hills on snow or ice.

squirm
[skwə:rm]

v. (몸을) 꿈틀대다; 몹시 창피해 하다
If you squirm, you move your body from side to side, usually because you are nervous or uncomfortable.

overcoat*
[óuvərkout]

n. 외투, 오버코트
An overcoat is a thick warm coat that you wear in winter.

sneeze*
[sni:z]

v. 재채기하다; n. 재채기
When you sneeze, you suddenly take in your breath and then blow it down your nose noisily without being able to stop yourself.

occupy*
[ákjupài]

v. (공간·지역·시간을) 차지하다; ~를 바쁘게 하다
If a room or something such as a seat is occupied, someone is using it, so that it is not available for anyone else.

blizzard
[blízərd]

n. 눈보라
A blizzard is a very bad snowstorm with strong winds.

drift*
[drift]

n. (눈이 바람에 휩쓸려 쌓인) 더미; 이동; v. (물·공기에) 떠가다; (서서히) 이동하다
(snowdrift n. 바람에 날려 쌓인 눈 더미)
A drift is a mass of snow that has built up into a pile as a result of the movement of wind.

broom*
[bru:m]

n. 비, 빗자루
A broom is a kind of brush with a long handle. You use a broom for sweeping the floor.

shovel*
[ʃʌvəl]

n. 삽; v. ~을 삽으로 뜨다
A shovel is a tool with a long handle that is used for lifting and moving earth, coal, or snow.

insist^{복습}
[insíst]

v. 고집하다, 주장하다, 우기다
If you insist that something should be done, you say so very firmly and refuse to give in about it.

go so far as to

idiom 심지어 ~하기까지 하다
If you go so far as to do something, you are willing to go to extreme or surprising limits in dealing with it.

basement**
[béismənt]

n. (건물의) 지하층
The basement of a building is a floor built partly or completely below ground level.

sprinkle*
[spriŋkl]

v. (액체·분말 등을) 뿌리다, 끼얹다; n. 소량, 조금
If you sprinkle a thing with something such as a liquid or powder, you scatter the liquid or powder over it.

smooth^{복습}
[smu:ð]

a. 매끈한; 순조로운; v. 매끈하게 하다; 고루 펴 바르다
A smooth surface has no roughness, lumps, or holes.

edge^{복습}
[edʒ]

n. 끝, 가장자리, 모서리; 우위; v. 조금씩 움직이다
The edge of something is the place or line where it stops, or the part of it that is furthest from the middle.

tremendous*
[triméndəs]

a. 엄청난, 굉장한, 대단한 (tremendously ad. 엄청나게)
You use tremendous to emphasize how strong a feeling or quality is, or how large an amount is.

pleased^{복습}
[pli:zd]

a. 기뻐하는, 만족해하는
If you are pleased, you are happy about something or satisfied with something.

flop
[flap]

v. 털썩 주저앉다, 드러눕다; (무겁게) 매달리다
If you flop into a chair, for example, you sit down suddenly and heavily because you are so tired.

stomach^{복습}
[stʌ́mək]

n. 복부, 배
You can refer to the front part of your body below your waist as your stomach.

slippery^{복습}
[slípəri]

a. 미끄러운
Something that is slippery is smooth, wet, or oily and is therefore difficult to walk on or to hold.

amuse*
[əmjú:z]

v. 즐겁게 하다, 재미있게 하다
If something amuses you, it makes you want to laugh or smile.

in turn

idiom 결국, 결과적으로
You use in turn to refer to actions or events that are in a sequence one after the other, for example because one causes the other.

slide^{복습}
[slaid]

v. 미끄러지다; 슬며시 움직이다; n. 떨어짐; 미끄러짐
When something slides somewhere or when you slide it there, it moves there smoothly over or against something.

freeze^{복습}
[fri:z]

v. (froze-frozen) 얼다; 얼리다; (두려움 등으로 몸이) 얼어붙다; n. 동결; 한파
If a liquid or a substance containing a liquid freezes, or if something freezes it, it becomes solid because of low temperatures.

melt**
[melt]

v. 녹다; (감정 등이) 누그러지다
When a solid substance melts or when you melt it, it changes to a liquid, usually because it has been heated.

go on^{복습}

idiom (어떤 상황이) 계속되다; 말을 계속하다
If something goes on, it continues to happen or exist without changing.

sleek^{복습}
[sli:k]

a. 윤이 나는; (모양이) 매끈한; 부티 나는; v. 윤이 나게 하다
Sleek hair or fur is smooth and shiny and looks healthy.

rosy*
[róuzi]

a. 장밋빛의, 발그레한; (전망 등이) 희망적인
If you say that someone has a rosy face, you mean that they have pink cheeks and look very healthy.

mop
[map]

v. 대걸레로 닦다, 청소하다; n. 대걸레
If you mop a surface such as a floor, you clean it with a mop.

flood^{**}
[flʌd]

n. 홍수; v. 물에 잠기게 하다; (감정·생각이) 밀려들다
If there is a flood, a large amount of water covers an area which is usually dry, for example when a river flows over its banks or a pipe bursts.

untidy^{복습}
[ʌntáidi]

a. 단정치 못한, 어수선한; 깔끔하지 못한
If you describe something as untidy, you mean that it is not neat or well arranged.

Check Your Reading Speed

1분에 몇 단어를 읽는지 리딩 속도를 측정해 보세요.

$$\frac{906 \text{ words}}{\text{reading time ( ) sec}} \times 60 = (\quad) \text{ WPM}$$

Build Your Vocabulary

plant***
[plænt]

n. 시설; 공장; 식물, 초목; v. 심다; (장소에) 놓다 (freezing plant n. 냉동 시설)
Plant is large machinery that is used in industrial processes.

install**
[instɔ́:l]

v. (장비·가구를) 설치하다; 자리를 잡게 하다
If you install a piece of equipment, you fit it or put it somewhere so that it is ready to be used.

cellar^{복습}
[sélər]

n. 지하 저장실
A cellar is a room underneath a building, which is often used for storing things in.

furnace*
[fɔ́:rnis]

n. 보일러
A furnace is a device which burns gas, oil, electricity, or coal in order to provide hot water, especially for the central heating in a building.

odd^{복습}
[ad]

a. 이상한, 특이한; 홀수의
If you describe someone or something as odd, you think that they are strange or unusual.

relief**
[rilí:f]

n. 안도, 안심; (고통·불안 등의) 완화
If you feel a sense of relief, you feel happy because something unpleasant has not happened or is no longer happening.

overcoat^{복습}
[óuvərkout]

n. 외투, 오버코트
An overcoat is a thick warm coat that you wear in winter.

refrigerate
[rifrídʒərèit]

v. (음식 등을) 냉장하다
If you refrigerate food, you make it cold, for example by putting it in a fridge, usually in order to preserve it.

practical**
[prǽktikəl]

a. 거의 완전한, 사실상의; 현실적인 (practically ad. 사실상, 거의)
Practically means almost, but not completely or exactly.

credit**
[krédit]

n. 신용 거래; (계좌) 잔고; 칭찬; v. 입금하다; ~의 공으로 믿다
(on credit idiom 외상으로)
If you are allowed credit, you are allowed to pay for goods or services several weeks or months after you have received them.

rookery^{복습}
[rúkəri]

n. (바다표범·펭귄 등의) 서식지, 번식지
A rookery is a breeding ground for gregarious birds such as rooks.

scarcely^{복습}
[skέərsli]

ad. ~하자마자; 겨우, 간신히; 거의 ~않다
If you say scarcely had one thing happened when something else happened, you mean that the first event was followed immediately by the second.

basement^{복습}
[béismənt]

n. (건물의) 지하층
The basement of a building is a floor built partly or completely below ground level.

astonish^{복습}
[əstániʃ]

v. 깜짝 놀라게 하다 (astonished a. 깜짝 놀란)
If you are astonished by something, you are very surprised about it.

climate^{복습}
[kláimit]

n. 기후; 분위기, 풍조
The climate of a place is the general weather conditions that are typical of it.

breed*
[bri:d]

v. 새끼를 낳다; n. (개·고양이·가축의) 품종
When animals breed, they have babies.

distribute*
[distríbju:t]

v. 분배하다, 배포하다, 배급하다
If you distribute things, you hand them or deliver them to a number of people.

chick*
[ʧik]

n. 새끼 새; 병아리
A chick is a baby bird.

hatch*
[hæʧ]

v. 부화하다; (계획 등을) 만들어 내다; n. (배·항공기의) 출입구
When a baby bird, insect, or other animal hatches, or when it is hatched, it comes out of its egg by breaking the shell.

mark***
[ma:rk]

v. 특징 짓다; 표시하다; n. 자국, 흔적
If something is marked by a particular quality or feature, it is a typical or important part of that thing.

fuzzy
[fʌzi]

a. 솜털이 보송보송한; 흐릿한, 어렴풋한
If something is fuzzy, it has a covering that feels soft and like fur.

droll
[droul]

a. 우스꽝스러운, 까부는
Something or someone that is droll is amusing or witty, sometimes in an unexpected way.

tremendous^{복습}
[triméndəs]

a. 엄청난; 굉장한, 대단한
You use tremendous to emphasize how strong a feeling or quality is, or how large an amount is.

rate**
[reit]

n. 속도; 비율; v. 평가하다
The rate at which something happens is the speed with which it happens.

relieve*
[rilí:v]

v. 안도하게 하다; (불쾌감·고통 등을) 없애 주다 (relieved a. 안도하는)
If you are relieved, you feel happy because something unpleasant has not happened or is no longer happening.

housework*
[háuswə:rk]

n. 가사, 집안일
Housework is the work such as cleaning, washing, and ironing that you do in your home.

curious^{복습}
[kjúəriəs]

a. 별난, 특이한; 궁금한; 호기심이 많은
If you describe something as curious, you mean that it is unusual or difficult to understand.

block^{복습}
[blak]

n. (단단한) 사각형 덩어리; (도로로 나뉘는) 구역, 블록; v. 막다, 차단하다
A block of a substance is a large rectangular piece of it.

dig**
[dig]

v. (dug-dug) (구멍 등을) 파다; (무엇을 찾기 위해) 뒤지다; n. 쿡 찌르기
If people or animals dig, they make a hole in the ground or in a pile of earth, stones, or rubbish.

dive^{복습}
[daiv]

v. (물 속으로 거꾸로) 뛰어들다; 잠수하다; n. (물 속으로) 뛰어들기
If you dive into some water, you jump in head-first with your arms held straight above your head.

refreshing
[rifréʃiŋ]

a. 신선한; 상쾌하게 하는
You say that something is refreshing when it is pleasantly different from what you are used to.

to tell the truth^{복습}

idiom 사실은
You say to tell you the truth or truth to tell in order to indicate that you are telling someone something in an open and honest way, without trying to hide anything.

coast**
[koust]

n. 해안
The coast is an area of land that is next to the sea.

unfortunately^{복습}
[ʌnfɔ́:rtʃənətli]

ad. 불행하게도, 유감스럽게도
You can use unfortunately to introduce or refer to a statement when you consider that it is sad or disappointing, or when you want to express regret.

spar
[spa:r]

v. 가볍게 치고 덤비다, 스파링하다; 말싸움하다
If you spar with someone, you box using fairly gentle blows instead of hitting your opponent hard.

flipper^{복습}
[flípər]

n. (바다표범·거북 등의) 지느러미발; (잠수·수영 때 신는) 오리발
The flippers of an animal that lives in water, for example a seal or a penguin, are the two or four flat limbs which it uses for swimming.

encourage^{복습}
[inkə́:ridʒ]

v. 격려하다, 용기를 북돋우다; 부추기다 (encouraging a. 격려하는)
Something that is encouraging gives people hope or confidence.

remark**
[rimá:rk]

n. 말, 언급; 주목; v. ~에 주목하다; 언급하다, 말하다
If you make a remark about something, you say something about it.

scene^{복습}
[si:n]

n. 장면, 광경; 현장; 풍경
You can describe an event that you see, or that is broadcast or shown in a picture, as a scene of a particular kind.

flood^{복습}
[flʌd]

v. 물에 잠기게 하다; (감정·생각이) 밀려들다; n. 홍수
If something such as a river or a burst pipe floods an area that is usually dry or if the area floods, it becomes covered with water.

drill*
[dril]

v. 반복 훈련시키다; 구멍을 뚫다; n. 훈련
If you drill people, you teach them to do something by making them repeat it many times.

march^{복습}
[ma:rʧ]

v. 행진하다; (단호한 태도로 급히) 걸어가다; n. 행진, 행군; 행진곡
When soldiers march somewhere, or when a commanding officer marches them somewhere, they walk there with very regular steps, as a group.

parade^{복습}
[pəréid]

n. 퍼레이드, 가두 행진; v. (과시하듯) 걸어 다니다; 행진하다
Parade is a formal occasion when soldiers stand in lines to be seen by an officer or important person, or march in a group.

fond^{복습}
[fand]

a. 애정을 느끼는, 좋아하는
If you are fond of something, you like it or you like doing it very much.

sight^{★★}
[sait]

n. 광경, 모습; 시력; 시야
A sight is something that you see.

flag^{★★}
[flæg]

n. 기, 깃발; v. 표시를 하다; 지치다; 약해지다
A flag is a piece of cloth which can be attached to a pole and which is used as a sign, signal, or symbol of something, especially of a particular country.

beak^{복습}
[bi:k]

n. (새의) 부리
A bird's beak is the hard curved or pointed part of its mouth.

mitten
[mitn]

n. 벙어리장갑
Mittens are gloves which have one section that covers your thumb and another section that covers your four fingers together.

distant^{★★}
[dístənt]

a. 먼, (멀리) 떨어져 있는; 다정하지 않은
Distant means very far away.

region^{복습}
[rí:dʒən]

n. 지방, 지역, 영역
A region is a large area of land that is different from other areas of land.

occupy^{복습}
[ákjupài]

v. ~를 바쁘게 하다; (공간·지역·시간을) 차지하다
If something occupies you, or if you occupy yourself, your time, or your mind with it, you are busy doing that thing or thinking about it.

dread[★]
[dred]

v. 몹시 무서워하다; 두려워하다; n. 두려움; 두려운 것
If you dread something which may happen, you feel very anxious and unhappy about it because you think it will be unpleasant or upsetting.

Chapters 13 & 14

1. Why was Mrs. Popper so worried one night that she stopped Mr. Popper on his way to the cellar?
   A. She was worried about keeping the cellar tidy.
   B. She was worried about the having enough money.
   C. She was worried about having the proper license for penguins.
   D. She was worried about the children being distracted from their studies.

2. What was Mr. Popper's idea to earn money with the penguins?
   A. He wanted to cook them.
   B. He wanted to sell them to the zoo.
   C. He wanted to sell them to somebody.
   D. He wanted to train the penguins to act.

3. Which of the following was NOT one of the tricks that Mr. Popper wanted to build an act around?
   A. Penguins playing the piano
   B. Penguins getting into a fight
   C. Penguins marching like an army
   D. Penguins climbing up steps and sliding down

4. How did Mrs. Popper learn to play the piano in the cellar?
   A. She learned to play with her eyes closed.
   B. She learned to play with her gloves on.
   C. She learned to play while standing up.
   D. She learned to play while dancing.

5. Why were the Popper family and their penguins going to find the Palace Theater?
   A. The Poppers were going to let the penguins explore the city without leashes.
   B. They were going to watch a performance of trained seals.
   C. They were going to see Mr. Greenbaum about starting an act.
   D. The penguins were going to live there instead of Mr. Popper's cellar.

6. Why did the passengers on the bus complain to the bus driver?
   A. Mr. Popper tried to show the passengers a trick.
   B. Mr. Popper opened all of the windows on the bus.
   C. The penguins sat on too many seats on the bus.
   D. The penguins were running around and making noise.

7. Why did Mr. Popper disapprove of the name suggested by Mr. Greenbaum?
   A. He thought that it should be longer.
   B. He wanted to have "Mr. Popper" in the name.
   C. He thought that someone else had already used that name.
   D. He thought it sounded too much like chorus girls or ballet dancers.

Check Your Reading Speed

1분에 몇 단어를 읽는지 리딩 속도를 측정해 보세요.

$$\frac{624 \text{ words}}{\text{reading time ( ) sec}} \times 60 = (\quad) \text{ WPM}$$

Build Your Vocabulary

cellar^{복습}
[sélər]

n. 지하 저장실
A cellar is a room underneath a building, which is often used for storing things in.

tidy^{복습}
[táidi]

a. 깔끔한, 잘 정돈된, 단정한; v. 치우다, 정돈하다
Something that is tidy is neat and is arranged in an organized way.

bill^{복습}
[bil]

n. 고지서, 청구서; 지폐; (새의) 부리; (극장 등의) 프로그램
A bill is a written statement of money that you owe for goods or services.

plant^{복습}
[plænt]

n. 시설; 공장; 식물, 초목; v. 심다; (장소에) 놓다 (freezing plant n. 냉동 시설)
Plant is large machinery that is used in industrial processes.

practical^{복습}
[prǽktikəl]

a. 거의 완전한, 사실상의; 현실적인 (practically ad. 사실상, 거의)
Practically means almost, but not completely or exactly.

break one's heart

idiom 몹시 실망시키다, 비탄에 잠기게 하다
If an event or situation breaks your heart, it makes you feel very sad.

thoughtful*
[θɔ́:tfəl]

a. (조용히) 생각에 잠긴; 사려 깊은 (thoughtfully ad. 생각에 잠겨)
If you are thoughtful, you are quiet and serious because you are thinking about something.

live on

idiom (얼마의 돈으로) 먹고 살다
To live on means to have a particular amount of money to buy the things that you need to live.

seal*
[si:l]

n. [동물] 바다표범; 직인, 도장; v. 봉인하다; 확정짓다, 다짐하다
A seal is a large animal with a rounded body and flat legs called flippers.

piece*
[pi:s]

n. (글·미술·음악 등의 작품) 하나; 조각, 단편, 파편, 일부분
You can refer to a work of art as a piece.

drill^{복습}
[dril]

v. 반복 훈련시키다; 구멍을 뚫다; n. 훈련
If you drill people, you teach them to do something by making them repeat it many times.

trick**
[trik]

n. 묘기; 속임수; 장난; v. 속이다, 속임수를 쓰다
A trick is a clever or skillful action that someone does in order to entertain people.

costume*
[kástjuːm]

n. 의상, 분장; 복장
An actor's or performer's costume is the set of clothes they wear while they are performing.

droll복습
[droul]

a. 우스꽝스러운, 까부는
Something or someone that is droll is amusing or witty, sometimes in an unexpected way.

figure복습
[fígjər]

n. 모습, 몸매; 수치; v. 생각하다; 판단하다
You refer to someone that you can see as a figure when you cannot see them clearly or when you are describing them.

tune*
[tjuːn]

n. 곡, 곡조, 선율; v. (악기의) 음을 맞추다; (기계를) 정비하다
You can refer to a song or a short piece of music as a tune.

military**
[mílitèri]

a. 군대의, 군사의; n. 군대
Military means relating to the armed forces of a country.

widow*
[wídou]

n. 미망인, 과부
A widow is a woman whose husband has died and who has not married again.

drag복습
[dræg]

v. 끌고 가다; 질질 끌리다; 힘들게 움직이다; n. 끌기; 장애물
If you drag something, you pull it along the ground, often with difficulty.

portable*
[pɔ́ːrtəbl]

a. 휴대가 쉬운, 휴대용의
A portable machine or device is designed to be easily carried or moved.

stepladder
[stéplædər]

n. 발판 사다리
A stepladder is a portable ladder that is made of two sloping parts that are hinged together at the top so that it will stand up on its own.

board복습
[bɔːrd]

n. 판자; 이사회; v. 승선하다, 탑승하다
A board is a flat, thin, rectangular piece of wood or plastic which is used for a particular purpose.

descriptive
[diskríptiv]

a. 서술하는, 묘사하는; 기술적인
Descriptive language or writing indicates what someone or something is like.

brook*
[bruk]

n. 개울
A brook is a small stream.

Check Your Reading Speed
1분에 몇 단어를 읽는지 리딩 속도를 측정해 보세요.

$$\frac{754 \text{ words}}{\text{reading time ( ) sec}} \times 60 = (\text{ }) \text{ WPM}$$

Build Your Vocabulary

chronicle^{복습}
[kránikl]
n. 신문; 연대기; v. 연대순으로 기록하다
Chronicle is sometimes used as part of the name of a newspaper.

string**
[striŋ]
n. 일련; 끈, 줄; v. 묶다, 매달다; (실 등에) 꿰다
A string of things or people is a series of things or people that come closely one after another.

flag^{복습}
[flæg]
n. 기, 깃발; v. 표시를 하다; 지치다; 약해지다
A flag is a piece of cloth which can be attached to a pole and which is used as a sign, signal, or symbol of something, especially of a particular country.

leash^{복습}
[liːʃ]
n. 가죽끈, 사슬; 속박, 통제; v. (개를) 줄에 매어 두다
A dog's leash is a long thin piece of leather or a chain, which you attach to the dog's collar so that you can keep the dog under control.

astonish^{복습}
[əstániʃ]
v. 깜짝 놀라게 하다 (astonished a. 깜짝 놀란)
If you are astonished by something, you are very surprised about it.

protest^{복습}
[próutest]
v. 항의하다, 이의를 제기하다; n. 항의
If you protest against something or about something, you say or show publicly that you object to it.

fare**
[fɛər]
n. (교통) 요금
A fare is the money that you pay for a journey that you make, for example, in a bus, train, or taxi.

hush*
[hʌʃ]
int. 쉿, 조용히 해; v. ~을 조용히 시키다
You say 'Hush!' to someone when you are asking or telling them to be quiet.

orderly^{복습}
[ɔ́ːrdərli]
a. 차례로 된, 규율 있는
If something is done in an orderly fashion or manner, it is done in a well-organized and controlled way.

fashion**
[fǽʃən]
n. 방법, 방식; (의상·머리형 등의) 유행(하는 스타일)
If you do something in a particular fashion or after a particular fashion, you do it in that way.

exhibit^{복습}
[igzíbit]
n. 전시품; v. 전시하다; 보이다, 드러내다
An exhibit is a painting, sculpture, or object of interest that is displayed to the public in a museum or art gallery.

80

to tell the truth^{복습}

idiom 사실은
You say to tell you the truth or truth to tell in order to indicate that you are telling someone something in an open and honest way, without trying to hide anything.

transfer*
[trænsfɔ́:r]

n. 환승표; (다른 장소로의) 이동; v. 이동하다, (장소를) 옮기다; (병을) 옮기다
A transfer is a ticket that allows a passenger to change routes or to change from one bus or train to another.

let well enough alone

idiom 현 상태에 만족하다
To leave well enough alone means to avoid trying to improve or change something that is satisfactory.

passenger^{복습}
[pǽsəndʒər]

n. 승객
A passenger in a vehicle such as a bus, boat, or plane is a person who is traveling in it, but who is not driving it or working on it.

address^{복습}
[ədrés]

v. 말을 하다; (~ 앞으로 우편물을) 보내다; 연설하다; n. 주소; 연설
If you address someone or address a remark to them, you say something to them.

Antarctic^{복습}
[æntá:rktik]

a. 남극의, 남극 지방의; n. 남극
The Antarctic is the area around the South Pole.

stuck
[stʌk]

a. 움직일 수 없는, 꼼짝 못하는; 무엇을 할지 모르는
If something is stuck in a particular position, it is fixed tightly in this position and is unable to move.

fast***
[fæst]

ad. 단단히; 완전히
If something is stuck fast, it is stuck very firmly and cannot move.

remark^{복습}
[rimá:rk]

n. 말, 언급; 주목; v. ~에 주목하다; 언급하다, 말하다
If you make a remark about something, you say something about it.

troop*
[tru:p]

v. 무리를 지어 걸어가다; n. (대규모의) 병력, 군대; 부대; 무리
If people troop somewhere, they walk there in a group, often in a sad or tired way.

backstage
[bækstéidʒ]

ad. 무대 뒤에서; 은밀히
In a theater, backstage refers to the areas behind the stage.

row*
[rou]

n. (사람·사물들의) 열, 줄; 노 젓기; v. 노를 젓다
A row of things or people is a number of them arranged in a line.

solemn^{복습}
[sáləm]

a. 엄숙한; 근엄한; 침통한
Someone or something that is solemn is very serious rather than cheerful or humorous.

conference*
[kánfərəns]

n. 회담, 협의; 학회
A conference is a meeting at which formal discussions take place.

pole^{복습}
[poul]

n. (지구의) 극; 기둥, 장대
The earth's poles are the two opposite ends of its axis, its most northern and southern points.

toe*
[tou]

n. 발가락 (toed a. 발가락이 ~한)
Your toes are the five movable parts at the end of each foot.

chorus[*]
[kɔ́ːrəs]

n. 합창단; 합창, 코러스; 후렴; v. 합창하다; 이구동성으로 말하다
A chorus is a large group of people who sing together.

coast^{복습}
[koust]

n. 해안 (coast to coast idiom 전국에 걸쳐)
Coast to coast means everywhere or all across a country.

Chapters 15 & 16

1. Why were the Poppers and Mr. Greenbaum interrupted by the manager?
    A. The manager wanted Mr. Greenbaum to pay him more.
    B. The manager wanted to see Mr. Popper's penguins practice.
    C. The manager told Mr. Greenbaum that the closing act hadn't arrived.
    D. The manager wanted Mr. Popper and his penguins to leave the theater.

2. Why did the other penguins get Nelson to look away?
    A. The other penguins liked Nelson to win.
    B. The other penguins liked Columbus to win.
    C. The other penguins wanted to fight, too.
    D. The other penguins liked Nelson and Columbus to have a draw.

3. What did Mr. Popper say was needed so that the penguins would be under control?
    A. The penguins needed ice cream cones.
    B. The music would have to stop playing.
    C. The audience would have to stop cheering.
    D. The ladders would have to be taken off the stage.

4. Why did the manager want Mrs. Popper to play the piano again after the act was over?

   A. The manager really liked the music she played.

   B. The manager missed seeing the performance on stage.

   C. The manager wanted to see her play with gloves on again.

   D. The manager wanted to have his ushers see the penguins march.

5. How did the two taxis get into an accident?

   A. They both wanted to get to the station first.

   B. They both wanted to pick up the penguins first.

   C. The drivers were distracted by the penguins making noise.

   D. The drivers were pecked by the penguins as they drove.

6. How was there trouble for the penguins in the sleeping cars?

   A. The penguins saw ladders and started climbing up them.

   B. The penguins were hungry and stopped to eat fish.

   C. The penguins started pecking sleeping passengers.

   D. The aisle was too narrow for the penguins to walk down.

7. How did the audience react to the penguins interfering with other acts in the program?

   A. The were upset and demanded their money back.

   B. They were pleased and liked them even more.

   C. They were confused and wanted them off the stage.

   D. They were surprised and embarrassed for Mr. Popper.

Check Your Reading Speed

1분에 몇 단어를 읽는지 리딩 속도를 측정해 보세요.

$$\frac{1{,}167 \text{ words}}{\text{reading time (\quad) sec}} \times 60 = (\quad) \text{ WPM}$$

Build Your Vocabulary

interrupt^{복습}
[ìntərápt]

v. (말·행동을) 방해하다; 중단시키다
If you interrupt someone who is speaking, you say or do something that causes them to stop.

groan*
[groun]

n. 신음, 끙 하는 소리; v. 신음하다, 끙끙거리다
A groan is a deep, long sound showing great pain or unhappiness.

marvelous*
[máːrvələs]

a. 놀라운, 믿기 어려운; 훌륭한, 우수한
If you describe someone or something as marvelous, you are emphasizing that they are very good.

turn up

idiom (사람이) 도착하다, 나타나다
If someone or something turns up, they arrive or appear somewhere, usually unexpectedly or in a way that was not planned.

rehearse
[rihə́ːrs]

v. 예행연습을 하다, 리허설을 하다 (rehearsal n. 리허설, 예행연습)
When people rehearse a play, dance, or piece of music, they practice it in order to prepare for a performance.

indulgence
[indʌ́ldʒəns]

n. (남의 결점에 대한) 관용
Indulgence means treating someone with special kindness, often when it is not a good thing.

novelty*
[návəlti]

n. 새로움, 참신함, 신기함; 새로운 것
Novelty is the quality of being different, new, and unusual.

number***
[nʌ́mbər]

n. (공연) 프로그램의 한 항목, 곡목; 수, 숫자; v. 번호를 매기다
You can refer to a short piece of music, a song, or a dance as a number.

unforeseen
[ʌ̀nfɔːrsíːn]

a. 예측하지 못한, 뜻밖의
If something that has happened was unforeseen, it was not expected to happen or known about beforehand.

dignify
[dígnəfài]

v. 위엄 있어 보이게 하다, 그럴듯하게 하다 (dignified a. 위엄 있는)
If you say that someone or something is dignified, you mean they are calm, impressive and deserve respect.

military^{복습}
[mílitèri]

a. 군대의, 군사의; n. 군대
Military means relating to the armed forces of a country.

march^{복습}
[maːrʧ]

n. 행진곡; 행진, 행군; v. 행진하다; (단호한 태도로 급히) 걸어가다
A march is a piece of music with a strong beat that matches the steps taken by marching people.

drill^{복습}
[dril]

v. 반복 훈련시키다; 구멍을 뚫다; n. 훈련
If you drill people, you teach them to do something by making them repeat it many times.

wheel^{복습}
[hwi:l]

v. 선회하다; (반대 방향으로) 홱 돌다; (바퀴 달린 것을) 밀다;
n. 바퀴; (자동차 등의) 핸들
If something such as a group of animals or birds wheels, it moves in a circle.

formation[*]
[fɔːrméiʃən]

n. (특정한) 대형; 형성 (과정)
If people or things are in formation, they are arranged in a particular pattern as they move.

precise[*]
[prisáis]

a. 정확한, 정밀한; 엄밀한, 꼼꼼한 (precision n. 정확성, 정밀성)
If you do something with precision, you do it exactly as it should be done.

piece^{복습}
[pi:s]

n. (글·미술·음악 등의 작품) 하나; 조각, 단편, 파편, 일부분
You can refer to a work of art as a piece.

clap[*]
[klæp]

v. 박수를 치다; (갑자기·재빨리) 놓다; n. 박수 (소리)
When you clap, you hit your hands together to show appreciation or attract attention.

vigorous^{복습}
[vígərəs]

a. 격렬한; 활발한; 활기찬, 건강한 (vigorously ad. 맹렬히, 힘차게)
Vigorous physical activities involve using a lot of energy, usually to do short and repeated actions.

hollow^{**}
[hálou]

a. (속이) 빈; 헛된; 공허한; v. 우묵하게 만들다
Something that is hollow has a space inside it, as opposed to being solid all the way through.

skip[*]
[skip]

v. (한 부분을) 건너뛰다; 깡충깡충 뛰다; n. 깡충깡충 뛰기
If you skip or skip over a part of something you are reading or a story you are telling, you miss it out or pass over it quickly and move on to something else.

widow^{복습}
[wídou]

n. 미망인, 과부
A widow is a woman whose husband has died and who has not married again.

semicircle
[sémisə̀:rkl]

n. 반원
A semicircle is one half of a circle.

midst[*]
[midst]

n. 한복판, 중앙, 한가운데
If someone or something is in the midst of a group of people or things, they are among them or surrounded by them.

spar^{복습}
[spa:r]

v. 가볍게 치고 덤비다, 스파링하다; 말싸움하다
If you spar with someone, you box using fairly gentle blows instead of hitting your opponent hard.

lean^{복습}
[li:n]

v. 기울이다, (몸을) 숙이다; ~에 기대다; a. 군살이 없는, 호리호리한
When you lean in a particular direction, you bend your body in that direction.

punch^{복습}
[pʌnʧ]

v. 주먹으로 치다; 구멍을 뚫다; n. 주먹으로 침
If you punch someone or something, you hit them hard with your fist.

stomach^{복습}
[stʌ́mək]

n. 복부, 배
You can refer to the front part of your body below your waist as your stomach.

flipper^{복습}
[flípər]

n. (바다표범·거북 등의) 지느러미발; (잠수·수영 때 신는) 오리발
The flippers of an animal that lives in water, for example a seal or a penguin, are the two or four flat limbs which it uses for swimming.

clinch
[klintʃ]

n. (권투 중에 서로) 끌어안음; v. 못박다, 고정시키다, 결말을 내다
A clinch is the act of one boxer holding onto the other to avoid being hit and to rest momentarily.

break loose

idiom 떨치다; 도망치다, 탈주하다
If people or animals break loose or are set loose, they are no longer held, tied, or kept somewhere and can move around freely.

applaud[*]
[əplɔ́:d]

v. 박수를 치다
When a group of people applaud, they clap their hands in order to show approval, for example when they have enjoyed a play or concert.

whereupon
[hwɛ̀ərəpán]

conj. 그래서, 그 때문에, 그 결과
You use whereupon to say that one thing happens immediately after another thing, and usually as a result of it.

retreat^{복습}
[ritrí:t]

v. 후퇴하다; 물러가다, 멀어져 가다; n. 후퇴, 철수; 물러섬
If you retreat, you move away from something or someone.

immediate^{복습}
[imí:diət]

a. 즉각적인; 당면한; 아주 가까이에 있는 (immediately ad. 즉시, 즉각)
If something happens immediately, it happens without any delay.

knock^{복습}
[nak]

v. 치다, 부딪치다; (문 등을) 두드리다; n. (문 등을) 두드리는 소리; 부딪침
(knock down idiom ~를 때려눕히다)
If you knock someone down, you hit or push them so that they fall to the ground or the floor.

prostrate
[prástreit]

a. (바닥에) 엎드린; (충격 등으로) 몸을 가누지 못하는; v. 엎드리다
If you are lying prostrate, you are lying flat on the ground, on your front.

sock
[sak]

v. 세게 치다, 강타하다; n. 양말
If you sock someone, you hit them with your fist forcefully.

row^{복습}
[rou]

n. (사람·사물들의) 열, 줄; 노 젓기; v. 노를 젓다
A row of things or people is a number of them arranged in a line.

bow[*]
[bau]

① v. (허리를 굽혀) 절하다; (고개를) 숙이다; n. 절, (고개 숙여 하는) 인사 ② n. 활
When you bow to someone, you briefly bend your body toward them as a formal way of greeting them or showing respect.

stepladder^{복습}
[stéplædər]

n. 발판 사다리
A stepladder is a portable ladder that is made of two sloping parts that are hinged together at the top so that it will stand up on its own.

stagehand
[stéidʒhænd]

n. 무대 담당자
A stagehand is a person whose job is to move the scenery and equipment on the stage in a theater.

88

ladder^{복습}
[lǽdər]

n. 사다리
A ladder is a piece of equipment used for climbing up something or down from something.

descriptive^{복습}
[diskríptiv]

a. 서술하는, 묘사하는; 기술적인
Descriptive language or writing indicates what someone or something is like.

brook^{복습}
[bruk]

n. 개울
A brook is a small stream.

discipline**
[dísəplin]

n. 규율, 훈육; 단련법, 수련법; v. 훈육하다
Discipline is the practice of making people obey rules or standards of behavior, and punishing them when they do not.

dreadful*
[drédfəl]

a. 끔찍한, 지독한; 무시무시한 (dreadfully ad. 몹시, 굉장히)
Dreadfully means extremely or very much.

shove^{복습}
[ʃʌv]

v. (거칠게) 밀치다; 아무렇게나 놓다; n. 힘껏 떠밂
If you shove someone or something, you push them with a quick, violent movement.

at once^{복습}

idiom 동시에, 한꺼번에; 즉시, 당장
If a number of different things happen at once or all at once, they all happen at the same time.

scramble*
[skrǽmbl]

v. 서로 밀치다; 재빨리 움직이다; n. (힘들게) 기어가기; 서로 밀치기
If a number of people scramble for something, they compete energetically with each other for it.

squawk
[skwɔːk]

v. (새가 크게) 꽥꽥 울다; (화·놀람 등으로) 시끄럽게 떠들다
When a bird squawks, it makes a loud harsh noise.

confuse^{복습}
[kənfjúːz]

v. (사람을) 혼란시키다; 혼동하다 (confusion n. 혼란; 혼동)
Confusion is a situation in which everything is in disorder, especially because there are lots of things happening at the same time.

toboggan^{복습}
[təbágən]

v. 썰매를 타다; n. 터보건 (썰매)
If you toboggan, you move along on a light wooden board with a curved front, to travel down hills on snow or ice.

noisy*
[nɔ́izi]

a. 시끌벅적한, 떠들썩한; 시끄러운
A noisy person or thing makes a lot of loud or unpleasant noise.

delicate**
[délikət]

a. 섬세한, 고운; 예민한, 민감한
Something that is delicate has a color, taste, or smell which is pleasant and not strong or intense.

hold one's sides

idiom 포복절도하다
If you hold your sides, you laugh a lot and uncontrollably.

signal**
[sígnəl]

n. (동작·소리로 하는) 신호; v. 신호를 보내다; 암시하다
A signal is a gesture, sound, or action which is intended to give a particular message to the person who sees or hears it.

congratulate[kəngrǽʧulèit]

v. 축하하다; 기뻐하다, 자랑스러워하다
If you congratulate someone, you say something to show you are pleased that something nice has happened to them.

absolute^{복습} [ǽbsəlùːt]

a. 완전한, 완벽한 (absolutely ad. 전적으로, 틀림없이)
Absolutely means totally and completely.

unique[*] [juːníːk]

a. 유일무이한, 독특한; 특별한; 고유의, 특유의
Something that is unique is the only one of its kind.

sensation[*] [senséiʃən]

n. 돌풍(을 불러일으키는 사람·것); 느낌; 감각
If a person, event, or situation is a sensation, it causes great excitement or interest.

trouper [trúːpər]

n. 믿음직한 동료; (극단 등의) 단원
If you describe someone as a trouper, you mean that they are people who you can always depend on or who never complains.

predict[*] [pridíkt]

v. 예측하다, 예견하다
If you predict an event, you say that it will happen.

term^{**} [təːrm]

n. (pl.) (합의·계약 등의) 조건, 조항; 용어; 기간; v. (특정한 이름·용어로) 칭하다
The terms of an agreement, treaty, or other arrangement are the conditions that must be accepted by the people involved in it.

contract^{**} [kántrækt]

n. 계약; v. 계약하다; 줄어들다, 수축하다
A contract is a legal agreement, usually between two companies or between an employer and employee, which involves doing work for a stated sum of money.

satisfactory^{**} [sæ̀tisfǽktəri]

a. 만족스러운, 더할 나위 없는
Something that is satisfactory is acceptable to you or fulfils a particular need or purpose.

parade^{복습} [pəréid]

v. 행진하다; (과시하듯) 걸어 다니다; n. 퍼레이드, 가두 행진
When people parade somewhere, they walk together in a formal group or a line, usually with other people watching them.

usher [ʌ́ʃər]

n. (교회·극장 등의) 좌석 안내원; v. 안내하다
An usher is a person who shows people where to sit, for example at a wedding or at a concert.

90

Check Your Reading Speed

1분에 몇 단어를 읽는지 리딩 속도를 측정해 보세요.

$$\frac{948 \text{ words}}{\text{reading time ( ) sec}} \times 60 = (\quad) \text{ WPM}$$

Build Your Vocabulary

on the road

idiom (장기간·장거리를) 여행 중인
If you are on the road, you are going on a long journey or a series of journeys by road.

scrub*
[skrʌb]

v. 문질러 씻다; 취소하다; n. 문질러 씻기
If you scrub something, you rub it hard in order to clean it, using a stiff brush and water.

polish*
[páliʃ]

v. 닦다, 윤내다; n. 광택; 세련
If you polish something, you rub it with a cloth to make it shine.

straighten^{복습}
[streitn]

v. 정리하다, 정돈하다; 똑바르게 하다; (자세를) 바로 하다
If you straighten something, you make it tidy or put it in its proper position.

housekeeper^{복습}
[háuskiːpər]

n. 주부; 가정부
A housekeeper is a married woman who does not have a paid job, but instead looks after her home and children.

at sixes and sevens

idiom 혼란스러운, 뒤죽박죽인
If things are at sixes and sevens, they are in a confused, badly organized, or difficult situation.

install^{복습}
[instɔ́ːl]

v. (장비·가구를) 설치하다; 자리를 잡게 하다
If you install a piece of equipment, you fit it or put it somewhere so that it is ready to be used.

freeze^{복습}
[friːz]

v. 얼다; 얼리다; (두려움 등으로 몸이) 얼어붙다; n. 동결; 한파
If a liquid or a substance containing a liquid freezes, or if something freezes it, it becomes solid because of low temperatures.

plant^{복습}
[plænt]

n. 시설; 공장; 식물, 초목; v. 심다; (장소에) 놓다 (freezing plant n. 냉동 시설)
Plant is large machinery that is used in industrial processes.

basement^{복습}
[béismənt]

n. (건물의) 지하층
The basement of a building is a floor built partly or completely below ground level.

uneasy*
[ʌníːzi]

a. (마음이) 불안한, 우려되는; 불편한; 어색한
If you are uneasy, you feel anxious, afraid, or embarrassed, because you think that something is wrong or that there is danger.

after all^{복습}

idiom 어쨌든; (예상과는 달리) 결국에는
You use after all when introducing a statement which supports or helps explain something you have just said.

ship^{복습}
[ʃip]

v. 실어 나르다, 운송하다; n. (큰) 배, 선박, 함선
If people or things are shipped somewhere, they are sent there on a ship or by some other means of transport.

railway**
[réilwei]

n. 철도; 선로, 철길
A railway is a route between two places along which trains travel on steel rails.

on account of

idiom ~ 때문에
You use on account of to introduce the reason or explanation for something.

traffic**
[trǽfik]

n. 차량들, 교통; 운항; 수송
Traffic refers to all the vehicles that are moving along the roads in a particular area.

pail*
[peil]

n. 들통, 양동이
A pail is a bucket, usually made of metal or wood.

race
[reis]

v. 경주하다; 쏜살같이 가다; n. 경주; 경쟁; 인종, 종족
If you race, you take part in a race.

block^{복습}
[blak]

n. (도로로 나뉘는) 구역, 블록; (단단한) 사각형 덩어리; v. 막다, 차단하다
A block in a town is an area of land with streets on all its sides.

tear**
[tɛər]

① v. (tore-torn) (거칠게 잡아 당겨) 찢어내다, 뜯어내다; 찢다, 뜯다; n. 구멍 (tear off idiom 떼어내다, 찢어내다) ② n. 눈물
If you tear something off, you remove it quickly by pulling violently.

annoyed^{복습}
[ənɔ́id]

a. 짜증이 난, 약이 오른
If you are annoyed, you are fairly angry about something.

pull out

idiom (역을) 떠나다, 출발하다
If a train or bus pulls out, it leaves a place.

brass*
[bræs]

n. 황동, 놋쇠
Brass is a yellow-colored metal made from copper and zinc.

rear*
[riər]

a. 뒤쪽의; n. (어떤 것의) 뒤쪽; v. (어린 아이·동물을) 기르다
Rear refers to at the back.

observation*
[àbzərvéiʃən]

n. 관찰, 관측, 감시
Observation is the action or process of carefully watching someone or something.

platform*
[plǽtfɔ:rm]

n. (객차의) 승강구; 연단, 강단
A platform is the area at the front or back of a bus or train where people stand to get off the bus or train.

barely^{복습}
[béərli]

ad. 간신히, 가까스로; 거의 ~아니게
You use barely to say that something is only just true or only just the case.

make it

idiom (간신히) 가다; (힘든 경험 등을) 버텨 내다
If you make it, you succeed in reaching a place.

92

gasp ^{복습}
[gæsp]

v. 헉 하고 숨을 쉬다, 숨이 턱 막히다; 숨을 제대로 못 쉬다; n. 헉 하는 소리를 냄
When you gasp, you take a short quick breath through your mouth, especially when you are surprised, shocked, or in pain.

porter*
[pɔ́:rtər]

n. (열차의) 승무원; (공항·호텔의) 짐꾼
A porter on a train is a person whose job is to make up beds in the sleeping car and to help passengers.

berth*
[bə:rθ]

n. (배·기차의) 침대
A berth is a bed on a boat, train, or caravan.

temptation*
[temptéiʃən]

n. 유혹(적인 것)
If you feel you want to do something or have something, even though you know you really should avoid it, you can refer to this feeling as temptation.

dozen**
[dʌzn]

n. 12개; 십여 개; 다수, 여러 개
If you have a dozen things, you have twelve of them.

ecstatic
[ekstǽtik]

a. 황홀한, 무아지경의
If you are ecstatic, you feel very happy and full of excitement.

discipline ^{복습}
[dísəplin]

n. 규율, 훈육; 단련법, 수련법; v. 훈육하다
Discipline is the practice of making people obey rules or standards of behavior, and punishing them when they do not.

clergyman*
[klɔ́:rdʒimən]

n. 남자 성직자
A clergyman is a male member of the clergy.

collar**
[kálər]

n. (윗옷의) 칼라, 깃; (개 등의) 목걸이
The collar of a shirt or coat is the part which fits round the neck and is usually folded over.

shoo
[ʃu:]

v. 쉬이 하고 쫓아내다; int. 저리 가
If you shoo an animal or a person away, you make them go away by waving your hands or arms at them.

conductor*
[kəndʌ́ktər]

n. (열차의) 차장; 승무원; 지휘자
On a train, a conductor is a person whose job is to travel on the train in order to help passengers and check tickets.

brakeman
[bréikmən]

n. (열차의) 제동수(制動手)
A brakeman is a railroad employee who assists the conductor and checks on the operation of a train's brakes.

rescue*
[réskju:]

n. 구출, 구조; v. 구하다, 구출하다 (come to rescue idiom 남을 구하러 오다)
If you go to someone's rescue or come to their rescue, you help them when they are in danger or difficulty.

distant ^{복습}
[dístənt]

a. 먼, (멀리) 떨어져 있는; 다정하지 않은
Distant means very far away.

broaden*
[brɔ́:dn]

v. (경험·지식 등을) 넓히다; 넓어지다, 퍼지다
When you broaden something such as your experience or popularity or when it broadens, the number of things or people that it includes becomes greater.

riotous
[ráiətəs]

a. 시끌벅적한; 소란을 피우는
You can describe someone's behavior or an event as riotous when it is noisy and lively in a rather wild way.

go off

idiom (일이) 진행되다; (경보기 등이) 울리다
If a performance goes off well, it is successful.

hitch
[hitʃ]

n. (잠깐 지체하게 하는) 문제
A hitch is a slight problem or difficulty which causes a short delay.

rehearse^{복습}
[rihə́:rs]

v. 예행연습을 하다, 리허설을 하다
If you rehearse something that you are going to say or do, you silently practice it by imagining that you are saying or doing it.

novelty^{복습}
[návəlti]

n. 새로움, 참신함, 신기함; 새로운 것
Novelty is the quality of being different, new, and unusual.

number^{복습}
[nʌ́mbər]

n. (공연) 프로그램의 한 항목, 곡목; 수, 숫자; v. 번호를 매기다
You can refer to a short piece of music, a song, or a dance as a number.

bill^{복습}
[bil]

n. (극장 등의) 프로그램; 지폐; (새의) 부리; 고지서, 청구서
The bill of a show or concert is a list of the entertainers who will take part in it.

clap^{복습}
[klæp]

v. 박수를 치다; (갑자기·재빨리) 놓다; n. 박수 (소리)
When you clap, you hit your hands together to show appreciation or attract attention.

stamp^{**}
[stæmp]

v. (발을) 구르다; 쾅쾅거리며 걷다; n. 우표; (발을) 쿵쾅거리기
If you stamp or stamp your foot, you lift your foot and put it down very hard on the ground, for example because you are angry or because your feet are cold.

roar^{복습}
[rɔ:r]

v. 함성을 지르다; 고함치다; 으르렁거리다; n. 으르렁거림, 포효
If someone roars, they shout something in a very loud voice.

herd[*]
[hə:rd]

v. (짐승을) 몰다; (특정 방향으로) 이동하다; n. (함께 사는 동종 짐승의) 떼
If you herd animals, you make them move along as a group.

tightrope
[táitroup]

n. (서커스에서 곡예사가 타는) 줄
A tightrope is a tightly stretched piece of rope on which someone balances and performs tricks in a circus.

wing^{**}
[wiŋ]

n. (연극 무대의 양쪽) 끝; (새·곤충의) 날개; v. 날아가다
In a theater, the wings are the sides of the stage which are hidden from the audience by curtains or scenery.

unfortunately^{복습}
[ʌnfɔ́:rtʃənətli]

ad. 불행하게도, 유감스럽게도
You can use unfortunately to introduce or refer to a statement when you consider that it is sad or disappointing, or when you want to express regret.

wire^{**}
[waiər]

n. 철사; (전화기 등의) 선; v. (건물·장비에) 전선을 연결하다
A wire is a long thin piece of metal that is used to fasten things or to carry electric current.

overhead*
[òuvərhéd]

ad. 머리 위에; a. 머리 위의
You use overhead to indicate that something is above you or above the place that you are talking about.

pleased^{복습}
[pli:zd]

a. 기뻐하는, 만족해하는
If you are pleased, you are happy about something or satisfied with something.

waddle^{복습}
[wadl]

v. 뒤뚱뒤뚱 걷다; n. 뒤뚱거리는 걸음걸이
To waddle somewhere means to walk there with short, quick steps, swinging slightly from side to side.

hurried*
[hə́:rid]

a. 서둘러 하는 (hurriedly ad. 황급히, 다급하게)
A hurried action is done quickly, because you do not have much time to do it in.

recover^{복습}
[rikÁvər]

v. (의식 등을) 되찾다; 회복되다; (손실 등을) 되찾다
If you recover a mental or physical state, it comes back again.

elbow**
[élbou]

n. 팔꿈치; v. (팔꿈치로) 밀치다
Your elbow is the part of your arm where the upper and lower halves of the arm are joined.

remark^{복습}
[rimá:rk]

n. 말, 언급; 주목; v. ~에 주목하다; 언급하다, 말하다
If you make a remark about something, you say something about it.

interfere*
[intərfíər]

v. 방해하다; 간섭하다, 개입하다
Something that interferes with a situation, activity, or process has a damaging effect on it.

Chapters 17 & 18

1. Why did the opera singer refuse to go on the stage in Minneapolis?
   A. She wanted the penguins put away.
   B. She wanted to sing with Mr. Popper's penguins.
   C. She wanted to go on the stage before Mr. Popper and his penguins.
   D. She wanted Mr. Popper and his penguins out of the theater completely.

2. Why could nobody hear the words of the opera singer's song?
   A. Her microphone was broken.
   B. The audience was laughing so hard.
   C. She lost her voice from yelling at the penguins.
   D. The penguins were making too much noise under the stage.

3. How could Mr. Popper feed the penguins for free?
   A. Hotels would give the penguins fish if they were well behaved.
   B. Local zoos would give Mr. Popper fish if he brought his penguins.
   C. A live fish company shipped Mr. Popper free fish all over the country.
   D. A shrimp company used Mr. Popper's testimonial and gave him free canned shrimp.

4. Why did Mr. Popper take the penguins to the roof of the hotel in New York?
   A. He wanted them to get some exercise.
   B. He wanted them to feel a cool breeze.
   C. He wanted them to slide down the steps.
   D. He wanted them to see the whole city.

5. Why was Mr. Popper so worried about the penguins and seals meeting?
   A. Mr. Popper was worried about the penguins hurting the seals.
   B. Mr. Swenson told Mr. Popper that the seals would eat the penguins
   C. Mr. Swenson told Mr. Popper that seals and penguins hated each other.
   D. Mr. Popper was worried about Mr. Swenson calling the police to arrest him.

6. How did the firefighters and policemen react to the penguins and seals?
   A. The firefighters put their hats on the penguins and the policemen put theirs on the seals.
   B. The policemen put their hats on the penguins and the firefighters put theirs on the seals.
   C. The firefighters and policemen stopped the penguins and seals from fighting each other.
   D. The firefighters and policemen stayed and bought tickets for the show.

7. Why did the theater manager want Mr. Popper arrested?
   A. Mr. Popper's penguins had injured Mr. Swenson's seals.
   B. Mr. Popper's penguins had injured audience members.
   C. Mr. Popper had caused a panic at the wrong theater.
   D. Mr. Popper needed a license to have his penguins.

Check Your Reading Speed

1분에 몇 단어를 읽는지 리딩 속도를 측정해 보세요.

$$\frac{1{,}081 \text{ words}}{\text{reading time ( ) sec}} \times 60 = (\quad) \text{ WPM}$$

Build Your Vocabulary

fame＊
[feim]
n. 명성
If you achieve fame, you become very well-known.

pleased복습
[pli:zd]
a. 기뻐하는, 만족해하는
If you are pleased, you are happy about something or satisfied with something.

celebrated＊
[séləbrèitid]
a. 유명한
A celebrated person or thing is famous and much admired.

annoyed복습
[ənɔ́id]
a. 짜증이 난, 약이 오른
If you are annoyed, you are fairly angry about something.

stagehand복습
[stéidʒhænd]
n. 무대 담당자
A stagehand is a person whose job is to move the scenery and equipment on the stage in a theater.

basement복습
[béismənt]
n. (건물의) 지하층
The basement of a building is a floor built partly or completely below ground level.

guard＊＊
[ga:rd]
v. 지키다, 보호하다; 감시하다; n. 경비 요원; 감시, 경호
If you guard a place, person, or object, you stand near them in order to watch and protect them.

entrance＊＊
[éntrəns]
n. 입구, 문; 입장
The entrance to a place is the way into it, for example a door or gate.

flight복습
[flait]
n. 계단, 층계; 비행; 항공기
A flight of steps or stairs is a set of steps or stairs that lead from one level to another without changing direction.

shriek복습
[ʃri:k]
v. (날카롭게) 비명을 지르다; 악을 쓰며 말하다; n. 날카로운 소리; 비명
When someone shrieks, they make a short, very loud cry, for example because they are suddenly surprised, are in pain, or are laughing.

pit＊
[pit]
n. (크고 깊은) 구덩이; 구멍; 함정 (orchestra pit n. 오케스트라 악단석)
In a theater, the orchestra pit is the space reserved for the musicians playing the music for an opera, musical, or ballet, immediately in front of or below the stage.

bite복습
[bait]
v. (이빨로) 물다; n. 물기; 한 입
If an animal or person bites you, they use their teeth to hurt or injure you.

98

peg[*]
[peg]

n. (현악기의) 줄감개; 못, 핀; 말뚝; v. 고정하다
A peg is a screw used for making the strings on a musical instrument tighter or looser.

string^{복습}
[striŋ]

n. 끈, 줄; 일련; v. 묶다, 매달다; (실 등에) 꿰다
The strings on a musical instrument such as a violin or guitar are the thin pieces of wire or nylon stretched across it that make sounds when the instrument is played.

fiddle[*]
[fidl]

n. 바이올린; v. 바이올린을 켜다; (세부 사항을) 조작하다; 만지작거리다
Some people call violins fiddles, especially when they are used to play folk music.

helpless[*]
[hélplis]

a. 무력한, 속수무책인 (helplessly ad. 무력하게)
If you are helpless, you do not have the strength or power to do anything useful or to control or protect yourself.

guilty^{복습}
[gílti]

a. 죄책감이 드는, 가책을 느끼는; 유죄의
If you feel guilty, you feel unhappy because you think that you have done something wrong or have failed to do something which you should have done.

shrill[*]
[ʃril]

a. 새된, 날카로운; v. 날카로운 소리를 내다
A shrill sound is high-pitched and unpleasant.

note^{***}
[nout]

n. 음, 음표; 메모
In music, a note is the sound of a particular pitch, or a written symbol representing this sound.

coast^{복습}
[koust]

n. 해안
The coast is an area of land that is next to the sea.

hold out

idiom 지속되다; 저항하다
If money or supplies hold out, they last or remain.

now and then

idiom 때때로, 가끔
If you say that something happens now and then or every now and again, you mean that it happens sometimes but not very often or regularly.

startle[*]
[sta:rtl]

v. 깜짝 놀라게 하다; 움찔하다; n. 깜짝 놀람 (startled a. 놀란)
If something sudden and unexpected startles you, it surprises and frightens you slightly.

object^{***}
[ábdʒikt]

v. 반대하다; n. 물건, 물체; 목적, 목표
If you object to something, you express your dislike or disapproval of it.

register[*]
[rédʒistər]

v. (공식 명부에 이름을) 등록하다, (출생·혼인 등을) 신고하다; n. 기록부, 명부
If you register to do something, you put your name on an official list, in order to be able to do that thing or to receive a service.

lap[*]
[læp]

n. 무릎; (경주에서 트랙의) 한 바퀴 (lap dog n. 작은 애완용 개)
A lap dog is a small pet dog that is given a lot of attention by its owner.

neat^{복습}
[ni:t]

a. 정돈된, 단정한; 깔끔한; 아기자기한
A neat place, thing, or person is tidy and smart, and has everything in the correct place.

mischief*
[místʃif]

n. 못된 짓, 장난
Mischief is playing harmless tricks on people or doing things you are not supposed to do.

on the whole^{복습}

idiom 전반적으로 보아, 대체로
You use on the whole to indicate that what you are saying is true in general but may not be true in every case.

occasional*
[əkéiʒənəl]

a. 가끔의, 때때로의 (occasionally ad. 때때로, 가끔)
Occasional means happening sometimes, but not regularly or often.

brass^{복습}
[bræs]

n. 황동, 놋쇠
Brass is a yellow-colored metal made from copper and zinc.

be far from

idiom ~와는 크게 동떨어져 있다
If you say that something is far from being the case, you are emphasizing that it is not at all the case, especially when people expect or assume that it is.

back and forth
[bæk ən fɔ́:rθ]

ad. 여기저기에, 왔다갔다; 좌우로; 앞뒤로
If someone moves back and forth, they repeatedly move in one direction and then in the opposite direction.

tie up

idiom 꼼짝 못 하게 하다; 묶어 놓다
If traffic is tied up, it is not moving very quickly.

traffic^{복습}
[træfik]

n. 차량들, 교통; 운항; 수송
Traffic refers to all the vehicles that are moving along the roads in a particular area.

nuisance*
[njú:sns]

n. 성가신 것, 골칫거리
If you say that someone or something is a nuisance, you mean that they annoy you or cause you a lot of problems.

cake**
[keik]

n. (일정한 모양의) 덩어리; 케이크; v. 두껍게 바르다
A cake is a small hard block of something, especially soap.

dreadful^{복습}
[drédfəl]

a. 끔찍한, 지독한; 무시무시한 (dreadfully ad. 몹시, 굉장히)
Dreadfully means extremely or very much.

fortunately^{복습}
[fɔ́:rʃənətli]

ad. 다행스럽게도, 운 좋게도
Fortunately is used to introduce or indicate a statement about an event or situation that is good.

expense*
[ikspéns]

n. 돈, 비용; 돈이 드는 일
Expense is the money that something costs you or that you need to spend in order to do something.

on the road^{복습}

idiom (장기간·장거리를) 여행 중인
If you are on the road, you are going on a long journey or a series of journeys by road.

give up

idiom 그만두다; 단념하다; 포기하다
If you give up, you stop doing or having something.

100

ship 복습
[ʃip]

v. 실어 나르다, 운송하다; n. (큰) 배, 선박, 함선
If people or things are shipped somewhere, they are sent there on a ship or by some other means of transport.

on time

idiom 시간에 맞추어서, 시간을 어기지 않고
If you are on time, you are not late.

feed 복습
[fi:d]

v. 먹이를 주다; 공급하다; n. (동물의) 먹이
If you feed a person or animal, you give them food to eat and sometimes actually put it in their mouths.

shrimp 복습
[ʃrimp]

n. 새우
Shrimps are small shellfish with long tails and many legs.

absolute 복습
[ǽbsəlù:t]

a. 완전한, 완벽한 (absolutely ad. 전적으로, 틀림없이)
Absolutely means totally and completely.

testimonial
[tèstəmóuniəl]

n. 추천서; 추천의 글; 기념물
A testimonial is a statement about the character or qualities of someone or something.

thrive 복습
[θraiv]

v. 잘 자라다; 번창하다
If someone or something thrives, they do well and are successful, healthy, or strong.

leading★★
[lí:diŋ]

a. 가장 중요한, 선두적인; 선두의
The leading person or thing in a particular area is the one which is most important or successful.

grocery 복습
[gróusəri]

n. 식료 잡화점; (pl.) 식료 잡화류
A grocery or a grocery store is a store where food and small items for the house are sold.

spinach
[spíniʧ]

n. 시금치
Spinach is a vegetable with large dark green leaves that you chop up and boil in water before eating.

association★★
[əsòusiéiʃən]

n. 연합, 협회, 단체
An association is an official group of people who have the same job, aim, or interest.

energetic★★
[ènərdʒétik]

a. 활기에 찬, 원기 왕성한
An energetic person is very active and does not feel at all tired.

oat★
[out]

n. (pl.) 귀리; 오트밀; a. 귀리로 만든
Oats are a cereal crop or its grains, used for making biscuits or a food called porridge, or for feeding animals.

handy★
[hǽndi]

a. 편리한, 유용한 (come in handy idiom 쓸모가 있다)
If something comes in handy, it is useful in a particular situation.

continent★
[kántənənt]

n. 대륙; 육지
A continent is a very large area of land, such as Africa or Asia, that consists of several countries.

reputation★
[rèpjutéiʃən]

n. 평판, 명성
Something's or someone's reputation is the opinion that people have about how good they are.

railway ^{복습}
[réilwei]

n. 철도; 선로, 철길
A railway is a route between two places along which trains travel on steel rails.

contract ^{복습}
[kántrækt]

n. 계약; v. 계약하다; 줄어들다, 수축하다
A contract is a legal agreement, usually between two companies or between an employer and employee, which involves doing work for a stated sum of money.

irritable
[írətəbl]

a. 화를 잘 내는, 성미가 급한
If you are irritable, you are easily annoyed.

Check Your Reading Speed

1분에 몇 단어를 읽는지 리딩 속도를 측정해 보세요.

$$\frac{1{,}062 \text{ words}}{\text{reading time ( ) sec}} \times 60 = (\quad) \text{ WPM}$$

Build Your Vocabulary

unseasonably
[ʌnsíːzənəbli]

ad. 계절에 맞지 않게
Unseasonably warm, cold, or mild weather is warmer, colder, or milder than it usually is at the time of year.

overlook*
[ouvərlúk]

v. (건물 등이) 바라보다, 내려다보다; 못 보고 넘어가다; 눈감아주다
If a building or window overlooks a place, you can see the place clearly from the building or window.

roof**
[ruːf]

n. 지붕; (터널·동굴 등의) 천장; v. 지붕을 씌우다
The roof of a building is the covering on top of it that protects the people and things inside from the weather.

breeze*
[briːz]

n. 산들바람, 미풍; v. 경쾌하게 움직이다
A breeze is a gentle wind.

charm**
[ʧaːrm]

v. 매혹하다, 매료하다; n. 매력
If you charm someone, you please them.

sparkle*
[spaːrkl]

v. 반짝이다; 생기 넘치다; n. 반짝거림; 생기 (sparkling a. 반짝거리는)
If something sparkles, it is clear and bright and shines with a lot of very small points of light.

confuse^{복습}
[kənfjúːz]

v. (사람을) 혼란시키다; 혼동하다 (confusion n. 혼란; 혼동)
Confusion is a situation in which everything is in disorder, especially because there are lots of things happening at the same time.

edge^{복습}
[edʒ]

n. 끝, 가장자리, 모서리; 우위; v. 조금씩 움직이다
The edge of something is the place or line where it stops, or the part of it that is furthest from the middle.

canyon*
[kǽnjən]

n. 협곡
A canyon is a long, narrow valley with very steep sides.

shove^{복습}
[ʃʌv]

v. (거칠게) 밀치다; 아무렇게나 놓다; n. 힘껏 떠밂
If you shove someone or something, you push them with a quick, violent movement.

pole^{복습}
[poul]

n. (지구의) 극; 기둥, 장대
The earth's poles are the two opposite ends of its axis, its most northern and southern points.

frighten**
[fraitn]

v. 겁먹게 하다, 놀라게 하다 (frightened a. 겁먹은, 무서워하는)
If you are frightened, you are anxious or afraid, often because of something that has just happened or that you think may happen.

concern[★★]
[kənsə́:rn]

v. (무엇에) 관한 것이다; 걱정스럽게 하다; n. 우려, 걱정; 관심사
You can say 'where something is concerned' to indicate the subject that you are talking about.

lack[★★]
[læk]

n. 부족, 결핍; v. ~이 없다, 부족하다
If there is a lack of something, there is not enough of it or it does not exist at all.

drowsy[★]
[dráuzi]

a. 졸리는, 꾸벅꾸벅 조는
If you feel drowsy, you feel sleepy and cannot think clearly.

absent-minded[복습]
[ǽbsənt-máindid]

a. 멍하니 있는, 넋놓은, 방심 상태의
Someone who is absent-minded forgets things or does not pay attention to what they are doing.

thread[복습]
[θred]

v. 요리조리 빠져나가다; (실 등을) 꿰다; n. 실; (이야기 등의) 맥락
If you thread your way through a group of people or things, or thread through it, you move through it carefully or slowly, changing direction frequently as you move.

traffic[복습]
[trǽfik]

n. 차량들, 교통; 운항; 수송
Traffic refers to all the vehicles that are moving along the roads in a particular area.

seal[복습]
[si:l]

n. [동물] 바다표범; 직인, 도장; v. 봉인하다; 확정짓다, 다짐하다
A seal is a large animal with a rounded body and flat legs called flippers.

pile[★★]
[pail]

v. 우르르 가다; (차곡차곡) 쌓다; n. 쌓아 놓은 것, 더미
If a group of people pile into or out of a vehicle, they all get into it or out of it in a disorganized way.

file[★]
[fail]

v. 줄지어 가다; (문서 등을) 보관하다; n. 파일, 서류철; 정보
When a group of people files somewhere, they walk one behind the other in a line.

entrance[복습]
[éntrəns]

n. 입구, 문; 입장
The entrance to a place is the way into it, for example a door or gate.

wing[복습]
[wiŋ]

n. (연극 무대의 양쪽) 끝; (새·곤충의) 날개; v. 날아가다
In a theater, the wings are the sides of the stage which are hidden from the audience by curtains or scenery.

burly
[bə́:rli]

a. 건장한; 억센
A burly man has a broad body and strong muscles.

apiece
[əpí:s]

ad. 각각, 하나에
If people have a particular number of things apiece, they have that number each.

hoarse
[hɔ:rs]

a. 목쉰, 쉰 목소리의
If your voice is hoarse, your voice sounds rough and unclear.

bark[★]
[ba:rk]

n. (개 등이) 짖는 소리; 나무껍질; v. (개가) 짖다; (명령·질문 등을) 내지르다
A bark is the loud, rough noise that a dog and some other animals make.

104

number ^{복습}
[nʌ́mbər]

n. (공연) 프로그램의 한 항목, 곡목; 수, 숫자; v. 번호를 매기다
You can refer to a short piece of music, a song, or a dance as a number.

dreadful ^{복습}
[drédfəl]

a. 끔찍한, 지독한; 무시무시한
If you say that something is dreadful, you mean that it is very bad or unpleasant, or very poor in quality.

uproar
[ʌ́prɔ̀ːr]

n. 대소동, 소란; 엄청난 논란
If there is uproar, there is a lot of shouting and noise because people are very angry or upset about something.

ring down the curtain

idiom (극장에서) 막을 내리다
To ring down the curtain means to lower the curtain at the end of a theatrical performance.

rush ^{**}
[rʌʃ]

v. 급(속)히 움직이다; 재촉하다; n. (감정이) 치밀어 오름; 혼잡, 분주함
If you rush somewhere, you go there quickly.

stairway ^{복습}
[stέərwèi]

n. (통로로서의) 계단
A stairway is a staircase or a flight of steps, inside or outside a building.

dressing room
[drésiŋ ruːm]

n. (극장의) 분장실; (선수들의) 탈의실
A dressing room is a room in a theater where performers can dress and get ready for their performance.

bear ^{복습}
[bɛər]

v. 참다, 견디다; 가지고 가다; (아이를) 낳다
If you can't bear someone or something, you dislike them very much.

shudder [*]
[ʃʌ́dər]

n. 몸이 떨림; 크게 흔들림; v. (공포·추위 등으로) 몸을 떨다; 마구 흔들리다
If you give a shudder, you are making a shaking movement because you are cold, frightened or disgusted.

insure [*]
[inʃúər]

v. 보험에 들다; 보증하다, 안전하게 하다
If you insure yourself or your property, you pay money to an insurance company so that, if you become ill or if your property is damaged or stolen, the company will pay you a sum of money.

clang
[klæŋ]

v. 쩽그랑 하는 소리를 내다
When a large metal object clangs, it makes a loud noise.

ladder ^{복습}
[lǽdər]

n. 사다리
A ladder is a piece of equipment used for climbing up something or down from something.

vex [*]
[veks]

v. 짜증나게 하다, 초조하게 하다, 애타게 하다
If someone or something vexes you, they make you feel annoyed, puzzled, and frustrated.

mustache [*]
[mʌ́stæʃ]

n. 콧수염 (mustached a. 콧수염을 기른)
A man's mustache is the hair that grows on his upper lip.

parade ^{복습}
[pəréid]

v. 행진하다; (과시하듯) 걸어 다니다; n. 퍼레이드, 가두 행진
When people parade somewhere, they walk together in a formal group or a line, usually with other people watching them.

gay^{복습}
[gei]

a. 명랑한, 쾌활한 (gaily ad. 명랑하게, 쾌활하게)
If you do something gaily, you do it in a lively, happy way.

patrol[*]
[pətróul]

n. 순찰대; 순찰; v. 순찰을 돌다; (특히 위협적으로) 돌아다니다
A patrol is a group of soldiers or vehicles that are moving around an area in order to make sure that there is no trouble there.

scarcely^{복습}
[skéərsli]

ad. 거의 ~않다; 겨우, 간신히; ~하자마자
You use scarcely to emphasize that something is only just true or only just the case.

delight^{복습}
[diláit]

v. 많은 기쁨을 주다, 아주 즐겁게 하다; n. 기쁨, 즐거움
(delighted a. 아주 즐거워하는)
If you are delighted, you are extremely pleased and excited about something.

silly^{**}
[síli]

a. 우스꽝스러운; 어리석은, 바보 같은
If you say that someone or something is silly, you mean that they are foolish, childish, or ridiculous.

friendly^{복습}
[fréndli]

a. (행동이) 친절한, 우호적인; 상냥한, 다정한
If you are friendly with someone, you like each other and enjoy spending time together.

take sides

idiom (불화 등이 있는 상황에서) 편을 들다
If you take sides in an argument or war, you support one of the sides against the other.

fierce[*]
[fiərs]

a. 사나운, 험악한; 맹렬한; 극심한
A fierce animal or person is very aggressive or angry.

relief^{복습}
[rilí:f]

n. 안도, 안심; (고통·불안 등의) 완화
If you feel a sense of relief, you feel happy because something unpleasant has not happened or is no longer happening.

slip[*]
[slip]

v. 슬며시 가다; 미끄러지다; 빠져 나가다
If you slip somewhere, you go there quickly and quietly.

part^{복습}
[pa:rt]

v. 헤어지다; (사물이) 갈라지다, 나뉘다 (parting a. 이별의, 작별의)
Your parting words or actions are the things that you say or do as you are leaving a place or person.

regretful
[rigrétfəl]

a. 유감스러워하는 (듯한); 후회하는 (듯한) (regretfully ad. 유감스러운 듯, 애석한 듯)
If you are regretful, you show that you regret something.

burst^{복습}
[bə:rst]

v. (burst-burst) 불쑥 움직이다; 터지다, 파열하다; n. 파열
To burst into or out of a place means to enter or leave it suddenly with a lot of energy or force.

warrant[*]
[wɔ́:rənt]

n. 근거, 이유; 영장; v. 정당화하다; 보증하다, 보장하다
A warrant is a reason for doing something.

arrest^{복습}
[ərést]

n. 체포; 저지, 정지; v. 체포하다; 막다; (시선·관심을) 끌다
An arrest is the action of seizing someone to take into legal custody, as by officers of the law.

daze
[deiz]

n. 멍한 상태; 눈이 부심; v. 멍하게 하다; 눈부시게 하다
(in a daze idiom 어리둥절한 상태인)
If someone is in a daze, they are feeling confused and unable to think clearly, often because they have had a shock or surprise.

break into

idiom (건물에) 침입하다; ~하기 시작하다
If you break into a building or a car, you enter a building or open a car illegally and by force.

panic[*]
[pǽnik]

n. 허둥지둥함, 공황 상태; 극심한 공포; v. 겁에 질려 어쩔 줄 모르다
Panic or a panic is a situation in which people are affected by a strong feeling of anxiety.

disturb^{복습}
[distə́:rb]

v. (작업·수면 등을) 방해하다; 건드리다; 불안하게 하다 (disturber n. 방해자)
If something disturbs a situation or atmosphere, it spoils it or causes trouble.

1. How could Mr. Popper get out of jail?

   A. He had to pay bail for him and each penguin.

   B. He had to return the penguins to Antarctica.

   C. He had to show the policemen his penguin act.

   D. He had to do performances for free at the Regal Theater.

2. Why was Mr. Popper surprised when he was freed from jail?

   A. Admiral Drake had shown up and freed him.

   B. Mr. Greenbaum had shown up and freed him.

   C. The mayor of New York had shown up and freed him.

   D. Mr. Popper was freed but he had to leave his penguins in jail.

3. How did Admiral Drake think that Mr. Popper's penguins would do in the North Pole?

   A. He worried that they might be eaten by polar bears.

   B. He worried that they would find it much colder than the South Pole.

   C. He thought that they would think it was just like the South Pole.

   D. He thought that they were clever enough to survive polar bears.

4. Why did Mr. Popper feel that putting the penguins in the movies was a bad idea?

A. He wanted to keep them for himself.

B. He thought that it would give people the wrong idea about them.

C. He thought that life in Hollywood would not be good for them.

D. He thought that they needed more training before they could act in front of cameras.

5. Which of the following was NOT a reason that Mr. Popper decided to give the penguins to Admiral Drake?

A. He knew the penguins belonged in a cold climate.

B. He felt sorry for the lonely men at the North Pole.

C. He was worried about the excitement and warm weather.

D. Admiral Drake was going to send him a polar bear in exchange.

6. Why did Mr. Popper go along with the penguins to the North Pole?

A. Admiral Drake thought that Mr. Popper was a scientist.

B. Admiral Drake needed Mr. Popper to keep the penguins well and happy.

C. Mr. Popper had already packed and brought his own fur suit for the journey.

D. Mr. Popper paid Admiral Drake the money he had earned from making movies.

7. How did Mrs. Popper feel about Mr. Popper going to the North Pole?

A. She would miss him but wished him good luck.

B. She worried that he would be eaten by a polar bear.

C. She worried about having enough money if Mr. Popper left.

D. She was happy to see him stop painting houses in Stillwater.

Check Your Reading Speed
1분에 몇 단어를 읽는지 리딩 속도를 측정해 보세요.

$$\frac{1,272 \text{ words}}{\text{reading time ( ) sec}} \times 60 = (\quad) \text{ WPM}$$

Build Your Vocabulary

bundle* [bʌndl]
v. ~을 마구 싸 보내다; 무리 지어 가다; n. 묶음, 다발; 꾸러미, 보따리
If someone is bundled somewhere, someone else pushes them there in a rough and hurried way.

patrol복습 [pətróul]
n. 순찰; 순찰대; v. 순찰을 돌다
A patrol is a group of soldiers or vehicles that are moving around an area in order to make sure that there is no trouble there.

wagon* [wǽgən]
n. 자동차; 수레; 화물 기차 (patrol wagon n. 범인 호송차)
A patrol wagon is a van or truck which the police use for transporting prisoners.

hustle [hʌsl]
v. (거칠게) 떠밀다; 재촉하다; n. 법석, 혼잡
If you hustle someone, you try to make them go somewhere or do something quickly, for example by pulling or pushing them along.

plea* [pliː]
n. 애원, 간청
A plea is an appeal or request for something, made in an intense or emotional way.

bust [bʌst]
v. (현장을) 덮치다; 고장 내다, 망치다; 파산하다
If you bust into a place, you suddenly enter that place.

hold*** [hould]
v. 사람을 유치하다, 감금하다; 붙들다; 유지하다
If someone holds you in a place, they keep you there as a prisoner and do not allow you to leave.

cell** [sel]
n. 감방; 작은 방; 휴대 전화
A cell is a small room in which a prisoner is locked.

furnish* [fə́ːrniʃ]
v. 공급하다, 제공하다; 갖추다, 비치하다
If you furnish someone with something, you provide or supply it.

bail [beil]
n. 보석(금); v. (급히) 떠나다; 보석으로 풀어 주다
Bail is a sum of money that an arrested person or someone else puts forward as a guarantee that the arrested person will attend their trial in a law court.

bill복습 [bil]
n. 고지서, 청구서; 지폐; (새의) 부리; (극장 등의) 프로그램
A bill is a written statement of money that you owe for goods or services.

salary* [sǽləri]
n. 급여, 봉급, 월급
A salary is the money that someone is paid each month by their employer.

110

jail*
[dʒeil]

n. 교도소, 감옥; v. 수감하다
A jail is a place where criminals are kept in order to punish them, or where people waiting to be tried are kept.

coast복습
[koust]

n. 해안
The coast is an area of land that is next to the sea.

dull복습
[dʌl]

a. 따분한, 지루한
If you describe someone or something as dull, you mean they are not interesting or exciting.

droop*
[dru:p]

v. 풀이 죽다; 아래로 처지다, 늘어지다
If your spirits droop, you start to feel less happy and energetic.

apparent복습
[əpǽrənt]

a. 분명한, 누가 봐도 알 수 있는
If something is apparent to you, it is clear and obvious to you.

lack복습
[læk]

n. 부족, 결핍; v. ~이 없다, 부족하다
If there is a lack of something, there is not enough of it or it does not exist at all.

prove**
[pru:v]

v. 입증하다, 증명하다 (prove too much idiom 감당할 수 없다)
If something proves to be true or to have a particular quality, it becomes clear after a period of time that it is true or has that quality.

trick복습
[trik]

n. 묘기; 속임수; 장난; v. 속이다, 속임수를 쓰다
A trick is a clever or skillful action that someone does in order to entertain people.

merry***
[méri]

a. 즐거운, 명랑한
If you describe someone's character or behavior as merry, you mean that they are happy and cheerful.

dismal*
[dízməl]

a. 음울한, 울적하게 하는; 형편없는
Something that is dismal is sad and depressing, especially in appearance.

turn up복습
[ ]

idiom (사람이) 도착하다, 나타나다
If someone or something turns up, they arrive or appear somewhere, usually unexpectedly or in a way that was not planned.

renew*
[rinjú:]

v. 갱신하다, 연장하다; 재개하다
When you renew something such as a license or a contract, you extend the period of time for which it is valid.

smooth복습
[smu:ð]

v. 매끈하게 하다; 고루 펴 바르다; a. 매끈한; 순조로운
If you smooth something, you move your hands over its surface to make it smooth and flat.

dust*
[dʌst]

v. 먼지를 털다; (고운 가루를) 뿌리다; n. (흙)먼지
When you dust something such as furniture, you remove dust from it, usually using a cloth.

presentable
[prizéntəbl]

a. (모습이) 남 앞에 내놓을 만한; 받아들여질 만한
If you say that someone looks presentable, you mean that they look fairly tidy or attractive.

footstep*
[fútstep]

n. 발소리; 발자국
A footstep is the sound or mark that is made by someone walking each time their foot touches the ground.

corridor*
[kɔ́:ridər]

n. 복도; 통로
A corridor is a long passage in a building or train, with doors and rooms on one or both sides.

jingle
[dʒíŋgl]

v. 딸랑거리다; n. 딸랑, 짤랑 (하고 울리는 소리)
When something jingles or when you jingle it, it makes a gentle ringing noise, like small bells.

barely복습
[béərli]

ad. 간신히, 가까스로; 거의 ~아니게
You use barely to say that something is only just true or only just the case.

in time

idiom (~에) 시간 맞춰, 늦지 않게
If you are in time for a particular event, you are not too late for it.

accustom*
[əkʌ́stəm]

v. 익히다, 익숙해지다 (accustomed a. 익숙해진)
When your eyes become accustomed to darkness or bright light, they adjust so that you start to be able to see things, after not being able to see properly at first.

beard*
[biərd]

n. (턱)수염 (bearded a. 수염이 있는)
A man's beard is the hair that grows on his chin and cheeks.

splendid복습
[spléndid]

a. 멋진, 화려한
If you say that something is splendid, you mean that it is very good.

gasp복습
[gæsp]

v. 헉 하고 숨을 쉬다, 숨이 턱 막히다; 숨을 제대로 못 쉬다; n. 헉 하는 소리를 냄
When you gasp, you take a short quick breath through your mouth, especially when you are surprised, shocked, or in pain.

Antarctic복습
[æntá:rktik]

n. 남극; a. 남극의, 남극 지방의
The Antarctic is the area around the South Pole.

expedition복습
[èkspədíʃən]

n. 탐험, 원정; 원정대
An expedition is an organized journey that is made for a particular purpose such as exploration.

reception*
[risépʃən]

n. 환영 연회; 환영, 응접; 평판; 청취(상태), 수신
A reception is a formal party which is given to welcome someone or to celebrate a special event.

anxious*
[ǽŋkʃəs]

a. 간절히 바라는; 불안해하는, 염려하는
If you are anxious to do something or anxious that something should happen, you very much want to do it or very much want it to happen.

cluster*
[klʌ́stər]

v. (소규모로) 모이다, 밀집하다; n. 무리, 집단, 떼
If people cluster together, they gather together in a small group.

get along복습

idiom 사이 좋게 지내다; 해나가다, 살아가다
If people get along, they like each other and are friendly to each other.

112

mayor^{복습}
[méiər]

n. (시·군 등의) 시장
The mayor of a town or city is the person who has been elected to represent it for a fixed period of time or to run its government.

on earth^{복습}

idiom 도대체 어떻게
On earth is used for emphasis in questions that begin with words such as 'how,' 'why,' 'what,' or 'where.' It is often used to suggest that there is no obvious or easy answer to the question being asked.

band**
[bænd]

n. 무리, 일행; 띠, 끈 v. 단결시키다; 묶다
A band of people is a group of people who have joined together because they share an interest or belief.

save the day

idiom 곤경을 면하게 하다
If someone or something saves the day in a situation which seems likely to fail, they manage to make it successful.

amazing*
[əméiziŋ]

a. 놀라운, 굉장한
You say that something is amazing when it is very surprising and makes you feel pleasure, approval, or wonder.

patience*
[péiʃəns]

n. 인내력, 인내심; 참을성
If you have patience, you are able to stay calm and not get annoyed.

get to the point

idiom 핵심에 이르다; 요점을 언급하다
When someone comes to the point or gets to the point, they start talking about the thing that is most important to them.

explore^{복습}
[iksplɔ́:r]

v. 탐험하다, 탐사하다; 분석하다
If you explore a place, you travel around it to find out what it is like.

Arctic^{복습}
[á:rktik]

n. 북극; a. 북극의, 북극 지방의
The Arctic is the area of the world around the North Pole.

on account of^{복습}

idiom ~ 때문에
You use on account of to introduce the reason or explanation for something.

pat^{복습}
[pæt]

v. 쓰다듬다; 가볍게 두드리다; n. 쓰다듬기, 토닥거리기
If you pat something or someone, you tap them lightly, usually with your hand held flat.

polar^{복습}
[póulər]

a. 북극의, 남극의, 극지의; 정반대되는
Polar means near the North and South Poles.

establish***
[istǽbliʃ]

v. (새로운 땅에) 정착시키다; (사실을) 규명하다, 밝히다; 설립하다
If someone establishes something such as an organization, a type of activity, or a set of rules, they create it or introduce it in such a way that it is likely to last for a long time.

breed^{복습}
[bri:d]

n. (개·고양이·가축의) 품종; v. 새끼를 낳다
A breed of a pet animal or farm animal is a particular type of it. For example, terriers are a breed of dog.

remarkable ^{복습}
[rimá:rkəbl]

a. 놀랄 만한, 놀라운, 주목할 만한
Someone or something that is remarkable is unusual or special in a way that makes people notice them and be surprised or impressed.

race ^{복습}
[reis]

n. 인종, 종족; 경주; 경쟁; v. 경주하다; 쏜살같이 가다
A race of animals or plants is a group of animals or plants that are similar to each other.

announce**
[ənáuns]

v. (도착을 알리기 위해) 이름을 말하다; 발표하다, 알리다
To announce means to say formally that someone has arrived or that something is about to happen.

mix-up
[míks-ʌp]

n. (특히 실수로 인한) 혼동
A mix-up is a mistake or a failure in the way that something has been planned.

colossal
[kəlásəl]

a. 거대한, 엄청난
If you describe something as colossal, you are emphasizing that it is very large.

fortune**
[fɔ́:rtʃən]

n. 거금; 재산, 부; 운
You can refer to a large sum of money as a fortune or a small fortune to emphasize how large it is.

pin money
[pín mʌni]

n. 소액의 돈; 용돈
Pin money is small amounts of extra money that someone earns or gets in order to buy things that they want but that they do not really need.

on easy street

idiom 풍족한 삶을 누리는
If you live on easy street, you are in a state of financial independence and comfort.

whisper*
[hwíspər]

v. 속삭이다, 소곤거리다; 은밀히 말하다; n. 속삭임, 소곤거리는 소리
When you whisper, you say something very quietly, using your breath rather than your throat, so that only one person can hear you.

ordinary**
[ɔ́:rdənèri]

a. 평범한; 보통의, 일상적인
Ordinary people or things are normal and not special or different in any way.

judicious
[dʒu:díʃəs]

a. 신중한, 판단력 있는 (judiciously ad. 사려 깊게)
If you describe an action or decision as judicious, you approve of it because you think that it shows good judgment and sense.

outwit
[àutwít]

v. ~보다 한 수 앞서다
If you outwit someone, you use your intelligence or a clever trick to defeat them or to gain an advantage over them.

114

Check Your Reading Speed

1분에 몇 단어를 읽는지 리딩 속도를 측정해 보세요.

$$\frac{1{,}082 \text{ words}}{\text{reading time ( ) sec}} \times 60 = (\quad) \text{ WPM}$$

Build Your Vocabulary

farewell*
[fέərwél]

int. 안녕!; n. 작별(인사), 고별
Farewell means the same as goodbye.

advantage**
[ædvǽntidʒ]

n. 유리한 점, 이점, 장점
An advantage is a way in which one thing is better than another.

influence**
[ínfluəns]

v. 영향을 미치다; n. 영향(력), 세력
If you influence someone, you use your power to make them agree with you or do what you want.

responsibility**
[rispànsəbíləti]

n. 책임; 의무(감)
If you have responsibility for something or someone, or if they are your responsibility, it is your job or duty to deal with them and to take decisions relating to them.

make up one's mind

idiom ~하기로 결심하다
If you make up your mind, you decide which of a number of possible things you will have or do.

pale**
[peil]

a. 창백한, 핼쑥한; (색깔이) 열은; v. 창백해지다
If someone looks pale, their face looks a lighter color than usual, usually because they are ill, frightened, or shocked.

haggard
[hǽgərd]

a. 초췌한; 여윈, 수척한
Someone who looks haggard has a tired expression and shadows under their eyes, especially because they are ill or have not had enough sleep.

announce복습
[ənáuns]

v. 발표하다, 알리다; (도착을 알리기 위해) 이름을 말하다
If you announce something, you tell people about it publicly or officially.

appreciate**
[əprí:ʃièit]

v. 고마워하다; 진가를 알아보다, 인정하다
If you appreciate something that someone has done for you or is going to do for you, you are grateful for it.

first of all

idiom 우선, 다른 무엇보다 먼저
You use first of all to introduce the first of a number of things that you want to say.

after all복습

idiom 어쨌든; (예상과는 달리) 결국에는
You use after all when introducing a statement which supports or helps explain something you have just said.

climate [복습]
[kláimit]
n. 기후; 분위기, 풍조
The climate of a place is the general weather conditions that are typical of it.

pole [복습]
[poul]
n. (지구의) 극; 기둥, 장대
The earth's poles are the two opposite ends of its axis, its most northern and southern points.

congratulate [복습]
[kəngrǽʧulèit]
v. 축하하다; 기뻐하다, 자랑스러워하다 (congratulations n. 축하해요!)
If you congratulate someone, you say something to show you are pleased that something nice has happened to them.

Arctic [복습]
[á:rktik]
n. 북극; a. 북극의, 북극 지방의
The Arctic is the area of the world around the North Pole.

foundation*
[faundéiʃən]
n. 기초, 토대; 설립, 창립
The foundation of something such as a belief or way of life is the things on which it is based.

expedition [복습]
[èkspədíʃən]
n. 원정대; 탐험, 원정
An expedition is an organized journey that is made for a particular purpose such as exploration.

fortune [복습]
[fɔ́:rʧən]
n. 거금; 재산, 부; 운
You can refer to a large sum of money as a fortune or a small fortune to emphasize how large it is.

contract [복습]
[kántrækt]
n. 계약; v. 계약하다; 줄어들다, 수축하다
A contract is a legal agreement, usually between two companies or between an employer and employee, which involves doing work for a stated sum of money.

comfort**
[kʌ́mfərt]
v. 위로하다, 위안하다; n. 안락, 편안; 위로, 위안
If you comfort someone, you make them feel less worried, unhappy, or upset, for example by saying kind things to them.

trick [복습]
[trik]
n. 묘기; 속임수; 장난; v. 속이다, 속임수를 쓰다
A trick is a clever or skillful action that someone does in order to entertain people.

meanwhile [복습]
[mí:nwàil]
ad. 그 동안에; 그 사이에
Meanwhile means while a particular thing is happening.

harbor*
[há:rbər]
n. 항구, 항만; 피난처, 은신처
A harbor is an area of the sea at the coast which is partly enclosed by land or strong walls, so that boats can be left there safely.

sail [복습]
[seil]
v. 항해하다; 미끄러지듯 나아가다; n. 돛; 항해 (sailing ship n. (대형) 범선)
A sailing ship is a large ship with sails, especially of the kind that were used to carry passengers or cargo.

supply**
[səplái]
n. (pl.) 보급품, 물자; 공급(량); 제공; v. 공급하다
You can use supplies to refer to food, equipment, and other essential things that people need, especially in large quantities.

hustle [복습]
[hʌsl]
v. (거칠게) 떠밀다; 재촉하다; n. 법석, 혼잡
If you hustle someone, you try to make them go somewhere or do something quickly, for example by pulling or pushing them along.

board^{복습}
[bɔːrd]

v. 승선하다, 탑승하다; n. 판자; 이사회 (on board idiom 승선한)
When you are on board a train, ship, or aircraft, you are on it or in it.

quarter**
[kwɔ́ːrtər]

n. (pl.) 숙소, 막사; 4분의 1; 구역; v. 4등분하다; 숙소를 제공하다
The rooms provided for soldiers, sailors, or servants to live in are called their quarters.

voyage*
[vɔ́iidʒ]

n. 여행, 항해; v. 여행하다, 항해하다
A voyage is a long journey on a ship or in a spacecraft.

vessel*
[vésəl]

n. (대형) 선박, 배; 그릇, 용기
A vessel is a ship or large boat.

delight^{복습}
[diláit]

n. 기쁨, 즐거움; v. 많은 기쁨을 주다, 아주 즐겁게 하다
If someone takes delight or takes a delight in something, they get a lot of pleasure from it.

curious^{복습}
[kjúəriəs]

a. 호기심이 많은; 별난, 특이한; 궁금한
If you are curious about something, you are interested in it and want to know more about it.

explore^{복습}
[iksplɔ́ːr]

v. 탐험하다, 탐사하다; 분석하다 (exploration n. 탐험, 탐사)
An exploration is a journey to a place to learn about it or to search for something valuable such as oil.

lively^{복습}
[láivli]

a. 활기 넘치는; 적극적인, 의욕적인; 선명한
A lively event or a lively discussion, for example, has lots of interesting and exciting things happening or being said in it.

live up to

idiom (다른 사람의 기대에) 부응하다
To live up to something means to behave as well as or be as good or successful as people expect.

reputation^{복습}
[rèpjutéiʃən]

n. 평판, 명성
Something's or someone's reputation is the opinion that people have about how good they are.

extraordinary*
[ikstrɔ́ːrdənèri]

a. 보기 드문, 비범한; 기이한, 놀라운
If you describe something as extraordinary, you mean that it is very unusual or surprising.

contribute**
[kəntríbjuːt]

v. 기여하다, 이바지하다; 기부하다 (contribution n. 기여, 이바지)
If you make a contribution to something, you do something to help make it successful or to produce it.

break down

idiom 감정을 주체하지 못하다; 고장 나다
If you break down, you lose control of your feelings and start crying.

lean^{복습}
[liːn]

v. 기울이다, (몸을) 숙이다; ~에 기대다; a. 군살이 없는, 호리호리한
When you lean in a particular direction, you bend your body in that direction.

wipe*
[waip]

v. (먼지·물기 등을) 닦다; 지우다; n. (행주·걸레를 써서) 닦기
If you wipe dirt or liquid from something, you remove it, for example by using a cloth or your hand.

straighten^{복습}
[stréitn]

v. (자세를) 바로 하다; 정리하다, 정돈하다; 똑바르게 하다
If you straighten from a relaxed or slightly bent position, you make your back or body straight and upright.

deck[*]
[dek]

n. (배의) 갑판; 층; v. 꾸미다, 장식하다
The deck of a ship is the top part of it that forms a floor in the open air which you can walk on.

keeper[*]
[kíːpər]

n. 사육사; (건물·귀중품 등을) 지키는 사람
A keeper at a zoo is a person who takes care of the animals.

roar^{복습}
[rɔːr]

v. 고함치다; 함성을 지르다; 으르렁거리다; n. 으르렁거림, 포효
If someone roars, they shout something in a very loud voice.

fur[*]
[fəːr]

n. 모피; (동물의) 털
Fur is the fur-covered skin of an animal that is used to make clothing or small carpets.

suit^{**}
[suːt]

n. (특정한 활동 때 입는) 옷; 정장; v. ~에게 어울리다; 편리하다
A particular type of suit is a piece of clothing that you wear for a particular activity.

anchor[*]
[ǽŋkər]

n. 닻; v. 닻을 내리다, 정박하다; 고정시키다
An anchor is a heavy hooked object that is dropped from a boat into the water at the end of a chain in order to make the boat stay in one place.

live on^{복습}

idiom (얼마의 돈으로) 먹고 살다
To live on means to have a particular amount of money to buy the things that you need to live.

tidy^{복습}
[táidi]

a. 깔끔한, 잘 정돈된, 단정한; v. 치우다, 정돈하다
Something that is tidy is neat and is arranged in an organized way.

missionary^{복습}
[míʃənèri]

a. 전도의, 선교(사)의; n. 선교사
Missionary is relating to or characteristic of a missionary or a religious mission.

in time^{복습}

idiom (~에) 시간 맞춰, 늦지 않게
If you are in time for a particular event, you are not too late for it.

echo[*]
[ékou]

v. 그대로 따라 하다; (소리가) 울리다, 메아리치다; n. (소리의) 울림, 메아리; 반복
If you echo someone's words, you repeat them or express agreement with their attitude or opinion.

scuttle
[skʌtl]

v. 허둥지둥 가다, 종종걸음을 치다
When people or small animals scuttle somewhere, they run there with short quick steps.

solemn^{복습}
[sáləm]

a. 엄숙한; 근엄한; 침통한 (solemnly ad. 엄숙하게, 진지하게)
Someone or something that is solemn is very serious rather than cheerful or humorous.

flipper^{복습}
[flípər]

n. (바다표범·거북 등의) 지느러미발; (잠수·수영 때 신는) 오리발
The flippers of an animal that lives in water, for example a seal or a penguin, are the two or four flat limbs which it uses for swimming.

wave^{★★}
[weiv]

v. (손·팔을) 흔들다; 손짓하다; n. 파도, 물결; (팔·손·몸을) 흔들기
If you wave or wave your hand, you move your hand from side to side in the air, usually in order to say hello or goodbye to someone.

수고하셨습니다!

드디어 끝까지 다 읽으셨군요! 축하드립니다! 여러분은 이 책을 통해 총 16,160 개의 단어를 읽으셨고, 800개 이상의 어휘와 표현들을 익히셨습니다. 이 책에 나온 어휘는 다른 원서를 읽을 때에도 빈번히 만날 수 있는 필수 어휘들입니다. 이 책을 읽었던 경험은 비슷한 수준의 다른 원서들을 읽을 때 큰 도움이 될 것 입니다.

이제 자신의 상황에 맞게 원서를 반복해서 읽거나, 오디오북을 들어 볼 수 있습니다. 혹은 비슷한 수준의 다른 원서를 찾아 읽는 것도 좋습니다. 일단 원서를 완독한 뒤에 어떻게 계속 영어 공부를 이어갈 수 있을지, 도움말을 꼼꼼히 살펴보고 각자 상황에 맞게 적용해 보세요!

리딩(Reading)을 확실하게 다지고 싶다면? 반복해서 읽어 보세요!

리딩 실력을 탄탄하게 다지고 싶다면, 같은 원서를 2-3번 반복해서 읽을 것을 권합니다. 같은 책을 여러 번 읽으면 지루할 것 같지만, 꼭 그렇지도 않습니다. 반복해서 읽을 때 처음과 주안점을 다르게 두면, 전혀 다른 느낌으로 재미있게 읽을 수 있습니다.

처음 원서를 읽을 때는 생소한 단어들과 스토리로 인해 읽으면서 곧바로 이해하기가 매우 힘들 수 있습니다. 전체 맥락을 잡고 읽어도 약간 버거운 느낌이지요. 하지만 반복해서 읽기 시작하면 달라집니다. 일단 내용을 파악한 상황이기 때문에 문장 구조나 어휘의 활용에 더 집중하게 되고, 조금 더 깊이 있게 읽을 수 있습니다. 좋은 표현과 문장을 수집하고 메모할 만한 여유도 생기게 되지요. 어휘도 많이 익숙해졌기 때문에 리딩 속도에도 탄력이 붙습니다. 처음 읽을 때는 '내용'에서 재미를 느꼈다면, 반복해서 읽을 때에는 '영어'에서 재미를 느끼게 되는 것입니다. 따라서 리딩 실력을 더욱 확고하게 다지고자 한다면, 같은 책을 2-3회 정도 반복해서 읽을 것을 권해 드립니다.

리스닝(Listening) 실력을 늘리고 싶다면?
귀를 통해서 읽어 보세요!

많은 영어 학습자들이 '리스닝이 안 돼서 문제'라고 한탄합니다. 그리고 리스닝 실력을 늘리는 방법으로 무슨 뜻인지 몰라도 반복해서 듣는 '무작정 듣기'를 선택합니다. 하지만 뜻도 모르면서 무작정 듣는 일에는 엄청난 인내력이 필요합니다. 그래서 대부분 며칠 시도하다가 포기해 버리고 말지요.

따라서 모르는 내용을 무작정 듣는 것보다는 어느 정도 알고 있는 내용을 반복해서 듣는 것이 더 효과적인 듣기 방법입니다. 그리고 이런 방식의 듣기에 활용할 수 있는 가장 좋은 교재가 오디오북입니다.

리스닝 실력을 향상하고 싶다면, 이 책에서 제공하는 오디오북을 이용해서 듣는 연습을 해 보세요. 활용법은 간단합니다. 일단 책을 한 번 완독했다면, 오디오북을 통해 다시 들어 보는 것입니다. 휴대 기기에 넣어 시간이 날 때 틈틈이 듣는 것도 좋고, 책상에 앉아 눈으로는 텍스트를 보며 귀로 읽는 것도 좋습니다. 이미 읽었던 내용이라 이해하기가 훨씬 수월하고, 애매했던 발음들도 자연스럽게 교정할 수 있습니다. 또 성우의 목소리 연기를 듣다 보면 내용이 더욱 생동감 있게 다가와 이해도가 높아지는 효과도 거둘 수 있습니다.

반대로 듣기에 자신 있는 사람이라면, 책을 읽기 전에 처음부터 오디오북을 먼저 듣는 것도 좋은 방법입니다. 귀를 통해 책을 쭉 읽어보고, 이후에 다시 눈으로 책을 읽으면서 잘 들리지 않았던 부분들을 보충하는 것이지요.

중요한 것은 내용을 따라가면서, 내용에 푹 빠져서 반복해 들어야 한다는 것입니다. 이렇게 연습을 반복해서 눈으로 읽지 않은 책이라도 '귀를 통해' 읽을 수 있을 정도가 되면, 리스닝으로 고생하는 일은 거의 없을 것입니다.

왼쪽의 QR코드를 스마트폰으로 인식하여 정식 오디오북을 들어 보세요!
더불어 롱테일북스 홈페이지(www.longtailbooks.co.kr)에서도
오디오북 MP3 파일을 다운로드 받을 수 있습니다.

스피킹(Speaking)이 고민이라면? 소리 내어 읽어 보세요!

스피킹 역시 많은 학습자들이 고민하는 부분입니다. 스피킹이 고민이라면, 원서를 큰 소리로 읽는 낭독 훈련(Voice Reading)을 해 보세요!

'소리 내어 읽는 것이 말하기에 정말로 도움이 될까?'라고 의아한 생각이 들 수도 있습니다. 하지만 인간의 두뇌 입장에서 봤을 때, 성대 구조를 활용해서 '발화'한다는 점에서는 소리 내어 읽기와 말하기에 큰 차이가 없다고 합니다. 소리 내어 읽는 것은 '타인의 생각'을 전달하고, 직접 말하는 것은 '자신의 생각'을 전달한다는 차이가 있을 뿐, 머릿속에서 문장을 처리하고 조음기관(혀와 성대 등)을 움직여 의미를 만든다는 점에서 같은 과정인 것이지요. 따라서 소리 내어 읽는 연습을 꾸준히 하는 것은 스피킹 연습에 큰 도움이 됩니다.

소리 내어 읽기를 하는 방법은 간단합니다. 일단 오디오북을 들으면서 성우의 목소리를 최대한 따라 하며 같이 읽어 보세요. 발음뿐 아니라 억양, 어조, 느낌까지 완벽히 따라 한다고 생각하면서 소리 내어 읽습니다. 따라 읽는 것이 조금 익숙해지면, 옆의 누군가에게 이 책을 읽어 준다는 생각으로 소리 내어 계속 읽어 나갑니다. 한 번 눈과 귀로 읽었던 책이기 때문에 보다 수월하게 진행할 수 있고, 자연스럽게 어휘와 표현을 복습하는 효과도 거두게 됩니다. 또 이렇게 소리 내어 읽은 것을 녹음해서 들어 보면 스스로에게도 좋은 피드백이 됩니다.

최근 말하기가 강조되면서 소리 내어 읽기가 크게 각광을 받고 있기는 하지만, 그렇다고 소리 내어 읽기가 무조건 좋은 것만은 아닙니다. 책을 소리 내어 읽다 보면, 무의식적으로 속으로 발음을 하는 습관을 가지게 되어 리딩 속도 자체는 오히려 크게 떨어지는 현상이 발생할 수 있습니다. 따라서 빠른 리딩 속도가 중요한 수험생이나 고학력 학습자들에게는 소리 내어 읽기가 적절하지 않은 방법입니다. 효과가 좋다는 말만 믿고 무턱대고 따라 하기보다는 자신의 필요에 맞게 우선순위를 정하고 원서를 활용하는 것이 좋습니다.

라이팅(Writing)까지 욕심이 난다면? 요약하는 연습을 해 보세요!

원서를 라이팅 연습에 직접적으로 활용하는 데에는 한계가 있지만, 적절히 활용하면 원서도 유용한 라이팅 자료가 될 수 있습니다.

특히 책을 읽고 그 내용을 요약하는 연습은 큰 도움이 됩니다. 요약 훈련의 방식도 간단합니다. 원서를 읽고 그날 읽은 분량만큼 혹은 책을 다 읽고 전체 내용을 기반으로, 책 내용을 한번 요약하고 나의 느낌을 영어로 적어보는 것입니다.

이때 그 책에 나왔던 단어와 표현을 최대한 활용하여 요약하는 것이 중요합니다. 영어 표현력은 결국 얼마나 다양한 어휘로 많은 표현을 해 보았느냐가 좌우하게 됩니다. 이런 면에서 내가 읽은 책을, 그 책에 나온 문장과 어휘로 다시 표현해 보는 것은 매우 효율적인 방법입니다. 책에 나온 어휘와 표현을 단순히 읽고 무슨 말인지 아는 정도가 아니라, 실제로 직접 활용해서 쓸 수 있을 만큼 확실하게 익히게 되는 것이지요. 여기에 첨삭까지 받을 수 있는 방법이 있다면 금상첨화입니다.

이러한 '표현하기' 연습은 스피킹 훈련에도 그대로 적용될 수 있습니다. 책을 읽고 그 내용을 3분 안에 다른 사람에게 영어로 말하는 연습을 해 보세요. 순발력과 표현력을 기르는 좋은 훈련이 될 것입니다.

꾸준히 원서를 읽고 싶다면? 뉴베리 수상작을 계속 읽어 보세요!

뉴베리 상이 세계 최고 권위의 아동 문학상인 만큼, 그 수상작들은 확실히 완성도를 검증받은 작품이라고 할 수 있습니다. 특히 '쉬운 어휘로 쓰인 깊이 있는 문장'으로 이루어졌다는 점이 영어 학습자들에게 큰 호응을 얻고 있습니다. 이렇게 '검증된 원서'를 꾸준히 읽는 것은 영어 실력 향상에 큰 도움이 됩니다.

아래에 수준별로 제시된 뉴베리 수상작 목록을 보며 적절한 책들을 찾아 계속 읽어 보세요. 꼭 뉴베리 수상작이 아니더라도 마음에 드는 작가의 다른 책을 읽어 보는 것 또한 아주 좋은 방법입니다.

• 영어 초보자도 쉽게 읽을 만한 아주 쉬운 수준. 소리 내어 읽기에도 아주 적합. Sarah, Plain and Tall★(Medal, 8,331단어), The Hundred Penny Box (Honor, 5,878단어), The Hundred Dresses★(Honor, 7,329단어), My Father's Dragon (Honor, 7,682단어), 26 Fairmount Avenue (Honor, 6,737단어)

• 중 · 고등학생 정도 영어 학습자라면 쉽게 읽을 수 있는 수준. 소리 내어 읽기에도 비교적 적합한 편.

Because of Winn-Dixie★(Honor, 22,123단어), What Jamie Saw (Honor, 17,203단어), Charlotte's Web (Honor, 31,938단어), Dear Mr. Henshaw (Medal, 18,145단어), Missing May (Medal, 17,509단어)

• 대학생 정도 영어 학습자라면 무난한 수준. 소리 내어 읽기에 적합하지 않음.

Number The Stars★(Medal, 27,197단어), A Single Shard (Medal, 33,726단어), The Tale of Despereaux★(Medal, 32,375단어), Hatchet★(Medal, 42,328단어), Bridge to Terabithia (Medal, 32,888단어), A Fine White Dust (Honor, 19,022단어), Jennifer, Hecate, Macbeth, William McKinley and Me, Elizabeth (Honor, 23,266단어)

• 원서 완독 경험을 가진 학습자에게 적절한 수준. 소리 내어 읽기에 적합하지 않음.

The Giver★(Medal, 43,617단어), From the Mixed-Up Files of Mrs. Basil E. Frankweiler (Medal, 30,906단어), The View from Saturday (Medal, 42,685단어), Holes★(Medal, 47,079단어), Criss Cross (Medal, 48,221단어), Walk Two Moons (Medal, 59,400단어), The Graveyard Book (Medal, 67,380단어)

뉴베리 수상작과 뉴베리 수상 작가의 좋은 작품을 엄선한 「뉴베리 컬렉션」에도 위 목록에 있는 도서 중 상당수가 포함될 예정입니다.

★「뉴베리 컬렉션」으로 이미 출간된 도서

어떤 책들이 출간되었는지 확인하려면, 지금 인터넷 서점에서 뉴베리 컬렉션을 검색해 보세요.

뉴베리 수상작을 동영상 강의로 만나 보세요!

영어원서 전문 동영상 강의 사이트 영서당(yseodang.com)에서는 뉴베리 컬렉션 『Holes』, 『Because of Winn-Dixie』, 『The Miraculous Journey of Edward Tulane』, 『Wayside School 시리즈』 등의 동영상 강의를 제공하고 있습니다. 뉴베리 수상 작이라는 최고의 영어 교재와 EBS 출신 인기 강사가 만난 명강의! 지금 사이트 를 방문해서 무료 샘플 강의를 들어 보세요!

'스피드 리딩 카페'를 통해 원서 읽기 습관을 길러 보세요!

일상에서 영어를 한마디도 쓰지 않는 비영어권 국가에서 살고 있는 우리가 영어 환경에 가장 쉽고, 편하고, 부담 없이 노출되는 방법은 바로 '영어원서 읽기' 입니다. 언제 어디서든 원서를 붙잡고 읽기만 하면 곧바로 영어를 접하는 환경이 만들어지기 때문이지요. 하루에 20분씩만 꾸준히 읽는다면, 1년에 무려 120시간 동안 영어에 노출될 수 있습니다. 이러한 이유 때문에 영어 교육 전문가들이 영어원서 읽기를 추천하는 것이지요.
하지만 원서 읽기가 좋다는 것을 알아도 막상 꾸준히 읽는 것은 쉽지 않습니다. 그럴 때에는 13만 명 이상의 회원을 보유한 국내 최대 원서 읽기 동호회 〈스피드 리딩 카페〉(cafe.naver.com/readingtc)를 방문해 보세요.
원서별로 정리된 무료 PDF 단어장과 수준별 추천 원서 목록 등 유용한 자료는 물론, 뉴베리 수상작을 포함한 다양한 원서의 리뷰와 정보를 무료로 확인할 수 있습니다. 특히 함께 모여서 원서를 읽는 '북클럽'은 중간에 포기하지 않고 원서 읽기 습관을 기르는 데 큰 도움이 될 것입니다.

Chapters 1 & 2

1. B   He was carrying his buckets, his ladders, and his boards so that he had rather a hard time moving along. He was spattered here and there with paint and calcimine, and there were bits of wallpaper clinging to his hair and whiskers, for he was rather an untidy man.

2. A   The reason Mr. Popper was so absent-minded was that he was always dreaming about far-away countries.

3. C   Mrs. Popper sighed. "I sometimes wish you had the kind of work that lasted all year, instead of just from spring until fall," she said. "It will be very nice to have you at home for a vacation, of course, but it is a little hard to sweep with a man sitting around reading all day." "I could decorate the house for you." "No, indeed," said Mrs. Popper firmly. "Last year you painted the bathroom four different times, because you had nothing else to do, and I think that is enough of that. But what worries me is the money. I have saved a little, and I daresay we can get along as we have other winters. No more roast beef, no more ice cream, not even on Sundays."

4. C   Mr. Popper was not worried, however. As he put on his spectacles, he was quite pleased at the prospect of a whole winter of reading travel books, with no work to interrupt him. He set his little globe beside him and began to read.

5. B   "Well, I didn't, and I don't think any of us will have any money for movies now," answered Mrs. Popper, a little sharply. She was not at all a disagreeable woman, but she sometimes got rather cross when she was worried about money.

6. D   "Penguins are very intelligent," continued Mr. Popper. "Listen to this, Mamma. It says here that when they want to catch some shrimps, they all crowd over to the edge of an ice bank. Only they don't just jump in, because a sea leopard might be waiting to eat the penguins. So they crowd and push until they manage to shove one penguin off, to see if it's safe. I mean if he doesn't get eaten up, the rest of them know it's safe for them all to jump in."

7. B   "Hello, Mr. Popper, up there in Stillwater. Thanks for your nice letter about

the pictures of our last expedition. Watch for an answer. But not by letter, Mr. Popper. Watch for a surprise. Signing off. Signing off."

Chapters 3 & 4

1. D   He had succeeded in removing the outer boards and part of the packing, which was a layer of dry ice, when from the depths of the packing case he suddenly heard a faint "*Ork*." His heart stood still. Surely he had heard that sound before at the Drake Expedition movies.

2. B   Mr. Popper had read that penguins are extremely curious, and he soon found that this was true, for stepping out, the visitor began to inspect the house.

3. C   "Perhaps," thought Mr. Popper, "all that white tiling reminds him of the ice and snow at the South Pole. Poor thing, maybe he's thirsty."

4. D   "*Gook! Gook!*" said the penguin, sliding down once more on his glossy white stomach. "It sounds something like 'Cook,'" said Mr. Popper. "Why, that's it, of course. We'll call him Cook—Captain Cook."

5. C   "He certainly is cute," she said. "I guess I'll have to forgive him for biting my ankle. He probably only did it out of curiosity. Anyway, he's a nice clean-looking bird."

6. B   Captain Cook had done it all right. He had discovered the bowl of goldfish on the dining-room window sill. By the time Mrs. Popper reached over to lift him away, he had already swallowed the last of the goldfish. "Bad, bad penguin!" reproved Mrs. Popper, glaring down at Captain Cook.

7. A   "Just a minute," answered Mr. Popper. "I just happened to think that Captain Cook will not feel right on the floor of that icebox. Penguins make their nests of pebbles and stones. So I will just take some ice cubes out of the tray and put them under him. That way he will be more comfortable."

Chapters 5 & 6

1. C   "It's my icebox, and I want some holes bored in the door," said Mr. Popper. … That is no way to talk. Believe it or not, I know what I'm doing. I mean, having you do. I want you to fix an extra handle on the inside of that box so it can be opened from the inside of the box."

2. A   Mr. Popper silently reached into his pocket and gave the service man his last five-dollar bill. He was pretty sure that Mrs. Popper would be annoyed at him for spending all that money, but it could not be helped.

3. B   "Mister," said the service man, "you win. I'll fix your extra handle. And while I am doing it, you sit down on that chair over there facing me, where I can keep an eye on you."

4. D   "Well, if it's only a bird . . ." said the policeman, lifting his cap to scratch his head in a puzzled sort of way. "From the way that fellow with a tool bag yelled at me outside, I thought there was a lion loose in here."

5. C   "It's certainly big enough for a license," said the policeman. "I tell you what to do. You call up the City Hall and ask them what the ruling about penguins is. And good luck to you, Popper. He's kind of a cute little fellow, at that. Looks almost human. Good day to you, Popper, and good day to you, Mr. Penguin."

6. D   "Then listen," roared Mr. Popper, now completely outraged. "If you folks at the City Hall don't even know what penguins are, I guess you haven't any rule saying they have to be licensed. I will do without a license for Captain Cook."

7. D   In a moment a new voice was speaking to Mr. Popper. "Good morning. This is the Automobile License Bureau. Did you have this same car last year, and if so, what was the license number?" Mr. Popper had been switched over to the County Building. He decided to hang up.

Chapters 7 & 8

1. D   Meanwhile Mr. Popper had abandoned his telephoning and was now busy shaving and making himself neat in honor of being the owner of such a splendid bird as Captain Cook.

2. C   Into the corners of every room he prowled and poked and pecked with a busy thoroughness; into every closet he stared with his white-circled eyes; under and behind all the furniture he crowded his plump figure, with little subdued cries of curiosity, surprise, and pleasure. And each time he found what he seemed to be looking for, he picked it up in the black end of his red beak, and carried it, waddling proudly on his wide, pink feet, into the kitchen, and into the icebox.

3. A   "I guess this is what you call the rookery," said Mr. Popper. "Only he couldn't find any stones to build his nest with."

4. B   Mr. Popper soon found that it was not so easy to take a penguin for a stroll. Captain Cook did not care at first for the idea of being put on a leash. However, Mr. Popper was firm. He tied one end of the clothesline to the penguin's fat throat and the other to his own wrist.

5. A   "*Gook!*" said Captain Cook, and raising his flippers, he leaned forward bravely

and tobogganed down the steps on his stomach.

6. C   "Yes," said Mr. Popper, realizing that his picture was about to be taken for the newspaper. The two young men had, as a matter of fact, heard about the strange bird from the policeman, and had been on their way to the Popper house, to get an interview, when they saw Captain Cook.

7. B   Still curious, Captain Cook started walking round and round the tripod, till the clothesline, the penguin, Mr. Popper and the tripod were all tangled up. At the advice of one of the bystanders, the tangle was finally straightened out by Mr. Popper's walking around the tripod three times in the opposite direction. At last, Captain Cook, standing still beside Mr. Popper, consented to pose.

Chapters 9 & 10

1. B   "Hey," said the barber to Mr. Popper. "Take that thing out of my shop. This is no zoo. What's the idea?"

2. A   "All right," said Mr. Popper, panting up the steps behind Captain Cook. "I suppose, being a bird, and one that can't fly, you have to go up in the air somehow, so you like to climb stairs. Well, it's a good thing this building has only three stories. Come on. Let's see what you can do."

3. D   When they reached the bottom, Captain Cook was so eager to go up again that Mr. Popper had to call a taxi, to distract him.

4. A   Next day the picture of Mr. Popper and Captain Cook appeared in the Stillwater *Morning Chronicle*, with a paragraph about the house painter who had received a penguin by air express from Admiral Drake in the faraway Antarctic. Then the Associated Press picked up the story, and a week later the photograph, in rotogravure, could be seen in the Sunday edition of the most important newspapers in all the large cities in the country.

5. D   "I will leave you some pills. Give him one every hour. Then you can try feeding him on sherbet and wrapping him in ice packs. But I cannot give you any encouragement because I am afraid it is a hopeless case. This kind of bird was never made for this climate, you know. I can see that you have taken good care of him, but an Antarctic penguin can't thrive in Stillwater."

6. C   It was addressed to Dr. Smith, the Curator of the great Aquarium in Mammoth City, the largest in the world. Surely if anyone anywhere had any idea what could cure a dying penguin, this man would.

7. D   "Unfortunately," he wrote, "it is not easy to cure a sick penguin. Perhaps you

do not know that we too have, in our aquarium at Mammoth City, a penguin from the Antarctic. It is failing rapidly, in spite of everything we have done for it. I have wondered lately whether it is not suffering from loneliness. Perhaps that is what ails your Captain Cook. I am, therefore, shipping you, under separate cover, our penguin. You may keep her. There is just a chance that the birds may get on better together."

Chapters 11 & 12

1. D   "I will go down in the cellar and get some white paint and paint their names on their black backs."

2. B   "Mamma," said Mr. Popper, "you put your food back in the icebox tonight, and we will just keep Greta and Captain Cook in the house. Captain Cook can help me move the nest into the other room. Then I will open all the windows and leave them open, and the penguins will be comfortable."

3. D   Mrs. Popper wanted to get her broom and have Mr. Popper bring his snow shovel to clear away the drifts, but the penguins were having so much fun in the snow that Mr. Popper insisted it should be left where it was.

4. C   So the next day Mr. Popper called an engineer and had a large freezing plant installed in the cellar, and took Captain Cook and Greta down there to live. Then he had the furnace taken out and moved upstairs into the living room.

5. B   Since Mr. Popper knew that penguins lay only two eggs a season, he was astonished when, a little later, the third egg was found under Greta. Whether the change in climate had changed the penguins' breeding habits, Mr. Popper never knew, but every third day a new one would appear until there were ten in all.

6. B   Mr. Popper also dug a large hole in the cellar floor and made a swimming and diving pool for the birds. From time to time he would throw live fish into the pool for the penguins to dive for.

7. A   Often, too, he thought how different his life had been before the penguins had come to keep him occupied. It was January now, and already he dreaded to think of the time when spring would come, and he would have to leave them all day and go back to painting houses.

Chapters 13 & 14

1. B   "Papa," said Mrs. Popper, "I'm glad to see you having such a nice vacation. And I must say that it's been easier than usual to keep the place tidy, with you down in the basement all the time. But, Papa, what are we to do for money?"

2. D   "Very well then," said Mr. Popper, "if there can be trained dogs and trained seals, why can't there be trained penguins?"

3. A   "What these penguins like to do most," said Mr. Popper, "is to drill like an army, to watch Nelson and Columbus get in a fight with each other, and to climb up steps and toboggan down. And so we will build our act around those tricks."

4. B   It was cold in the cellar, of course, so that Mrs. Popper had to learn to play the piano with her gloves on.

5. C   "Look here" said Mr. Popper at breakfast one morning. "It says here in the *Morning Chronicle* that Mr. Greenbaum, the owner of the Palace Theater, is in town. He's got a string of theaters all over the country; so I guess we had better go down and see him."

6. B   "Sorry," said Mr. Popper, addressing everyone in the bus, "but I'll have to open all the windows. These are Antarctic penguins and they're used to having it a lot colder than this." It took Mr. Popper quite a while to open the windows, which were stuck fast. When he had succeeded, there were plenty of remarks from the other passengers.

7. D   "Couldn't we call them Popper's Pink-toed Penguins?" asked Mr. Greenbaum. Mr. Popper thought for a moment. "No," he said, "I'm afraid we couldn't. That sounds too much like chorus girls or ballet dancers, and these birds are pretty serious. I don't think they'd like it."

Chapters 15 & 16

1. C   "The Marvelous Marcos, who close the program, haven't turned up, and the audience are demanding their money back."

2. B   "That's part of the act," explained Janie. "The other penguins all like Columbus to win, and so they all say '*Gook!*' at the end. That always makes Nelson look away, so Columbus can sock him good."

3. D   "You'll have to get those ladders off the stage, or I'll never get these birds under control," said Mr. Popper. "The curtain is supposed to fall at this point."

4. D   "And thanks again," said the manager. "Would you mind putting on your gloves again for just a minute, Mrs. Popper? I'd like you to start playing that 'Military March' again and let the penguins parade for a minute. I want to get my ushers in here to look at those birds. It would be a lesson to them."

5. A   Each of the taxi-drivers was eager to be the first to get to the station and surprise the people there by opening the door of his cab and letting out six penguins. So they raced each other all the way, and in the last block they tried to pass each other, and

one of the fenders got torn off.

6. A   The porters' ladders offered too much temptation to the penguins. There were a dozen happy *Orks* from a dozen ecstatic beaks. Popper's Performing Penguins, completely forgetting their discipline, fought to climb the ladders and get into the upper berths.

7. B   And whenever they appeared, the more they interfered with the other acts on the program the better the audiences liked them.

Chapters 17 & 18

1. A   The other actors on the program were not always so pleased, however. Once, in Minneapolis, a celebrated lady opera singer got very much annoyed when she heard that the Popper Penguins were to appear on the same program. In fact, she refused to go on the stage unless the penguins were put away.

2. B   The musicians kept on playing, and the lady on the stage, when she saw the penguins, sang all the louder to show how angry she was. The audience was laughing so hard that nobody could hear the words of her song.

3. D   This statement, with a picture of the twelve penguins, was printed in all the leading magazines, and the Owens Oceanic Shrimp Company gave Mr. Popper an order that was good for free cans of shrimps at any grocery store anywhere in the country.

4. B   Mr. Popper took them up to the roof garden to catch whatever cool breeze might be blowing.

5. B   In the wings stood a large, burly, red-faced man. "So these are the Popper Performing Penguins, huh?" he said. "Well, I want to tell you, Mr. Popper, that I'm Swen Swenson, and those are my seals in there on the stage now, and if your birds try any funny business, it'll be too bad for them. My seals are tough, see? They'd think nothing of eating two or three penguins apiece."

6. A   The penguins under their firemen's helmets were parading in front of the policemen, while the seals, in their policemen's caps, were barking at the firemen, when Mr. Popper and Mr. Swenson finally opened the door.

7. C   "You've broken into my theater and thrown the place into a panic, that's what you've done. You're a disturber of the peace." ... "Mr. Greenbaum's theater is the Royal, not the Regal. You've come to the wrong theater. Anyway, out you go, you and your Performing Penguins. The patrol is waiting outside."

1. A   "That theater manager is pretty mad at the way you busted into his theater, so I'm holding you. I'm going to give you all a nice quiet cell — unless you furnish bail. I'm putting the bail at five hundred dollars for you and one hundred dollars for each of the birds."

2. A   It was not Mr. Greenbaum who stood there. It was a great, bearded man in a splendid uniform. Smiling, he held out his hand to Mr. Popper. "Mr. Popper," he said, "I am Admiral Drake." "Admiral Drake!" gasped Mr. Popper. "Not back from the South Pole!"

3. D   "But if there were penguins up there, mightn't the polar bears eat them?" "Oh, ordinary penguins, yes," said the Admiral judiciously; "but not such highly-trained birds as yours, Mr. Popper. They could outwit any polar bear, I guess."

4. C   "Mr. Klein," he said, "I want you to know how much I appreciate your offer of putting my birds in the movies. But I am afraid I have to refuse. I do not believe the life in Hollywood would be good for the penguins."

5. D   Then he turned to Admiral Drake. "Admiral Drake, I am going to give you the birds. In doing this, I am considering the birds first of all. I know that they have been comfortable and happy with me. Lately, though, with the excitement and the warm weather, I've been worried about them. The birds have done so much for me that I have to do what is best for them. After all, they belong in a cold climate. And then I can't help being sorry for those men up at the North Pole, without any penguins to help them pass the time."

6. B   "But how could I go with you? I'm not an explorer or a scientist. I'm only a house painter." "You're the keeper of the penguins, aren't you?" roared the Admiral. "Man alive, aren't those penguins the reason for this whole Expedition? And who's going to see that they're well and happy if you're not along? Go put on one of those fur suits, like the rest of us. We're pulling anchor in a minute."

7. A   "Oh, as to that," said Mrs. Popper, "I'll miss you very much, my dear. But we have money to live on for a few years. And in winter it will be much easier to keep the house tidy without a man sitting around all day. I'll be getting back to Stillwater. Tomorrow is the day for the meeting of the Ladies' Aid and Missionary Society, and I'll be just in time. So good-by, my love, and good luck."

1장 스틸워터

9월 말의 어느 오후였습니다. 스틸워터 (Stillwater)라는 아름답고 작은 도시에서, 주택 도장공인 파퍼 씨가 일을 마치고 집으로 가고 있었습니다.

그는 자신의 양동이, 사다리, 그리고 자신의 판자들을 들고 있었기 때문에 움직이는 데 꽤 힘들어하고 있었습니다. 페인트와 백색 도료가 그의 몸 여기저기에 튀겨져 있었고 그의 머리카락과 구레나룻에는 벽지 조각들이 달라붙어 있었는데, 이는 그가 약간 깔끔하지 못한 남자이기 때문이었습니다.

그가 지나가자 아이들은 놀다가 고개를 들어 그에게 미소를 지어 보였고, 주부들은 그를 보고서는 말했습니다. "오 이런, 저기 파퍼 씨가 가네. 나는 봄에 집을 새로 페인트칠해 달라고 존 (John)에게 부탁하는 것을 꼭 기억해야겠어."

아무도 파퍼 씨가 머릿속으로 무슨 생각을 하고 있는지 알지 못했고, 어느 누구도 그가 어느 날 스틸워터에서 가장 유명한 사람이 될 것이라고 생각조차 하지 못했습니다.

그는 몽상가였습니다. 심지어 그가 벽지에 풀을 펴 바르거나, 혹은 다른 사람들의 집 외관을 칠하느라 가장 바쁠 때에도, 그는 자신이 무엇을 하고 있는

지 잊어버렸습니다. 한번은 그가 한 부엌의 세 면은 초록색으로, 나머지 한 면은 노란색으로 칠했던 적이 있었습니다. 그 집의 주부는, 화를 내고 그에게 일을 다시 하라고 시키는 대신에, 그것을 몹시 마음에 들어 해서 그에게 부엌을 그 상태로 두게 했습니다. 그리고 모든 다른 주부들도, 그들이 그것을 보았을 때, 역시 그것을 좋아해서, 곧 스틸워터의 모든 사람이 두 가지 색을 칠한 부엌을 가지게 되었습니다.

파퍼 씨가 그토록 멍한 이유는 그가 항상 멀리 떨어진 나라들에 대해 몽상하고 있기 때문이었습니다. 그는 스틸워터를 벗어난 적이 없었습니다. 그가 불행하다는 것이 아닙니다. 그에게는 자기 소유의 괜찮고 아담한 집, 그가 정말 사랑하는 아내, 그리고 제이니 (Janie)와 빌(Bill)이라고 불리는 두 아이들이 있었습니다. 하지만, 그랬다면 좋았을 거라고, 그는 종종 생각했습니다. 만약 그가 파퍼 부인을 만나 정착하기 전에 그가 세상의 무언가를 볼 수 있었더라면 하고 말이에요. 그는 인도 (India)에서 호랑이를 사냥하거나, 히말라야 산맥(Himalayas)의 정상을 오르거나, 혹은 남양(South Seas)에서 진주를 찾아 잠수를 한 적이 없었습니다. 무엇보다도, 그는 남극과 북극을 한 번도 본 적이 없었습니다.

그것이 바로 그가 그중에서 가장 후회하는 일이었습니다. 그는 얼음과 눈이 반짝거리며 하얗게 펼쳐진 그 엄청난 땅을 본 적이 없었습니다. 자신이 스틸워터의 주택 도장공이 아니라, 과학자여서 중요한 극지방 탐험 가운데 몇몇에 참여할 수 있었으면 좋겠다고 그가 얼마나 바랐는지 모릅니다. 그가 갈 수 없었기에, 그는 항상 그것들에 대해 생각하고 있었습니다.

극지방에 대한 영화가 마을에 개봉한다는 이야기를 들을 때마다, 그는 가장 먼저 매표소 앞에 있는 사람이었고, 종종 그는 연달아 세 편을 보기도 했습니다. 마을 도서관에 'Arctic' 또는 'Antarctic'—북극 또는 남극—에 대한 새로운 책이 들어올 때마다 파퍼 씨는 가장 먼저 그것을 빌렸습니다. 정말이지, 그는 극지방 탐험가들에 대해서 너무 많이 읽어서 그는 그들 모두의 이름을 말할 수 있었고 각자가 무슨 일을 했는지 말할 수 있었습니다. 그는 그 주제에 있어서 꽤 권위자였습니다.

그의 저녁은 하루 중 최고의 시간이었습니다. 그때는 그가 자신의 아담한 집 안에 앉아서 지구의 위와 아래에 있는 추운 지역에 대해 읽을 수 있었습니다. 그가 읽을 때 그는 제이니와 빌이 지난 크리스마스에 그에게 준 작은 지구본을 가져와서, 자신이 읽고 있는 정확한 장소를 찾아 볼 수 있었습니다.

그래서 지금, 그가 거리를 지나 나아가는 동안, 그는 하루가 끝나서, 그리고 9월의 마지막 날이어서 행복했습니다.

프라우드풋 에비뉴(Proudfoot Avenue) 432번지에 있는 깔끔하고 아담한 단층집(bungalow)의 문에 도착하자, 그는 안으로 들어섰습니다.

"후유, 여보." 그가 말하면서, 자신의 양동이와 사다리와 판자들을 내려놓았고, 파퍼 부인에게 키스했습니다. "실내 장식하는 기간이 끝났어요. 난 스틸워터에 있는 모든 부엌을 칠했어요; 나는 엘름 스트리트(Elm Street)에 있는 새 아파트 건물의 모든 방들을 도배했지요. 사람들이 자신들의 집을 페인트칠하기를 원하는 봄이 오기 전까지 더는 일이 없을 거예요."

파퍼 부인이 한숨을 쉬었습니다. "나는 가끔 당신이 봄부터 가을까지가 아니라, 일 년 내내 할 수 있는 종류의 직업을 가졌으면 해요." 그녀가 말했습니다. "물론, 휴가 기간 동안에 당신이 집에 있게 되는 것은 매우 좋을 거예요, 하지만 사람이 하루 종일 책을 보느라 앉아 있는 가운데 쓸고 청소하는 것은 힘들어요."

"난 당신을 위해서 집을 장식할 수도 있어요."

"안 돼요, 정말이에요." 파퍼 부인이 단호하게 말했습니다. "작년에 당신은 화장실을 네 번이나 칠했잖아요, 당신에게 다른 할 일이 아무것도 없다고 하면서요, 그리고 나는 그걸로 충분하다고 봐요. 하지만 나를 걱정하게 하는 것은 바로 돈이에요. 나는 약간 저축해 놓앉고, 나는 아마도 우리가 다른 겨울을 보내던 것처럼 지낼 수 있을 거라고 생각해요. 더 이상 로스트 비프(roast beef)요리도 없고, 아이스크림도 없지만요. 심지어 일요일에도요."

"우리 매일 콩을 먹게 되는 거예요?" 놀다가 돌아온 제이니와 빌이 물었습니다.

"유감스럽게도 그럴 것 같구나." 파퍼 부인이 말했습니다. "어쨌거나, 저녁을 먹어야 하니까, 가서 너희들 손을 씻으렴. 그리고 애들 아빠, 이 어질러져 있는 페인트 좀 치워 줘요. 왜냐하면 당신은 한동안 그것들이 필요하지 않을 테니까요."

2장 라디오에서 들려오는 목소리

그날 저녁, 파퍼 씨네 아이들이 잠자리에 들었을 때, 파퍼 씨와 파퍼 부인은 길고, 조용한 저녁을 보내려고 자리를 잡고 앉았습니다. 프라우드풋 에비뉴 432번지에 있는 깔끔한 거실은 벽에 내셔널 지오그래픽 잡지(*National Geographic Magazine*)에서 나온 사진들이 걸려 있다는 것을 제외한다면, 스틸워터의 모든 다른 거실과 비슷했습니다. 파퍼 부인이 수선할 것을 들어 올리는 동안, 파퍼 씨는 담배 파이프, 책, 그리고 그의 지구본을 챙겼습니다.

때때로 파퍼 부인은 작게 한숨 쉬면서 앞으로 올 긴 겨울에 대해 생각했습니다. 정말로 쓸 수 있을 만큼 충분한

양의 콩이 있는 걸까, 그녀는 궁금해했습니다.

하지만, 파퍼 씨는 걱정스럽지 않았습니다. 그가 자신의 안경을 꼈을 때, 그는 자신을 방해할 아무런 일도 없이, 겨울 내내 여행 책을 읽는다는 기대에 상당히 기뻤습니다. 그는 자신의 작은 지구본을 옆에 놓았고 읽기 시작했습니다.

"당신 무엇을 읽고 있어요?" 파퍼 부인이 물었습니다.

"난 *남극의 모험*(*Antarctic Adventures*)이라고 불리는 책을 읽고 있어요. 그건 정말 흥미로워요. 그 책은 남극에 갔었던 다양한 사람들과 그들이 그곳에서 무엇을 찾았는지에 대해서 모두 말해 주고 있어요."

"당신은 남극에 대해 읽는 게 지겹지도 않아요?"

"아니, 난 그렇지 않아요. 물론 난 그곳에 대해 읽는 것보다는 차라리 그곳에 가고 싶지만 말이에요. 하지만 읽는 것이 차선책이지요."

"내 생각에는 그곳은 분명히 매우 지겨울 거예요." 파퍼 부인이 말했습니다. "몹시 따분하고 춥게 들리는 걸요, 그 모든 얼음과 눈 때문에요."

"오, 아니에요." 파퍼 씨가 대답했습니다. "만약 당신이 나랑 같이 작년에 비쥬(Bijou) 극장에서 상영한 드레이크 탐험대(Drake Expedition)에 대한 영화를 보러 갔다면 당신은 따분하다고 생각하지 않았을 거예요."

"흠, 난 보러 가지 않았죠. 그리고 난 우리 가운데 어느 누구도 이제 영화를 볼 돈이 있을 것 같진 않네요." 파퍼 부인이 약간 날카롭게 대답했습니다. 그녀는 결코 무례한 여성이 아니었지만, 돈에 대해 걱정을 할 때면 그녀는 가끔 약간 짜증을 내고는 했습니다.

"당신이 갔었다면 말이에요, 여보." 파퍼 씨가 계속 말했습니다. "당신은 남극이 얼마나 아름다운지 봤을 거예요. 하지만 난 그중에서 가장 멋진 부분은 펭귄이라고 생각해요. 그 탐험대에 있던 모든 사람들이 그들과 노는 데 그렇게 즐거운 시간을 보낸 것도 당연해요. 그것들은 세상에서 가장 우스꽝스러운 새들이에요. 그것들은 다른 조류처럼 날지 못해요. 그것들은 작은 아이처럼 똑바로 서서 걸어 다니지요. 그것들이 걷는 것에 싫증이 나면 그것들은 그냥 자신들의 배로 엎드려서 미끄러져 버려요. 한 마리를 애완동물로 삼으면 정말 좋을 거예요."

"애완동물이라니요!" 파퍼 부인이 말했습니다. "처음에는 빌이 개를 원하더니 그다음에는 제이니가 새끼 고양이를 가지고 싶다고 조르고. 이제는 당신과 펭귄들까지! 하지만 나는 어떤 애완동물도 두지 않을 거예요. 그것들은 집 안에 너무 많은 먼지를 일으키고, 지금 이 집을 깔끔하게 유지하는 것만으로도 나는 할 일이 충분해요. 애완동물을 먹이느라 들어가는 비용은 말할 것도 없고요. 어쨌든, 우리는 어항에 사는 금붕어가 있잖아요."

"펭귄은 정말 똑똑해요." 파퍼 씨가 말을 이어나갔습니다. "이것 좀 들어 봐요, 애들 엄마. 여기에서 말하기를 그것들이 새우를 잡으려고 할 때, 그것들은 모두 얼음으로 된 둑의 가장자리로 우르르 몰려간대요. 다만 그것들은 그냥 뛰어들지는 않는데, 왜냐하면 얼룩무늬 물범(sea leopard)이 펭귄을 잡아먹으려고 기다리고 있을지도 모르기 때문이에요. 그래서 그것들은 펭귄 한 마리를 떨어지게 할 때까지 몰려들고 밀쳐요, 안전한지 확인하기 위해서 말이에요. 내 말은 만약 떨어진 펭귄이 잡아 먹히지 않는다면, 나머지 펭귄도 자신들이 모두 뛰어들어도 안전하다는 것을 알게 되는 거죠."

"세상에 맙소사!" 파퍼 부인이 충격받은 말투로 말했습니다. "그것들은 내게 마치 꽤 야만적인 새처럼 들리는 걸요."

"그것은 독특한 일이에요." 파퍼 씨가 말했습니다. "모든 북극곰들이 북극에 살고 모든 펭귄들은 남극에 산다는 것이요. 나는 펭귄들이 또한, 북극도 좋아할 것이라고 생각해요, 만약에 그것들이 그곳에 어떻게 가는지만 안다면 말이지요."

열 시에 파퍼 부인은 하품을 했고 그녀의 수선할 거리를 내려놓았습니다. "뭐, 당신은 계속 그 야만적인 새들에 대해 읽도록 해요, 하지만 나는 자러 가야겠어요. 내일은 9월 30일, 목요일이고, 나는 교회 여성 단체의 첫 모임에 나가야 해요."

"9월 30일이라고!" 파퍼 씨가 흥분한 어조로 말했습니다. "당신은 오늘 밤이 9월 29일 수요일이라고 말하는 게 아니겠지요?"

"어머, 네, 난 그렇게 말한 거예요. 그래서 뭐가 어쨌다는 거예요?"

파퍼 씨는 그의 책 남극의 모험을 내려놓았고 서둘러서 라디오로 다가갔습니다.

"그래서 뭐가 어쨌다니요!" 그가 반복해서 말하며, 스위치를 눌렀습니다. "아니, 오늘은 드레이크 남극 탐험대가 방송을 시작하는 밤이잖아요."

"그건 아무것도 아니에요." 파퍼 부인이 말했습니다. "그저 세계의 아래에 있는 많은 사람들이 '안녕하세요, 엄마. 안녕하세요, 아빠.'라고 말하는 것뿐이잖아요."

"쉿!" 파퍼 씨가 명령하며, 그의 귀를 라디오에 가까이 대었습니다.

지지직거리는 소리가 들리더니, 그러다 갑자기, 남극으로부터 희미한 목소리가 파퍼 씨네 거실로 흘러들어 왔습니다.

"전 드레이크 제독(Admiral Drake)입니다. 안녕하세요, 엄마. 안녕하세요, 아빠. 안녕하세요, 파퍼 씨."

"어머나 세상에." 파퍼 부인이 외쳤습니다. "그가 '아빠(Papa)'라고 말했어요, 아님 '파퍼(Popper)'라고 했어요?"

"안녕하세요, 저 위에 있는 스틸워터에 사는 파퍼 씨. 우리의 지난 탐험을 담은 사진에 대한 당신의 훌륭한 편지에 대해 감사합니다. 답장을 기다리세요. 하지만 편지 형식은 아닐 겁니다, 파퍼 씨. 깜짝 놀랄 만한 일을 기다리세요. 방송을 종료합니다. 방송을 종료합니다."

"당신이 드레이크 제독에게 편지를 썼어요?"

"네, 내가 그랬지요." 파퍼 씨가 인정했습니다. "내가 편지를 써서 그에게 내가 얼마나 펭귄이 우스꽝스럽다고 생각하는지 말했어요."

"오, 맙소사." 정말로 몹시 감명 받아서, 파퍼 부인이 말했습니다.

파퍼 씨는 그의 작은 지구본을 집었고 남극을 찾았습니다. "그리고 그가 저 멀리 떨어진 곳에서 나에게 말을 걸었다고 생각해 봐요. 그리고 그는 심지어 내 이름도 언급했어요. 애들 엄마, 당신은 그가 말하는 깜짝 놀랄 일이 무엇이라고 생각해요?"

"나는 전혀 모르겠어요." 파퍼 부인이 말했습니다. "하지만 난 자러 가야겠어요. 난 내일 있을 교회 여성 단체 모임에 늦고 싶지 않거든요."

3장 남극에서 보내온 물건

위대한 드레이크 제독이 라디오 너머로 그에게 말을 걸었다는 흥분과 그에게 올 제독의 메시지에 대한 호기심으로 인해, 파퍼 씨는 그날 밤 잠을 제대로 잘 수 없었습니다. 그는 제독의 말이 무엇을 의미하는지 알아내기 위해 도저히 기다릴 수 없을 것 같았습니다. 아침이 왔을 때, 그는 그에게 아무데도 갈 곳이 없고, 페인트칠할 집도 없고, 도배할 방도 없다는 것에 유감스러워질 정도였습니다. 그것은 시간을 때우는 데 도움이 되었을 것입니다.

"당신 거실을 새로 도배하면 어때요?" 그가 파퍼 부인에게 물었습니다. "나에게 벽지 넘버 88번이 꽤 많아요, 시장님의 집을 하고 남은 것이지요."

"하지 않았으면 좋겠어요." 파퍼 부인이 단호하게 말했습니다. "지금 있는 벽지도 충분히 꽤 괜찮아요. 나는 오늘 교회 여성 단체의 첫 모임에 갈 예정이고 난 내가 집에 왔을 때 치워야 할 어떤 엉망진창인 상황도 원하지 않는다고요."

"잘 알겠어요, 여보." 파퍼 씨가 온순하게 말했고 그는 자신의 담배 파이프, 지구본, 그리고 남극의 모험이라는 책을 갖고 자리를 잡았습니다. 하지만 어째서인지, 오늘 그가 읽는 동안, 그는 인쇄된 단어들에 그의 주의를 기울일 수가 없었습니다. 그의 생각은 자꾸 옆길로 새어 드레이크 제독에게로 흘러갔습니다. 그가 파퍼 씨를 위한 깜짝 놀랄 만한 일이라고 말한 것이 과연 무엇일까요?

그의 마음의 평화를 위해서는 다행스럽게도, 그는 그렇게 오랫동안 기다리지 않아도 되었습니다. 그날 오후, 파퍼 부인이 여전히 그녀의 모임에 나가 있었고, 제이니와 빌이 아직 학교에서 집으로 돌아오지 않은 동안에, 현관문에서 큰 초인종 소리가 났습니다.

"그건 그냥 우편배달부인 것 같군. 난 문을 열어주려고 신경 쓰지 않겠어." 그가 혼잣말했습니다.

초인종이 이번에는 조금 더 크게, 다시 울렸습니다. 혼자서 투덜거리면서, 파퍼 씨는 문으로 갔습니다.

그곳에 서 있는 사람은 우편배달부가 아니었습니다. 그건 파퍼 씨가 여태껏 본 가장 큰 상자를 가진 속달 택배 배달원이었습니다.

"파퍼라는 이름을 가진 사람이 여기에 사나요?"

"전데요."

"흠, 저 멀리 남극 대륙에서 항공 속달 우편으로 온 소포가 여기 있습니다. 엄청난 여정이지요, 그렇고말고요."

파퍼 씨는 영수증에 서명했고 상자를 살펴보았습니다. 그것은 표시들로 온통 덮여 있었습니다. "한 번에 개봉." 하나는 그렇게 쓰여 있었습니다. "냉장 보관." 다른 것은 그렇게 말했습니다. 그는 상자 여기저기에 공기구멍이 뚫어져 있다는 것을 알아차렸습니다.

여러분은 일단 그가 상자를 집 안으로 들이자, 파퍼 씨가 스크루 드라이버를 가져오는 데 시간을 지체하지 않았다는 것을 짐작할 수 있겠죠. 이때쯤에는, 물론, 그가 그것이 드레이크 제독에게서 온 깜짝 놀랄 만한 것을 추측해 냈기 때문입니다.

그는 외부 판자들과 한 층의 드라이 아이스로 된 포장재의 일부를 떼어내는 데 성공해냈을 때, 포장 상자의 안쪽에서 그는 갑자기 희미한 "오크"라는 소리를 들었습니다. 그의 심장이 우뚝 멈췄습니다. 분명하게 그는 전에 드레이크 탐험대 영화에서 그 소리를 들었습니다. 그의 손이 떨려 그는 간신히 남은 포장재들을 들어 올릴 수 있었습니다.

그것에 대해서는 일말의 의혹도 없었습니다. 그것은 펭귄이었습니다.

파퍼 씨는 기뻐서 말을 잃었습니다.

하지만 펭귄은 말을 잃지 않았습니다. "오크." 그것이 다시 말했고, 이번에는 그것은 자신의 날개를 내밀면서 포장물의 잔재를 뛰어 넘었습니다.

그것은 대략 2.5피트 정도의 키를 가진 통통하고 작은 녀석이었습니다. 비록 그것은 작은 아이의 체구와 비슷했지만, 그것은 앞쪽에 있는 그것의 매끄럽고 하얀 조끼와 뒤에서 살짝 끌리고 있는 길고 검은색의 연미복 때문에 작은 신사에 더 가까워 보였습니다. 그것의 눈들은 그것의 검은 머리에 두 하얀 원으로 박혀 있었습니다. 그것은 자신의 머리를 이쪽저쪽으로 기울이며, 처음에는 한쪽 눈으로 그다음에는 반대쪽 눈으로, 파퍼 씨를 살펴보았습니다.

파퍼 씨는 펭귄이 굉장히 호기심이 많다는 것을 읽은 적이 있었고, 그는 곧 이것이 사실이라는 것을 알게 되었습니다. 앞으로 나오면서, 그 손님이 집

을 관찰하기 시작했기 때문이었습니다. 복도를 따라서 그것이 자신의 이상하고, 거만하고 작은 뽐내는 듯한 걸음걸이로 나아갔고 침실들로 들어갔습니다. 그것이, 또는 그가 —파퍼 씨는 이미 그것을 수컷이라고 생각하기 시작했습니다 —화장실에 다다랐을 때, 그것은 자신의 얼굴에 흡족한 표정을 지은 채 주위를 둘러 보았습니다.

"아마도." 파퍼 씨가 생각했습니다. "저 모든 하얀 타일들이 깔린 것이 그에게 남극에 있는 얼음과 눈을 떠올리게 하는지도 몰라. 가여운 것, 아마도 그는 목이 마를 거야."

조심스럽게 파퍼 씨는 욕조에 차가운 물을 채우기 시작했습니다. 이 일은 약간 어려웠습니다. 왜냐하면 궁금한 것이 많은 새가 계속 몸을 뻗어 자신의 날카로운 붉은 부리로 수도꼭지를 물으려고 했기 때문입니다. 하지만, 마침내, 그는 욕조를 모두 채우는 데 성공했습니다. 펭귄이 계속 들여다보았기 때문에, 파퍼 씨는 그것을 들어 올렸고 안에 내려놓았습니다. 펭귄은 신경 쓰는 것 같지 않았습니다.

"어쨌거나, 너는 부끄러움이 없구나." 파퍼 씨가 말했습니다. "너는 남극에서 그 탐험가들과 노는 것에 익숙해진 것 같네."

그가 펭귄이 충분히 목욕을 했다고 생각했을 때, 그는 마개를 뽑았습니다. 그가 막 다음에 무엇을 할지 생각하고 있을 때 제이니와 빌이 학교에서 돌아

와 불쑥 들어왔습니다.

"아빠." 그들이 화장실 문 앞에서 함께 외쳤습니다. "그게 뭐예요?"

"그것은 드레이크 제독이 나에게 보내준 남극 펭귄이란다."

"보세요!" 빌이 말했습니다. "그것이 행진하고 있어요."

아주 즐거워하는 펭귄은 정말로 행진하고 있었습니다. 그의 잘생긴 검은 머리로 작게 만족해하는 고갯짓을 하면서 그는 욕조 안에서 왔다 갔다 행진하고 있었습니다. 때때로 그는 몇 걸음이 걸리는지 세고 있는 것 같았습니다—길이로는 여섯 걸음, 너비로는 두 걸음, 다시 길이로는 여섯 걸음, 그리고 너비로는 두 걸음이 걸렸습니다.

"저렇게 커다란 새 치고는 그는 몹시 작은 보폭을 지녔어." 빌이 말했습니다.

"그리고 그의 작고 검은 코트가 뒤로 끌리는 것 좀 봐. 거의 마치 그것이 그에게 너무 큰 것처럼 보여." 제이니가 말했습니다.

하지만 펭귄은 행진하는 것에 싫증이 났습니다. 이번에, 그것이 욕조의 끝에 다다르자, 그것은 미끄럽고 굴곡진 곳을 뛰어 넘기로 했습니다. 그다음에 그것은 돌아섰고, 날개를 쭉 뻗고서, 자신의 하얀 배로 엎드려 터보건 썰매를 타듯 미끄러져 갔습니다. 그들은 그 날개들을 볼 수 있었는데, 마치 연미복의 소매처럼, 바깥쪽은 검은색이었고, 그 안쪽은 흰색이었습니다.

"꽥! 꽥!" 펭귄이 말하면서, 자신의 새로운 게임을 몇 번이고 계속했습니다.

"그의 이름은 뭐예요, 아빠?" 제이니가 물었습니다.

"꽥! 꽥!" 펭귄이 말하면서, 다시 한번 그의 윤기 나는 하얀 배로 엎드려 미끄러져 갔습니다.

"그것은 마치 'Cook'이라는 소리처럼 들리는 구나." 파퍼 씨가 말했습니다. "이런, 물론, 바로 그거야. 우리는 그를 쿡(Cook)이라고 부를 거란다—캡틴 쿡(Captain Cook)이라고 말이야."

4장 캡틴 쿡

"누구를 캡틴 쿡이라고 부른다고요?" 파퍼 부인이 물었는데, 그녀는 너무나 조용히 들어와서 그들 가운데 어느 누구도 그녀가 들어오는 소리를 듣지 못했습니다.

"아니, 펭귄을 말이에요." 파퍼 씨가 말했습니다. "나는 그냥 말하는 거예요." 그가 계속 말하는 동안, 파퍼 부인은 자신의 당혹감에서 회복하기 위해 갑자기 바닥에 주저앉았습니다. "우리가 그를 캡틴 쿡에게서 이름을 따서 지을 수도 있다고 말이지요. 그는 미국 독립 혁명 시절에 살았던 유명한 영국의 탐험가예요. 그는 아무도 이전에는 가본 적이 없었던 모든 곳을 항해했지요. 물론, 그는 사실 남극에는 가지 않았지만, 그는 남극 지역에 대한 중요한 과학적인 발견들을 했어요. 그는 용감한 사람이자 친절한 지도자였지요. 그래서 나는 캡틴 쿡이 여기 우리의 펭귄에게 매우 잘 어울리는 이름이라고 생각했어요."

"세상에 맙소사!" 파퍼 부인이 말했습니다.

"꽥!" 갑자기 다시 활발해지며, 캡틴 쿡이 말했습니다. 그의 날개들을 펄럭거리면서 그는 욕조에서 세면대로 뛰어갔고, 그곳에 잠시 서서 바닥을 살펴보았습니다. 그러더니 그는 뛰어내렸고, 파퍼 부인에게로 걸어가서, 그녀의 발목을 조기 시작했습니다.

"그를 말려요, 애들 아빠!" 파퍼 부인이 비명을 지르며, 복도로 도망치자 캡틴 쿡이 그녀를 쫓아갔고, 파퍼 씨와 아이들이 따라갔습니다. 거실에서 그녀는 잠시 멈췄습니다. 캡틴 쿡도 역시 멈췄는데, 왜냐하면 그는 그 방에 몹시 흡족했기 때문입니다.

이제 펭귄이 거실에 있는 것이 아마 아주 이상하게 보일 테지만, 거실은 펭귄에게 아주 이상하게 보일 것입니다. 캡틴 쿡이 자신의 흥분한 둥근 두 눈에 호기심 어린 기색을 담고서, 그의 검은 연미복이 거만하게 그의 작은 분홍빛 발의 뒤로 끌리면서, 천을 씌운 의자에서 다른 의자로 뽐내듯 걸으며, 그것이 무엇으로 만들어졌는지 확인하려고 각각을 쪼아 보는 것을 보게 되자, 심지어 파퍼 부인조차도 미소 지을 수밖에 없었습니다. 그러더니 그는 갑자기 돌아섰고 부엌으로 급히 걸어갔습니다.

"어쩌면 그는 배고픈가 봐요." 제이니

가 말했습니다.

캡틴 쿡은 곧장 냉장고로 급히 걸어갔습니다.

"꽥?" 그가 물으면서, 자신의 고개를 현명하게 파퍼 부인을 향해 기울였고, 그의 오른쪽 눈으로 애원하듯이 그녀를 쳐다보았습니다.

"그는 확실히 귀엽네요." 그녀가 말했습니다. "그가 내 발목을 문 것을 난 용서해 줘야만 할 것 같네요. 그는 아마도 호기심에 그런 행동을 했을 거예요. 어쨌든, 그는 착하고 깨끗해 보이는 새이네요."

"오크?" 펭귄이 반복해서 말하며, 냉장고 문에 달린 금속 손잡이를 그의 위로 뻗친 부리로 조금씩 깨물었습니다.

파퍼 씨가 그를 위해 문을 열어 주었고, 캡틴 쿡은 아주 꼿꼿이 서서 그의 윤이 나는 검은색 머리를 뒤로 젖혀 자신이 안을 볼 수 있게 했습니다. 파퍼 씨의 일이 겨울에는 없기 때문에, 냉장고는 평소처럼 꽉 차 있지는 않았지만, 펭귄은 그 사실을 몰랐습니다.

"당신은 그가 무엇을 먹기를 좋아한다고 생각해요?" 파퍼 부인이 물었습니다.

"어디 보자." 파퍼 씨가 말하면서, 그는 모든 음식물을 꺼냈고 그것을 부엌 탁자 위에 두었습니다. "그럼 이제, 캡틴 쿡, 한 번 봐봐."

펭귄은 의자 위로 뛰어올랐고 거기에서 다시 탁자의 가장자리 위로 뛰어오르면서, 자기 몸의 균형을 되찾으려고 그의 날개들을 다시 퍼덕거렸습니다. 그다음에 그는 진지하게 탁자 주변, 그리고 음식이 담긴 접시들 사이를 걸어 다니면서, 비록 그가 아무것도 건드리지 않았지만, 모든 것을 큰 흥미를 가지고 살펴보았습니다. 마침내 그는 우뚝, 굉장히 꼿꼿하게 서서, 그의 부리를 천장을 가리키도록 들어 올렸고, 크고, 마치 기분 좋게 그르렁거리는 듯한 소리를 내었습니다. "오-오-오-오-오-오, 오-오-오-오-오." 그가 지저귀었습니다.

"저건 그것이 얼마나 기쁜지에 대해서 말하는 펭귄의 방식이에요." 그의 남극에 관한 책에서 그것에 대해 읽었던, 파퍼 씨가 말했습니다.

하지만, 보아하니, 캡틴 쿡이 보여주고자 했던 것은 그가 그들의 음식에 대해서라기보다는, 그들의 친절함에 대해 만족스럽다는 것이었습니다. 이제는, 그들에게는 놀랍게도, 그가 뛰어내렸고 식당으로 걸어갔습니다.

"알겠어요." 파퍼 씨가 말했습니다. "우리는 그를 위해 새우 통조림이나 뭐 그런 것과 같은, 약간의 해산물을 마련해야겠어요. 또는 아마도 그는 아직 배고프지 않을지도 몰라요. 나는 펭귄들이 음식을 먹지 않고도 한 달을 버틸 수 있다는 것을 읽은 적이 있어요."

"엄마! 아빠!" 빌이 불렀습니다. "와서 캡틴 쿡이 무슨 짓을 했는지 보세요."

캡틴 쿡은 제대로 일을 저질렀습니다. 그는 식당의 창틀 위에 있는 어항에 담긴 금붕어를 발견했습니다. 파퍼 부인이 그를 들어 올려서 떼어 놓으려고 손을 뻗었을 때쯤에는, 그는 이미 금붕어의 남은 몸을 삼켰습니다.

"못된, 못된 펭귄!" 파퍼 부인이 꾸짖으며, 캡틴 쿡을 노려보았습니다.

캡틴 쿡은 카펫 위에서 죄책감을 느끼는 듯이 쪼그리고 앉았고 자신의 몸을 작아 보이게 하려고 했습니다.

"그는 자기가 잘못했다는 것을 알아요." 파퍼 씨가 말했습니다. "그가 똑똑하지 않아요?"

"어쩌면 우리는 그를 훈련시킬 수 있을 거예요." 파퍼 부인이 말했습니다. "못된, 버릇없는 캡틴." 그녀는 펭귄에게 큰 목소리로 말했습니다. "금붕어를 먹다니, 참 못됐구나." 그리고 그녀는 그의 둥글고 검은 머리를 찰싹 때렸습니다.

그녀가 다시 그러기 전에, 캡틴 쿡은 서둘러서 부엌으로 뒤뚱뒤뚱 걸어갔습니다.

그곳에서 파퍼 가족은 여전히 열려 있는 냉장고 속에 숨으려고 하는 그를 발견했습니다. 그는 얼음칸 코일 아래 쪼그리고 있었는데, 그 아래 공간에 그는 겨우 비집고 들어가서 앉아 있었습니다. 그의 둥글고, 하얀−원형의 두 눈이 냉장고 안의 어둑함 속에서 그들을 신비롭게 바라보았습니다.

"내 생각에는 저게 그에게 적절한 온도인 것 같아요, 게다가." 파퍼 씨가 말했습니다. "우리는 그를 저기에서 자게 할 수 있어요, 밤에요."

"하지만 난 어디에 음식을 보관하라

고요?" 파퍼 부인이 물었습니다.

"오, 난 우리가 음식을 넣을 다른 냉장고를 살 수 있을 것 같아요." 파퍼 씨가 말했습니다.

"보세요." 제이니가 말했습니다. "그가 잠들었어요."

파퍼 씨는 냉방 조절 스위치를 최대로 돌려서 캡틴 쿡이 더 편안하게 잘 수 있게 했습니다. 그리고는 그는 문을 살짝 열어 놔서 펭귄이 숨을 쉴 수 있는 신선한 공기가 충분히 있을 수 있게 했습니다.

"그가 숨을 쉴 수 있게, 내일 내가 냉장고 서비스 부서에서 사람을 보내게 해서 문에 구멍 몇 개를 뚫게 할게요." 그가 말했습니다. "그러고 나서 그가 문의 안쪽에 손잡이를 달 수 있다면 캡틴 쿡은 자기가 원하는 대로 그의 냉장고를 들락날락거릴 수 있을 거예요."

"이런, 맙소사, 난 우리가 펭귄을 애완동물로 기르게 될 거라고는 생각해보지도 않았어요." 파퍼 부인이 말했습니다. "그래도, 전반적으로, 그는 꽤 얌전하게 행동하네요, 그리고 그는 정말 멋있고 깨끗해서 어쩌면 그는 당신과 아이들에게 좋은 모범이 될지도 모르죠. 그리고 이제, 내가 분명히 말하건대, 우리는 서둘러야만 해요. 우리는 저 새를 보는 것 외에 아무것도 하지 않았잖아요. 애들 아빠, 당신은 내가 식탁에 콩을 차리는 것을 도와주겠어요?"

"잠깐만요." 파퍼 씨가 대답했습니다. "나는 막 캡틴 쿡이 냉장고의 바닥 위에 있는 것이 불편할 거라는 생각이 들었어요. 펭귄은 조약돌과 돌멩이로 그들의 둥지를 만들거든요. 그래서 난 얼음 조각을 틀에서 꺼내서 그것들을 그의 밑에 둘 거예요. 그러면 그도 더 편안해질 거예요."

5장 펭귄이 일으킨 문제들

다음 날에 프라우드풋 에비뉴 432번지는 꽤 다사다난했습니다. 처음에는 서비스 기사가 그다음에는 경찰이 그다음에는 면허와 관련된 문제가 있었습니다.

캡틴 쿡은 아이들의 방에서, 제이니와 빌이 바닥에서 직소 퍼즐을 맞추는 것을 보고 있었습니다. 조각 하나를 먹어서 빌이 벌로 그를 때린 이후에 그는 조각들을 건드리지 않는 일을 매우 잘 해내고 있었습니다. 그는 냉장고 서비스 기사가 뒷문으로 오는 것을 듣지 못했습니다.

파퍼 부인이 펭귄을 위해 새우 통조림을 사러 시장에 나갔기에, 파퍼 씨는 혼자서 부엌에서 서비스 기사에게 그가 냉장고에 무엇을 하기를 원하는지 설명했습니다.

서비스 기사는 그의 도구 가방을 부엌 바닥에 내려놓고, 냉장고를 보더니, 솔직히 말하자면, 아직 면도도 하지 않았고 그다지 단정하지도 않은 파퍼 씨를 보았습니다.

"선생님." 그가 말했습니다. "선생님

144

은 저 문에 환기 구멍이 필요하지 않을 겁니다."

"그건 내 냉장고이고, 난 문에 몇 개의 구멍이 나기를 원해요." 파퍼 씨가 말했습니다.

그들은 그것에 대해 꽤 오랫동안 말다툼을 했습니다. 파퍼 씨는 자신이 원하는 일을 서비스 기사가 하게 하려면, 그가 살아 있는 펭귄을 냉장고에 두려고 하고, 비록 문이 밤중에 내내 닫혀 있더라도, 그는 자신의 애완동물이 신선한 공기를 충분히 마시기를 원한다는 것을 설명하기만 하면 된다는 것을 알았습니다. 하지만, 그는 설명하는 것에 약간 고집을 부리고 싶었습니다. 그는 벌써 파퍼 씨가 약간 제정신이 아닌 것 같다고 생각하는 것처럼 자신을 바라보고 있는, 이 인정 없는 서비스 기사와 캡틴 쿡에 대해 이야기하고 싶지 않았습니다.

"어서요, 내가 말하는 대로 해요." 파퍼 씨가 말했습니다. "내가 그 일에 대해 당신에게 돈을 줄 거예요."

"무슨 돈으로요?" 서비스 기사가 물었습니다.

파퍼 씨는 그에게 5달러 지폐를 건넸습니다. 그 돈이면 파퍼 부인과 아이들을 위해 얼마나 많은 콩을 살 수 있는지 생각하는 것은 그를 약간 슬프게 했습니다.

서비스 기사는 마치 그가 파퍼 씨를 하나도 신뢰할 수 없다는 듯이 그 지폐를 신중하게 살펴보았습니다. 하지만

결국에 그는 그것을 자신의 주머니 속에 넣었고, 그의 도구 가방에서 드릴을 꺼냈고, 냉장고 문에 깔끔한 형태로 다섯 개의 작은 구멍을 냈습니다.

"이제." 파퍼 씨가 말했습니다. "일어나지 말아요. 잠시만 기다려요. 한 가지 일이 더 있어요."

"이번에는 또 뭐예요?" 서비스 기사가 말했습니다. "제 생각엔 이제 선생님은 제가 그 경첩에서 문을 떼어내서 약간 더 많은 공기가 들어가게 하길 원하는 것 같은데요. 아니면 선생님은 제가 선생님의 냉장고를 가지고 라디오 세트를 만들기를 바라요?"

"장난치지 마세요." 파퍼 씨가 분을 내며 말했습니다. "그런 말 하는 게 아닙니다. 믿거나 말거나, 나는 내가 무슨 일을 하고 있는지 알아요. 내 말은, 당신에게 무엇을 하라고 시키는지 말이에요. 나는 당신이 냉장고 안쪽에 추가로 손잡이를 달아서 문이 냉장고 안에서도 열릴 수 있게 했으면 좋겠군요."

"그건." 서비스 기사가 말했습니다. "좋은 생각이에요. 선생님은 안쪽에 추가 손잡이를 원하는 군요. 알았어요, 알았어." 그가 자신의 도구 가방을 들었습니다.

"당신은 나를 위해 그 일을 하지 않을 건가요?" 파퍼 씨가 물었습니다.

"오, 물론이죠, 물론이에요." 서비스 기사가 말하면서, 뒷문을 향해 조금씩 나아갔습니다.

파퍼 씨는 그가 하는 모든 동의의 말

에도 불구하고, 서비스 기사가 안쪽 손잡이를 달아줄 어떤 의사도 없다는 것을 알았습니다.

"난 당신이 서비스 기사인줄 알았는데요." 그가 말했습니다.

"서비스 기사 맞아요. 그건 선생님이 이제까지 말한 것 가운데 처음으로 상식적인 말이네요."

"당신이 심지어 냉장고 문의 안쪽에 추가 손잡이를 다는 방법도 모른다면 당신은 참 훌륭한 서비스 기사이겠군요."

"오, 제가 모른다고요, 그런가요? 제가 할 줄 모른다고 생각하지 마세요. 그것에 대해 말하자면, 저는 심지어 제 도구 가방에 여분의 손잡이도 있고, 나사도 충분히 있어요. 선생님은 제가 그 일을 할 줄 모른다고 생각할 필요가 없어요, 만약에 제가 하기를 원한다면 말이에요."

파퍼 씨는 말없이 그의 주머니로 손을 뻗었고 자신의 마지막 남은 5달러 지폐를 서비스 기사에게 주었습니다. 그는 파퍼 부인이 그 돈을 다 써버린 것에 대해 그에게 짜증을 내리란 것을 꽤 확신했지만, 어쩔 도리가 없었습니다.

"선생님." 서비스 기사가 말했습니다. "선생님이 이겼네요. 제가 당신을 위한 추가 손잡이를 달아드리지요. 그리고 제가 그 일을 하는 동안에, 선생님은 제가 선생님을 지켜볼 수 있는 곳에, 저기에 제 방향에 놓인 저 의자에 앉아 있으세요."

"좋아요." 파퍼 씨가 말하면서, 앉았습니다.

서비스 기사가 여전히 바닥에서, 새 손잡이를 고정할 마지막 나사를 끼우고 있었을 때, 펭귄이 자신의 분홍색 발로 조용히 걸어서 부엌으로 들어섰습니다.

낯선 남자가 바닥 위에 앉아 있는 것을 보고 놀라서, 캡틴 쿡은 조용히 걸어갔고 신기한 듯이 그를 쪼기 시작했습니다. 하지만 서비스 기사는 캡틴 쿡보다 훨씬 더 놀랐습니다.

"오크." 펭귄이 말했습니다. 혹은 아마도 서비스 기사가 말한 것일지도 모릅니다. 파퍼 씨는 그가 잠시 후 자신의 몸과 의자를 일으켜 세웠을 때 방금 무슨 일이 일어났는지 확신할 수 없었습니다. 날아가는 도구들이 쏟아졌고, 문이 난폭하게 쾅 하고 닫혔고, 서비스 기사는 사라졌습니다.

이 갑작스러운 소리에, 물론, 아이들이 뛰쳐나왔습니다. 파퍼 씨는 그들에게 어떻게 냉장고가 이제 펭귄을 위해 다 개조되었는지 보여 주었습니다. 그는 또한, 캡틴 쿡에게도, 그를 그 안에 가둬 두면서 보여 주었습니다. 펭귄은 즉시 반짝이는 새로운 안에 달린 손잡이를 알아챘고 그것을 자신의 평소와 같은 호기심으로 물었습니다. 문이 열렸고, 캡틴 쿡이 뛰어 나왔습니다.

파퍼 씨는 재빠르게 캡틴 쿡을 다시 안에 넣었고 문을 다시 닫아서, 펭귄이 그의 경험으로 배웠는지 확인하려고 했습니다. 얼마 지나지 않아, 캡틴 쿡은 나오는 데 꽤 능숙해졌고 문이 닫혔을 때 안으로 들어가는 방법을 배울 준비가 되었습니다.

경찰이 뒷문으로 왔을 때쯤에는, 캡틴 쿡은 마치 그가 그 안에서 평생 살았던 것처럼 쉽게 냉장고 안팎을 드나들고 있었습니다.

6장 더 많은 골칫거리들

아이들이 경찰을 눈치 챈 첫 번째 사람이었습니다.

"봐요, 아빠." 빌이 말했습니다. "경찰이 뒷문에 있어요. 그가 아빠를 체포할 거예요?"

"꽥." 캡틴 쿡이 말하며, 품위 있게 문으로 걸어갔고, 방충망 사이로 그의 부리를 쑥 내밀려고 했습니다.

"여기가 프라우드풋 에비뉴 432번지인가요?"

"그렇습니다." 파퍼 씨가 대답했습니다.

"글쎄, 제 생각에도 여기가 맞는 것 같군요." 경찰이 말했고, 캡틴 쿡을 가리켰습니다. "저것이 당신의 것인가요?"

"네, 그런데요." 자랑스러워하며, 파퍼 씨가 말했습니다.

"그리고 당신은 무슨 일을 하죠?" 경찰이 엄격하게 물었습니다.

"아빠는 예술가예요." 제이니가 말했습니다.

"아빠는 항상 페인트와 백색 도료를 온통 그의 옷에 묻히고 다녀요." 빌이 말했습니다.

"전 주택 도장공이자, 도배업자입니다." 파퍼 씨가 말했습니다. "안으로 들어오지 않을래요?"

"그러지 않겠어요." 경찰이 말했습니다. "제가 꼭 그래야 하는 게 아니라면 말이에요."

"하, 하!" 빌이 말했습니다. "경찰이 캡틴 쿡을 무서워해요."

"꾸엑!" 펭귄이 말하며, 그의 붉은 부리를 크게 벌려, 마치 그가 경찰을 보고 웃고 싶어 하는 것 같았습니다.

"그게 말할 수 있나요?" 경찰이 물었습니다. "그게 뭐예요—거대한 앵무새인가요?"

"그건 펭귄이에요." 제이니가 말했습니다. "우리는 그것을 애완동물로 삼고 있어요."

"뭐, 그게 단지 새라면…" 경찰이 말하면서, 당혹스럽다는 듯이 자신의 이마를 긁기 위해 그의 모자를 들어 올렸습니다. "도구 가방을 가진 남자가 밖에서 저에게 소리쳤던 것으로는, 저는 여기에 풀려난 사자라도 있다고 생각했어요."

"엄마는 아빠의 머리카락이 가끔 사자의 것처럼 보인다고 말하기도 해요." 빌이 말했습니다.

"조용히 해, 빌." 제이니가 말했습니다. "경찰은 아빠의 머리카락이 어떻게 보이는지 신경 쓰지 않아."

경찰은 이제 그의 턱을 긁었습니다. "그게 단지 새일 뿐이라면, 당신이 그를 우리 안에 둔다면 전 괜찮을 것 같네요."

"우리는 그를 냉장고 안에 둘 거예요." 빌이 말했습니다.

"당신이 그것을 냉장고에 두든지 말든지, 내 알 바 아닙니다." 경찰이 말했습니다. "당신이 그것이 어떤 종류의 새라고 말했죠?"

"펭귄이요." 파퍼 씨가 대답했습니다. "그건 그렇고, 저는 그를 데리고 저와 같이 산책을 가기를 원할 수도 있어요. 만약 제가 그에게 줄을 채운다면, 그래도 괜찮을까요?"

"정말지." 경찰이 말했습니다. "솔직히 전 펭귄에 대한 지방 조례가 무엇인지 모르겠네요, 공용 도로에서, 줄이 매여 있어야 하는지 아닌지 말이에요. 제가 제 경사에게 물어보죠."

"아마도 전 그에 대한 면허를 얻어야 할 수도 있겠네요." 파퍼 씨가 말했습니다.

"그건 확실히 면허가 있어야 할 만큼 충분히 커다랗죠." 경찰이 말했습니다. "제가 당신에게 무엇을 해야 할지 알려줄게요. 당신이 시청에 전화를 걸어서 그들에게 펭귄에 대한 판례가 무엇인지 물어보세요. 그리고 행운을 빌어요, 파퍼 씨. 그는 좀 귀엽고 작은 녀석이네요, 더구나. 거의 사람처럼 보이고 말이에요. 좋은 하루 보내세요, 파퍼 씨, 그리고 좋은 하루 보내요, 펭귄 군."

파퍼 씨가 캡틴 쿡을 위한 면허에 대해 알아보려고 시청에 전화를 걸었을

때, 펭귄은 초록색 선을 물어뜯어서 전화를 끊으려고 최선을 다했습니다. 아마 그는 그것을 새로운 종류의 장어라고 생각했을지도 모릅니다. 하지만 바로 그때 파퍼 부인이 시장에서 돌아왔고 새우 통조림 한 캔을 땄기에, 파퍼 씨는 곧 전화 옆에 혼자 남겨졌습니다.

그렇다 하더라도, 그는 자신이 이상한 애완동물을 위해 면허를 얻어야만 하는지 아닌지에 대해 알아내는 것이 그렇게 쉽지 않다는 것을 알게 되었습니다. 매번 그가 자신이 무엇을 원하는지 설명할 때마다, 그는 잠시 기다리라는 말을 듣게 되었고, 한참 후에 새로운 목소리가 그에게 무엇을 원하는지 물었습니다. 이런 일이 상당히 오랜 시간 동안 계속 되었습니다. 마침내 새로운 목소리가 이 경우에 약간의 관심을 가진 듯했습니다. 이 친절한 목소리에 만족해하며, 파퍼 씨는 다시 캡틴 쿡에 대해 말하기 시작했습니다.

"그는 육군 대위인가요, 경찰 서장인가요, 아니면 해군 대령인가요?"

"아니에요." 파퍼 씨가 말했습니다. "그는 펭귄이라고요."

"다시 말씀해주시겠어요?" 목소리가 말했습니다.

파퍼 씨가 그 말을 반복했습니다. 목소리는 그가 그것의 철자를 말하는 것이 더 낫겠다고 제안했습니다.

"P-e-n-g-u-i-n." 파퍼 씨가 말했습니다. "펭귄이라니까요."

"오!" 목소리가 말했습니다. "당신 말

148

은 캡틴 쿡의 이름이 벤자민(Benjamin)이라는 건가요?"

"벤자민이 아니에요. 펭귄이에요. 그건 새라고요." 파퍼 씨가 말했습니다.

"당신 말은." 그의 귓가의 전화기에서 말했습니다. "캡틴 쿡이 새들을 총으로 사냥할 수 있는 면허를 원한다는 건가요? 죄송해요. 조류-사냥 기간은 11월까지는 시작되지 않습니다. 그리고 좀 더 명확하게 말하려고 해주세요, 성함이—토퍼 씨(Mr. Topper)라고 말했었죠?"

"제 이름은 파퍼입니다, 토퍼가 아니에요." 파퍼 씨가 소리쳤습니다.

"그래요, 포터 씨(Mr. Potter). 이제 제가 당신의 말을 꽤 분명하게 들을 수 있네요."

"그렇다면 잘 들어요." 파퍼 씨가 이제 완전히 분노해서, 으르렁거리듯 말했습니다. "만약에 시청에 있는 당신들이 펭귄이 무엇인지도 모른다면, 당신들은 그것들에게 면허가 있어야 하는지에 대한 어떠한 규칙도 없을 것 같군요. 난 캡틴 쿡에 대한 면허 없이 지내겠어요."

"잠시 만요, 포프웰 씨(Mr. Popwell). 우리들의 호수, 강, 연못, 그리고 하천 항해 부서의 트레드보텀 씨(Mr. Treadbottom)가 막 들어왔어요. 제가 당신이 그에게 직접 이야기할 수 있도록 해드릴게요. 아마 그는 당신의 이 벤자민 쿡에 대해서 알지도 몰라요."

잠시 후 새로운 목소리가 파퍼 씨에게 말을 했습니다. "안녕하세요. 여기는 자동차 면허국입니다. 당신은 작년과 같은 차를 가지고 있나요, 만약 그렇다면, 자동차 번호가 어떻게 되시죠?"

파퍼 씨는 군청 건물로 전화가 넘겨진 것이었습니다.

그는 전화를 끊기로 했습니다.

7장 캡틴 쿡 둥지를 짓다

몹시 내키지 않아하며, 제이니와 빌은 캡틴 쿡을 두고 학교에 가야만 했습니다. 파퍼 부인은 부엌에서, 다소 늦게 아침 설거지를 하느라 바빴고; 그녀는 어렴풋이 펭귄이 꽤 자주 냉장고를 들락날락 하는 것을 깨달았지만, 처음에는 그것에 대해 별다른 생각이 없었습니다.

그동안에 파퍼 씨는 그가 전화하던 것을 내버려두고 이제는 캡틴 쿡처럼 훌륭한 새의 주인이 된 것을 기리며 면도를 하고 자신의 몸을 깔끔하게 하느라 바빴습니다.

그러나 펭귄은, 비록 지금은 다소 방치되었지만, 결코 한가하지 않았습니다.

특이하고 흥분되는 일과 평소보다 더 일찍 시장에 가야 했기 때문에, 파퍼 부인은 아직 집안을 정리할 짬이 나지 않았습니다. 그녀는 훌륭한 살림꾼이었습니다. 그럼에도 불구하고, 제이니와 빌과 같은 두 아이들과 저렇게 깔끔하지 못한 남편이 있다면, 그녀가 다소 자주 방을 치워야만 한다는 사실을 부인할 수 없었습니다.

캡틴 쿡은 이제 물건을 치우는 것에 주의를 기울이고 있었습니다.

모든 방의 구석구석으로 그는 돌아다녔고 쿡쿡 찔렀고 쉬지 않고 철저하게 쪼아 보았습니다; 모든 벽장 속을 그는 그의 하얀-원형의 두 눈으로 바라보았습니다; 모든 가구의 아래와 뒤로 그는 작고 조용한 호기심 어리고, 놀라워하고, 감탄하는 울음소리를 내며, 자신의 통통한 몸으로 비집고 들어갔습니다.

그리고 매번 그가 찾고 있는 듯했던 것을 그가 발견했을 때마다, 그는 그것을 자신의 붉은 부리의 검은색 끝으로 집어 올렸고, 그것을 들고 가며, 자랑스럽게 그의 넓적하고, 분홍색 발로 뒤뚱거리며, 부엌으로, 그리고 냉장고로 갔습니다.

결국에는 파퍼 부인이 도대체 그 분주한 새가 무슨 짓을 하고 있는지 궁금해하기에 이르렀습니다. 그녀가 보았을 때, 그녀는 빨리 와서 캡틴 쿡이 지금 무엇을 했는지 보라고 파퍼 씨에게 소리칠 수밖에 없었습니다.

나중에 파퍼 부인이 알아차렸듯이, 그 자신도 꽤나 멋지게 보이는, 파퍼 씨도 그녀와 같이 깜짝 놀라서 냉장고 안을 쳐다보게 되었습니다.

캡틴 쿡도 역시 다가왔고, 그들이 보는 것을 도와주었습니다. "오크, 오크." 그가 의기양양해하며 말했습니다.

파퍼 부인이 웃었고, 파퍼 씨는 그들이 캡틴 쿡이 집안을 휘젓고 다닌 것의 결과를 보게 되자 숨을 헉 하고 들이마셨습니다.

두 타래의 감은 실, 흰색 체스 비숍(bishop) 하나, 그리고 직소 퍼즐 여섯 조각...티스푼과 닫힌 안전성냥갑...래디시 무(radish), 페니 두 개, 니켈 한 개, 그리고 골프 공 한 개. 두 개의 몽당연필, 구부러진 게임용 카드 한 장, 그리고 작은 재떨이.

머리핀 다섯 개, 올리브 하나, 두 개의 도미노 조각(domino), 그리고 양말 한 짝...손톱 다듬는 줄, 다양한 크기의 단추 네 개, 공중전화용 동전, 아이들의 장난감 구슬 일곱 개, 그리고 작은 인형 의자...

체커 말(checker) 다섯 개, 그레이엄 크래커(graham cracker) 조각 약간, 파치시(parcheesi) 컵, 그리고 지우개 하나...문 열쇠, 단춧고리, 그리고 구겨진 은박지 뭉치...매우 오래된 레몬 반쪽, 자기 인형의 머리, 파퍼 씨의 담배 파이프, 그리고 진저에일(ginger-ale) 뚜껑...잉크병 마개, 나사 두 개, 그리고 벨트 버클...

아이용 목걸이에서 나온 구슬 여섯 개, 블록 쌓기 조각 다섯 개, 바느질용 달걀 모양 받침(darning egg), 뼈, 작은 하모니카(harmonica), 그리고 조금 먹은 막대사탕. 치약 뚜껑 두 개와 작은 빨간 수첩까지.

"이게 바로 번식지라고 부르는 것인 듯해요." 파퍼 씨가 말했습니다. "단지 그는 자신의 둥지를 지을 어떤 돌멩이도 찾을 수 없었던 것뿐이에요."

"뭐." 파퍼 부인이 말했습니다. "그 펭귄들은 남극에서는 야만스러운 방식으로 지낼지 모르지만, 내가 분명히 말하건대 난 이 녀석이 집안에서는 꽤 도움이 될 것 같네요."

"오크!" 캡틴 쿡이 말했고, 거실로 뽐내듯 걸어가다가, 그는 가장 좋은 램프를 쳐서 떨어뜨리고 말았습니다.

"내 생각에는, 애들 아빠." 파퍼 부인이 말했습니다. "당신이 캡틴 쿡을 밖으로 데리고 나가서 약간의 운동이라도 시키는 것이 좋을 것 같아요. 이럴수가, 그런데 당신 완전히 멋을 부렸잖아요. 아니, 당신은 거의 마치 당신 자신이 펭귄처럼 보여요."

파퍼 씨는 자신의 머리카락을 매끈하게 만졌고 그의 구레나룻을 면도했습니다. 두 번 다시 파퍼 부인이 그가 사자처럼 정신 사나워 보인다고 잔소리하지 않을 것입니다. 그는 하얀 셔츠에 하얀 타이를 하고 하얀 플란넬(flannel) 바지를 입었고, 한 켤레의 선명한 황갈색의, 거무스름한 짙은 붉은색 구두를 신었습니다. 그는 자신의 낡은 검은색 연미복을 삼나무 장롱에서 꺼냈는데, 그것은 그가 결혼할 때 입었던 것이었고, 조심스럽게 그것을 털어서, 입었습니다.

그는 정말로 약간 펭귄처럼 보였습니다. 그는 돌아서서 파퍼 부인을 위해, 지금의 펭귄처럼 뽐내듯이 걸어 보았습니다.

하지만 그는 캡틴 쿡에 대한 자신의 의무를 잊지 않았습니다.

"애들 엄마, 빨랫줄 몇 야드만 좀 줄래요?" 파퍼 씨가 물었습니다.

8장 펭귄의 산책

파퍼 씨는 곧 펭귄을 데리고 산책을 가는 것이 그렇게 쉽지만은 않다는 것을 알게 되었습니다.

캡틴 쿡은 처음에는 줄에 매어진다는 것에 대해 좋아하지 않았습니다. 하지만, 파퍼 씨는 단호했습니다. 그는 빨랫줄의 한쪽 끝을 펭귄의 두꺼운 목에 묶었고 반대쪽 끝을 자신의 손목에 묶었습니다.

"오크!" 캡틴 쿡이 분해하며 말했습니다. 그럼에도 불구하고, 그는 매우 합리적인 새였고, 그가 저항하는 것이 그에게 아무 이익이 되지 않는다는 것을 알았을 때, 그는 자기 원래대로의 품위를 되찾았고 파퍼 씨가 자신을 이끌게 하기로 했습니다.

파퍼 씨는 자신의 가장 좋은 나들이용 중산모(derby)를 썼고 그의 곁에서 뒤뚱거리며 걷고 있는 캡틴 쿡과 함께 현관문을 열었습니다.

"꾹." 펭귄이 말하며, 현관 입구의 가장자리에서 멈춰 계단을 내려다보았습니다.

파퍼 씨는 그에게 넉넉한 길이의 빨랫줄로 된 목줄을 주었습니다.

"꽥!" 캡틴 쿡이 말했고, 그의 날개를 들어 올리며, 그는 용감하게 앞으로 몸을 기울였고 그의 배로 터보건 썰매를 타듯 계단을 내려갔습니다.

파퍼 씨도 비록 같은 방법은 아니었지만, 따라갔습니다. 캡틴 쿡은 재빨리 다시 일어났고 그의 고개를 이리저리 빠르게 돌리고 새로운 광경에 대해 기뻐하는 듯한 말을 하며 파퍼 씨보다 앞서서 거리로 활보하며 갔습니다.

프라우드풋 에비뉴를 따라서 파퍼 씨네 가족의 이웃인 캘러핸 부인(Mrs. Callahan)이 그녀의 팔 한가득 식료품을 안고 왔습니다. 그녀가 캡틴 쿡과 그의 검은색 연미복을 입은 모습이 마치 더 커다란 펭귄처럼 보이는 파퍼 씨를 보았을 때 그녀는 깜짝 놀라서 쳐다보았습니다.

"어머나!" 새가 그녀의 실내복 아래에 있는 줄무늬 스타킹을 살펴보기 시작하자 그녀가 외쳤습니다. "그건 부엉이도 아니고 그건 거위도 아니잖아요."

"아니지요." 파퍼 씨가 말하며, 자신의 나들이용 중산모를 기울였습니다. "그건 남극 펭귄이에요, 캘러핸 부인."

"나한테서 떨어져." 캘러핸 부인이 캡틴 쿡에게 말했습니다. "개미핥기(anteater)라고요, 그게?"

"개미핥기가 아니에요." 파퍼 씨가 설명했습니다. "남극(Antarctic)이요. 그건 남극에서 내게 보내졌어요."

"당장 당신의 남극 거위를 나한테서 떼어 놔요." 캘러핸 부인이 말했습니다.

파퍼 씨가 고분고분하게 빨랫줄을 당기는 동안, 캡틴 쿡은 캘러핸 부인의 줄무늬 스타킹을 마지막으로 쪼았습니다.

"맙소사!" 캘러핸 부인이 말했습니다. "난 당장 잠깐 들려서 파퍼 부인을 봐야겠어요. 난 절대 이 일을 믿지 못할 것 같군요. 난 이제 가겠어요."

"나도 가야겠네요." 파퍼 씨가 말하는 동안 캡틴 쿡은 그를 거리를 따라서 끌고 갔습니다.

그들이 다음에 도착한 곳은 프라우드풋 에비뉴와 메인 스트리트(Main Street)가 만나는 모퉁이에 있는 약국이었습니다. 여기에서 캡틴 쿡은 창문가에 진열된 것을 들여다보겠다고 고집을 부렸는데, 그것은 반짝거리는 하얀 붕소 결정체가 담긴 봉투를 여러 개 풀어 놓은 것으로 이루어져 있었습니다. 이것들을 그가 극지방의 눈으로 착각한 것이 분명했는데, 왜냐하면 그가 창문을 격렬하게 쪼기 시작했기 때문입니다.

갑자기 자동차가 그것의 브레이크에서 날카로운 소리를 내면서 가까이에 있는 연석을 향해 휙 돌아서 왔고, 두 젊은 남자가 뛰어 나왔는데, 그들 가운데 한 사람은 카메라를 들고 있었습니다.

"이게 분명히 그것일 거야." 첫 번째 젊은 남자가 다른 사람에게 말했습니다.

"그들이야, 틀림없어." 두 번째 젊은 남자가 말했습니다.

사진사는 그의 삼각대를 보도 위에 세웠습니다. 이때쯤에는 약간의 군중이 주위에 모여들었고, 하얀 가운을 입은 두 남자도 심지어 구경하러 약국에

152

서 나왔습니다. 캡틴 쿡은, 하지만, 여전히 창문에 진열된 것에 지나치게 정신이 팔려서 돌아보려고도 하지 않았습니다.

"당신이 프라우드풋 에비뉴 432번지에 사는 파퍼 씨이지요, 그렇죠?" 두 번째 젊은 남자가 물으면서, 자신의 주머니에서 수첩을 꺼냈습니다.

"그런데요." 파퍼 씨가 말하면서, 자신의 사진이 곧 신문에 실리기 위해 찍힐 참이라는 것을 깨달았습니다. 두 젊은 남자들은, 사실은, 경찰에게서 그 이상한 새에 대해서 들었었고, 인터뷰를 하러 파퍼 씨의 집으로 가던 중이었는데, 마침 그들이 캡틴 쿡을 봤던 것입니다.

"이봐, 펠리컨(pelican)아, 돌아서서 여기 좀 보렴." 사진사가 말했습니다.

"저건 펠리컨이 아니야." 기자인 다른 사람이 말했습니다. "펠리컨은 그들의 부리 안에 주머니가 있다고."

"난 그것이 도도(dodo)라고 생각했었는데, 단지 도도는 멸종했지만 말이야. 이건 우아한 사진이 나올 것 같아, 내가 그녀를 돌아서게만 할 수 있다면."

"그건 펭귄이에요." 파퍼 씨가 자랑스럽게 말했습니다. "그 녀석의 이름은 캡틴 쿡이지요."

"꽥!" 펭귄이 말하며, 이제 그들이 그에 대해 말하고 있자, 돌아섰습니다. 카메라 삼각대를 발견하자, 그는 걸어와서 그것을 살폈습니다.

"아마도 그것이 세 발 달린 황새라고

여기는 것 같아." 사진사가 말했습니다.

"당신의 이 새 말이에요—" 기자가 말했습니다. "그건 수컷이에요 아님 암컷이에요? 사람들이 알고 싶어 할 거예요."

파퍼 씨는 망설였습니다. "글쎄요, 전 그것을 캡틴 쿡이라고 불러요."

"그렇다면 그건 수컷이 되겠네요." 기자가 말하면서, 빠르게 자신의 수첩에 적었습니다.

여전히 신기해하며, 캡틴 쿡은 삼각대 주위를 계속 돌면서 걸어 다니다가, 결국 빨랫줄, 펭귄, 파퍼 씨 그리고 삼각대가 모두 엉켜버렸습니다. 구경꾼 가운데 한 사람의 조언을 따라서, 엉켜있던 것은 파퍼 씨가 삼각대 주위를 반대 방향으로 세 번이나 걸어 다니고 나서야 마침내 풀렸습니다. 드디어, 캡틴 쿡은, 파퍼 씨의 옆에 가만히 서서, 포즈를 취하는 걸 허락했습니다.

파퍼 씨는 자신의 타이를 바로 했고, 사진사는 사진을 찍었습니다. 캡틴 쿡은 그의 눈을 감았고, 이러한 상태로 그의 사진이 나중에 모든 신문에 실렸습니다.

"마지막으로 질문 하나만 더 하겠습니다." 기자가 물었습니다. "당신은 어디에서 당신의 이상한 애완동물을 얻었나요?"

"남극 탐험가, 드레이크 제독으로부터요. 그가 저에게 선물로 그를 보내줬어요."

"그래요." 기자가 말했습니다. "어쨌

거나, 이건 좋은 이야기네요."

두 젊은 남자는 그들의 차에 뛰어 올랐습니다. 파퍼 씨와 캡틴 쿡은 그들의 산책을 계속 했는데, 꽤 많은 군중이 따라오며 질문을 했습니다. 군중이 너무 많아졌고, 도망치기 위해서, 파퍼 씨는 캡틴 쿡을 이발소로 데려갔습니다.

이발소를 운영하던 남자는, 이때까지만 해도, 파퍼 씨의 아주 절친한 친구였습니다.

9장 이발소 안에서

이발소 안은 매우 조용했습니다. 이발사는 나이든 신사에게 면도를 해주고 있었습니다.

캡틴 쿡은 이 광경을 매우 흥미롭게 여겼고, 더 잘 보려고, 그는 거울 아래 선반 위로 뛰어 올랐습니다.

"맙소사!" 이발사가 말했습니다.

이발사의 의자에 앉은 신사는, 그의 얼굴이 이미 거품으로 하얗게 덮여 있었는데, 그의 고개를 반쯤 들어서 무슨 일이 일어났는지 보려고 했습니다.

"꽥!" 펭귄이 말하며, 그의 날개를 퍼덕거렸고 그 신사의 얼굴의 위에 있는 거품을 향해 자신의 긴 부리를 뻗었습니다.

비명을 지르고 펄쩍 뛰면서, 신사가 자신의 기대어 누운 자세에서 일어나, 이발소의 의자에서 나왔고, 심지어 그의 코트와 모자를 챙기려고 멈추지도

못한 채, 거리로 도망쳤습니다.

"꾹! 캡틴이 말했습니다.

"이봐." 이발사가 파퍼 씨에게 말했습니다. "저것을 내 가게에서 치워. 여기는 동물원이 아니라고. 도대체 무슨 생각을 한 거야?"

"내가 그를 자네 가게의 뒷문으로 데리고 나가도 될까?" 파퍼 씨가 물었습니다.

"아무 문이나 괜찮아." 이발사가 말했습니다. "그것이 빨리만 된다면. 지금 그건 내 빗에서 빗살들을 물어뜯고 있단 말이야."

파퍼 씨는 캡틴 쿡을 자신의 팔로 들었고, "꾸엑?" "꾸욱!" 그리고 "오크!" 하는 울음소리가 난무하는 와중에 가게 밖으로 그리고 가게의 뒷방으로 그리고 문을 나가 골목길로 나아갔습니다.

캡틴 쿡은 이제 그의 첫 번째 건물 뒷 계단을 발견했습니다.

파퍼 씨는 펭귄이 어딘가로 향하는 계단을 발견했을 때, 그가 그것들을 오르지 못하게 막는 것이 절대로 불가능하다는 것을 알게 되었습니다.

"좋아." 파퍼 씨가 말하며, 캡틴 쿡의 뒤에서 헐떡이며 계단을 올랐습니다. "그렇겠지, 새이기도 하고, 더구나 날 수 없는 새인데, 너도 어떻게 해서든지 공중으로 올라가야만 하겠지, 그래서 네가 계단을 오르는 것을 좋아하는 거야. 뭐, 이 건물이 고작 3층이라서 다행이야. 어서. 네가 뭘 할 수 있는지 보자."

천천히 하지만 지지치 않고, 캡틴 쿡

은 분홍색 발을 하나씩 하나씩 한 계
단에서 그 다음 계단으로 올렸고, 빨랫
줄의 반대쪽 끝에서 파퍼 씨가 따라가
고 있었습니다.

마침내 그들은 꼭대기 층계참에 다
다랐습니다.

"자 이제 뭐?" 파퍼 씨가 캡틴 쿡에
게 물었습니다.

더는 올라갈 계단이 없다는 것을 알
게 되자, 캡틴 쿡은 돌아섰고 이제는
내려가는 계단을 살펴보았습니다.

그때 그가 자신의 날개를 들었고 앞
으로 몸을 기울였습니다.

파퍼 씨는, 여전히 숨을 쉬려고 헐떡
이고 있었는데, 단단히 결심한 새가 그
토록 빨리 몸을 내던지리라고 생각하지
못했었습니다. 그는 펭귄이 그들에게
기회가 있을 때마다 터보건 썰매를 타
듯 미끄러진다는 것을 기억했었어야만
했습니다.

아마도 그가 어리석게도 자신의 손
목에 빨랫줄의 한쪽 끝을 묶었나 봅
니다.

어쨌든, 이번에는 파퍼 씨가 갑자기
미끄러지며, 하얀 옷을 입은 자신의 배
로 엎드린 채, 3층의 계단을 내려가는,
자신의 모습을 발견하게 되었습니다.
이는 파퍼 씨 바로 앞에서 자신의 미끄
럼 타기를 즐기고 있는, 펭귄을 기쁘게
했습니다.

그들이 바닥에 도착했을 때, 캡틴 쿡
이 다시 올라가기를 몹시 바랐기 때문
에 파퍼 씨는 그의 관심을 돌리기 위

해, 택시를 불러야만 했습니다.

"프라우드풋 에비뉴 432번지요." 파
퍼 씨가 운전사에게 말했습니다.

운전사는, 친절하고 예의 바른 남자
여서, 그가 요금을 받을 때까지는 그의
특이하게 조화를 이룬 승객들을 비웃
지 않았습니다.

"오 저런!" 그녀가 자신의 남편에게
문을 열었을 때, 파퍼 부인이 말했습니
다. "당신이 산책을 나갈 때만해도 당
신은 정말 깔끔하고 멋있어 보였는데.
지금 당신의 앞을 봐요!"

"미안해요, 여보." 파퍼 씨가 겸손한
어조로 말했습니다. "하지만 당신은 펭
귄이 다음에 무슨 행동을 할지 예측할
수가 없어요."

그렇게 말하며, 그는 모든 평소와 다
른 운동으로 인해 꽤나 지쳐있었기 때
문에, 누워 있으려고 갔고, 반면에 캡
틴 쿡은 목욕을 하고 냉장고에서 낮잠
을 잤습니다.

10장 불행의 어두운 그림자

다음 날 파퍼 씨와 캡틴 쿡의 사진이 스
틸워터의 아침 신문에, 멀리 떨어진 남
극에 사는 드레이크 제독에게서 항공
속달 우편으로 펭귄을 받은 주택 도색
공에 대한 문단과 함께, 실렸습니다. 그
러더니 연합 통신사가 그 이야기를 알
게 되었고, 한 주 뒤에 그라비어 인쇄
술로 찍힌 사진을 나라에 있는 모든 대
도시에서 가장 중요한 신문들의 일요일

판에서 볼 수 있었습니다.

자연스럽게 파퍼 가족은 모두 무척 자랑스러워했고 행복해했습니다.

하지만, 캡틴 쿡은 행복하지 않았습니다. 그는 갑자기 집을 돌아다니던 그의 활기차고, 탐색하는 작은 산책을 멈췄고, 하루의 대부분을 냉장고 안에서 부루퉁해하며 앉아있었습니다. 파퍼 부인은 모든 이상한 물건들을 치웠고, 단지 구슬과 체커 말을 남겨서, 캡틴 쿡이 이제 좋고, 정돈된 아담한 번식지를 가질 수 있게 했습니다.

"그가 더 이상 우리랑 놀지 않아요." 빌이 말했습니다. "제가 그에게서 제 구슬 몇 개를 가져가려고 했더니, 그가 저를 물려고 했어요."

"못된 캡틴 쿡." 제이니가 말했습니다.

"그를 혼자 내버려두는 것이 좋겠구나, 애들아." 파퍼 부인이 말했습니다. "그가 시무룩해하는 것 같구나, 내 생각엔."

하지만 풀이 죽은 것보다 훨씬 더 심각한 무언가가 캡틴 쿡을 병들게 했다는 것이 곧 분명해졌습니다. 하루 종일 그는 냉장고에서 그의 작고 하얀 원형의 두 눈으로 밖을 슬프게 내다보면서 앉아 있었습니다. 그의 털은 그 사랑스럽고, 반짝이는 빛을 잃었습니다; 그의 둥그스름한 작은 배는 매일 홀쭉해졌습니다.

파퍼 부인이 그에게 통조림 새우 몇 마리를 주면 이제 그는 돌아섰습니다.

어느 저녁에 그녀가 그의 체온을 쟀습니다. 화씨104도(40℃)였습니다.

"글쎄, 애들 아빠." 그녀가 말했습니다. "내 생각엔 당신이 수의사를 부르는 것이 좋을 것 같아요. 난 캡틴 쿡이 정말로 아픈 것일까 봐 걱정이에요."

하지만 수의사가 왔을 때, 그는 그저 자신의 고개를 저었습니다. 그는 아주 훌륭한 동물 의사였고, 비록 그는 이전에 결코 펭귄을 치료한 적이 없었지만, 그는 이 녀석이 심각하게 아프다는 것을 한눈에 알아차릴 만큼 새에 대해 충분히 알고 있었습니다.

"제가 당신에게 약 몇 가지를 놓고 갈게요. 그에게 매시간에 하나씩 주세요. 그리고는 당신은 그에게 셔벗(sherbet)을 먹여보고 그를 아이스 팩으로 감싸보기도 하세요. 하지만 전 이게 아무 희망도 없는 상황인 듯해서 당신에게 어떤 격려의 말도 해줄 수가 없군요. 이런 종류의 새는 절대 이런 기후와 맞지 않아요, 당신도 알겠지만. 전 당신이 그를 잘 돌봐왔다는 것을 알겠어요, 하지만 남극 펭귄은 스틸워터에서 잘 지낼 수 없어요."

그날 밤 파퍼 가족은 밤을 지새우면서, 돌아가며 아이스 팩을 갈아 주었습니다.

전혀 소용이 없었습니다. 아침에 파퍼 부인이 캡틴 쿡의 체온을 다시 쟀습니다. 그것은 화씨 105도(40.5℃)로 올라갔습니다.

모든 사람이 매우 동정적이었습니다.

아침 신문의 기자는 들려서 펭귄에 대해 물어보았습니다. 이웃들은 온갖 종류의 육수와 젤리를 가져와서 이 작은 녀석을 유혹해보려고 했습니다. 심지어 캡틴 쿡에 대해 결코 높이 사지 않았던, 캘러핸 부인도 그를 위해 멋진 냉동 커스터드를 만들어왔습니다. 아무것도 소용이 없었습니다. 캡틴 쿡은 너무 많이 악화되었습니다.

그는 이제 하루 종일 깊은 혼수상태에 빠져 잠을 잤고, 모두 끝이 멀지 않았다고 말하고 있었습니다.

모든 파퍼 씨네 가족은 이 우스꽝스럽고, 진지한 작은 친구를 몹시 좋아하게 되었고, 파퍼 씨의 마음은 두려움으로 얼어붙었습니다. 그에게 있어서 캡틴 쿡이 죽는다면 그의 삶이 매우 공허할 것 같았습니다.

분명히 누군가는 아픈 펭귄을 위해 무엇을 해야 할지 알고 있을 것이었습니다. 그는 멀리 떨어진 남극에 있는, 드레이크 제독에게 조언을 요청할 어떤 방법이라도 있기를 바랐지만, 시간이 없었습니다.

그가 절망하다가, 파퍼 씨는 어떤 생각을 해냈습니다. 편지가 그에게 그의 애완동물을 가져다 주었습니다. 그는 앉아서 또 다른 편지를 썼습니다.

그것은 세계에서 가장 큰 도시인, 매머드 시(Mammoth City)에 있는 대형 수족관의 전시 책임자, 스미스 박사(Dr. Smith)에게 보내는 것이었습니다. 분명 어딘가에 있는 누군가가 죽어가는 펭귄을 치료할 수 있는 것에 대해 어떤 생각이 있다면, 바로 이 사람일 것입니다.

이틀 후에 그 전시 책임자에게서 답장이 왔습니다. "유감스럽지만." 그가 썼습니다. "아픈 펭귄을 치료하는 것은 쉽지 않습니다. 아마도 당신은 우리도 역시, 매머드 시에 있는 우리의 수족관에, 남극에서 온 펭귄이 있다는 사실을 몰랐을 겁니다. 그것은 우리가 그것에게 하는 모든 것에도 불구하고, 급속도로 약해지고 있어요. 나는 최근에 그것이 외로움 때문에 고통스러워하는 게 아닐까 생각했었습니다. 아마도 그게 바로 당신의 캡틴 쿡을 아프게 한 것일지도 모릅니다. 나는, 그래서, 당신에게, 별도의 우편으로, 우리의 펭귄을 보냅니다. 당신이 그녀를 가져도 됩니다. 이 새들이 함께 더 나아질 기회가 있을 수도 있어요."

그리고 그렇게 그레타(Greta)는 프라우드풋 에비뉴에 와서 살게 되었습니다.

11장 그레타

그래서 결국엔, 캡틴 쿡은 죽지 않았습니다.

냉장고에는 펭귄 두 마리가 있었는데, 한 마리는 서 있었고 다른 한 마리는 얼음칸 아래에 있는 둥지 위에 앉아 있었습니다.

"그들은 콩깍지에 든 두 개의 콩처럼

꼭 닮았어요." 파퍼 부인이 말했습니다.

"두 마리의 펭귄처럼이겠지요, 당신 말은." 파퍼 씨가 대답했습니다.

"맞아요, 그런데 누가 누구란 말이에요?"

이때 서 있던 펭귄이 냉장고에서 뛰어 나와, 안으로 부리를 뻗었고 자느라고 눈이 감겨 있는, 앉아 있는 펭귄의 밑에서 체커 말을 하나 꺼냈고, 그것을 파퍼 씨의 발 옆에 놓았습니다.

"이것 봐요, 애들 엄마, 그가 나에게 고마워하고 있어요." 파퍼 씨가 말하면서, 펭귄을 쓰다듬었습니다. "남극에서는 그것이 바로 펭귄이 그 우정을 표현하는 방식이에요, 단지 체커 말 대신 돌멩이를 사용하겠지만요. 이 녀석이 분명히 캡틴 쿡일 거예요, 그리고 그는 우리가 자기에게 그레타를 데려다 주고 녀석을 구해준 것에 대해 고마워하고 있다는 것을 보여 주려고 하고 있어요."

"그래요, 하지만 우리가 어떻게 그 녀석들을 구분하죠? 매우 헷갈리네요."

"내가 지하 저장고로 내려가서 흰색 페인트를 좀 가져와서 그들의 이름을 녀석들의 검은 등에 칠해 놓을게요."

그리고 그는 지하 저장고의 문을 열었고 내려가기 시작하다가, 캡틴 쿡이 갑작스럽게 그를 따라서 터보건 썰매를 타듯 미끄러져 내려갔을 때 거의 발을 헛디딜 뻔했습니다. 그가 다시 올라왔을 때, 파퍼 씨는 자신의 손에 붓과 작은 페인트 통을 들고 있었고, 동시에 펭귄은 그의 등에 하얀 글씨로 캡틴 쿡 (CAPT. COOK)이라고 써져 있었습니다.

"꽥!" 캡틴 쿡이 말하며, 자랑스럽게 자신의 이름을 냉장고에 있는 펭귄에게 보여주었습니다.

"꾹!" 앉아 있는 펭귄이 말했고, 그러더니 자신의 둥지에서 몸을 꿈틀거리며 움직여서, 그녀가 자신의 등을 파퍼 씨에게 돌렸습니다.

그래서 파퍼 씨는 냉장고 앞에 있는 바닥 위에 앉았고, 그러는 동안에 캡틴 쿡은 처음에는 한쪽 눈으로, 다음에는 반대쪽 눈으로, 지켜보았습니다.

"당신은 뭐라고 그녀를 부를 거예요?" 파퍼 부인이 물었습니다.

"그레타라고 부를 거예요."

"그건 좋은 이름이네요." 파퍼 부인이 말했습니다. "그리고 그녀도 또한, 착한 새처럼 보여요. 하지만 그들 둘이 냉장고를 꽉 채우고 있고, 곧 알들을 낳게 될 거고, 정신을 차리고 보면, 냉장고는 당신의 펭귄들에게 충분히 크지 않을 거예요. 게다가, 당신은 내가 어떻게 하면 음식을 차갑게 보관할 수 있는지에 대해서는 하나도 일을 하지 않았잖아요."

"할 거예요, 여보." 파퍼 씨가 약속했습니다. "이미 10월 중순치고는 꽤 추워졌어요, 그리고 곧 캡틴 쿡과 그레타가 바깥에 있기에도 충분히 추워질 거예요."

"그래요." 파퍼 부인이 말했습니다. "하지만 당신이 그들을 집 바깥에 둔다면, 그들이 도망갈지도 몰라요."

158

"애들 엄마." 파퍼 부인이 말했습니다. "당신은 오늘 밤에 당신의 음식을 냉장고에 다시 넣도록 해요. 그리고 우리는 그냥 그레타와 캡틴 쿡을 집 안에 둘 거예요. 캡틴 쿡은 내가 둥지를 다른 방으로 옮기는 것을 도와줄 수 있어요. 그다음에 내가 모든 창문을 열고 그것들을 열어둔 채로 놔 두면, 펭귄들은 편안해질 거예요."

"그들은 편안하겠죠, 분명히." 파퍼 부인이 말했습니다. "그런데 우리는 어떡하고요?"

"우리는 우리의 겨울 오버코트와 모자를 집 안에서 입으면 되잖아요." 파퍼 씨가 말하면서, 그는 일어나서 돌아다니면서 모든 창문을 열었습니다.

"확실히 더 춥네요." 파퍼 부인이 재채기하며, 말했습니다.

다음 며칠은 훨씬 더 추웠지만, 파퍼 씨네 가족은 곧 자신들의 오버코트를 입고서 앉아 있는 것에 익숙해졌습니다. 그레타와 캡틴 쿡은 항상 열린 창문에서 제일 가까운 의자들을 사용했습니다.

11월의 이른 초순, 어느 밤에, 눈보라가 내리쳤고, 파퍼 씨네 가족들이 아침에 일어났을 때, 커다란 눈 더미들이 집 안 곳곳에 있었습니다.

파퍼 부인은 자신의 빗자루를 가져오고 파퍼 씨에게 그의 눈삽을 가져오게 해서 그 눈 더미들을 치우고 싶었지만, 펭귄들이 그 눈 속에서 몹시 즐거운 시간을 보내고 있었기에 파퍼 씨는

눈을 있는 그 자리에 두자고 주장했습니다.

사실은, 그는 심지어 그날 밤에 지하실에서 오래된 정원 호스를 가져와서 모든 바닥에 물이 1인치 깊이가 될 때까지 물을 뿌리기도 했습니다. 다음 날 아침이 되자 모든 파퍼 씨네 집 바닥은 열린 창문 근처의 가장자리 주위로는 눈 더미가 있고, 매끈한 얼음으로 덮여 있었습니다.

그레타와 캡틴 쿡 둘 다 엄청나게 이 모든 얼음에 기뻐했습니다. 그들은 거실의 한쪽 끝에 있는 눈 더미에 올라갔고, 서로를 뒤따르며, 얼음 위로, 그들이 너무 빨리 달려서 그들의 몸의 균형을 유지하지 못할 때까지, 달려 내려왔습니다. 그러더니 그들은 그들의 배로 털썩 엎드렸고 미끄러운 얼음을 가로지르며 터보건 썰매를 타듯 미끄러졌습니다.

이는 빌과 제니를 몹시 재미있게 해서 그들도 역시, 그들의 오버코트의 배 부분으로 엎드려서, 이 놀이를 해 보았습니다. 이는 결국 펭귄을 몹시 즐겁게 했습니다. 그러자 파퍼 씨가 거실에 있는 모든 가구를 한쪽으로 옮겨서, 펭귄들과 아이들이 진정한 미끄럼 타기를 할 수 있는 충분한 공간을 만들어 주었습니다. 처음에는 가구를 옮기는 것이 약간 어려웠는데, 왜냐하면 의자들의 아랫부분이 얼음으로 얼어붙어 있었기 때문이었습니다.

오후가 되면서 날씨는 따뜻해졌고 얼음이 녹기 시작했습니다. "이제, 애들

아빠." 파퍼 부인이 말했습니다. "당신이 정말로 무언가를 해야만 해요. 우리는 계속 이렇게 할 수 없어요."

"하지만 캡틴 쿡과 그레타가 둘 다 통통하고 윤기가 흐르고, 아이들도 이렇게 뺨이 발그레한 적이 없잖아요."

"정말 건강에 좋을지는 몰라요." 파퍼 부인이 말하는 동안에, 그녀는 바닥을 마루걸레로 닦았습니다. "하지만 매우 깔끔하지 않다고요."

"내가 내일 그것에 대해 무언가를 할게요." 파퍼 씨가 말했습니다.

12장 먹여 살려야 할 새로운 식구들

그래서 다음 날 파퍼 씨는 기술자를 불렀고 지하 저장고에 냉동 시설을 설치하게 했고, 캡틴 쿡과 그레타를 아래로 데려가 그곳에서 살게 했습니다. 그리고는 그는 난방기를 꺼서 그것을 위층으로 가져가 거실로 옮겼습니다. 거기에 있는 것은 매우 이상하게 보였지만, 파퍼 부인이 말했듯이, 적어도 항상 그들의 오버코트를 입지 않아도 되어서 다행이었습니다.

파퍼 씨는 이 모든 개조가 몹시 비싸다는 것을 알았을 때 다소 걱정스러웠습니다. 냉동 기술자도 또한, 그가 파퍼 씨가 사실상 돈이 없다는 것을 알았을 때, 걱정했습니다. 하지만, 파퍼 씨는 그가 할 수 있는 한 빨리 돈을 주겠다고 약속했고, 그 남자는 그가 모든 것을 외상으로 살 수 있게 했습니다.

파퍼 씨가 펭귄들을 옮긴 것은 잘한 일이었는데 그가 옮겨주자, 파퍼 부인의 알들에 대한 생각이 옳았기 때문입니다. 번식지가 지하실로 옮겨지자마자 그레타는 첫 번째 알을 낳았습니다. 3일 후에 두 번째 알이 나타났습니다.

펭귄은 한 계절에 단지 두 개의 알만을 낳는다고 파퍼 씨가 알고 있었기 때문에, 얼마 있다가, 세 번째 알이 그레타의 밑에서 발견되었을 때, 그는 깜짝 놀랐습니다. 기후의 변화가 펭귄의 번식 습관을 바꾸어놓았는지 아닌지, 파퍼 씨는 절대 알 수 없었지만, 알들이 총 10개가 될 때까지 3일마다 새로운 알들이 생겼습니다.

이제 펭귄 알들이 너무 커서 엄마 펭귄은 한 번에 단지 두 개의 알 위에만 앉을 수 있었고, 이는 상당한 문제를 일으켰습니다. 하지만, 파퍼 씨가 남는 알들을 펭귄의 체온에 딱 맞게 유지되는, 뜨거운 물병들과 전기 보온 패드 밑에 나누어 넣어서, 그 문제를 해결했습니다.

새끼 펭귄들은, 그들이 부화하기 시작했을 때는, 그들의 엄마와 아빠처럼 그렇게 훌륭하게 색이 두드러지지 않았습니다. 그들은 엄청난 속도로 자라는 솜털이 보송보송하고, 우스꽝스러운 작은 생물들이었습니다. 캡틴 쿡과 그레타는, 비록, 물론 파퍼 씨네 가족들도 또한, 모두 도와주었지만, 그들에게 음식을 나르느라 매우 바빴습니다.

언제나 너무나 대단한 독서가였던

파퍼 씨는, 새끼 펭귄들의 이름을 떠올리는 데 아무 어려움을 겪지 않았습니다. 그 이름들은 넬슨(Nelson), 콜럼버스(Columbus), 루이자(Louisa), 제니(Jenny), 스콧(Scott), 마젤란(Magellan), 아델리나(Adelina), 이자벨라(Isabella), 퍼디난드(Ferdinand), 그리고 빅토리아(Victoria)였습니다. 그럼에도 불구하고, 그는 이름을 지어야 할 펭귄이 10마리가 넘지 않는다는 것에 다소 안도했습니다.

파퍼 부인도 또한, 그것들이 실제로 그녀가 집안일을 하는 데 그녀에게 별로 큰 차이를 주진 않았지만, 모두에게 충분한 펭귄의 수라고 생각했습니다—파퍼 씨와 아이들이 부엌에 있는 지하 저장고로 가는 문을 닫는 것만 기억한다면 말이지요.

펭귄들은 모두 부엌으로 올라가는 계단을 오르는 것을 좋아했고, 그들이 부엌문이 닫혀 있는 것을 보게 되지 않는 한 언제 멈춰야 할지를 몰랐습니다. 그러면, 당연하게도, 그들은 돌아서서 다시 계단을 썰매를 타듯 미끄러져 내려갔습니다. 파퍼 부인이 부엌에서 일하고 있을 때, 이로 인해 때때로 약간 별난 소리가 나곤 했지만, 그녀는 자신이 올해 겨울에 너무나 많은 다른 이상한 것들에 익숙해졌듯이, 그것에도 익숙해졌습니다.

파퍼 씨가 펭귄을 위해 아래층에 설치한 냉동 시설은 크고 좋은 것이었습니다. 그것은 작은 얼음 조각들 대신에, 매우 큰 얼음 덩어리를 만들었기 때문에, 곧 파퍼 씨는 12마리의 펭귄들이 살고 올라갈 수 있는 일종의 얼음 성을 그 아래에 만들어 주었습니다.

파퍼 씨는 또 지하 저장고 바닥에 커다란 구멍을 팠고 새들을 위한 수영하고 잠수할 수 있는 수영장을 만들었습니다. 때때로 그는 수영장 안에 펭귄들이 잠수해서 잡도록 살아 있는 물고기를 던져놓기도 했습니다. 그들은 이를 몹시 새롭고 신나는 것으로 여겼는데, 왜냐하면, 솔직히 말해서, 그들은 새우 통조림에 약간 질렸기 때문이었습니다. 살아 있는 생선은 특별히 주문되어 수조차와 유리 상자에 실려 저 멀리 해안에서부터 프라우드풋 에비뉴 432번지로 가져온 것이었습니다. 불행하게도, 그것들은 꽤 비쌌습니다.

그렇게 많은 펭귄들이 있다는 것은 좋은 일이었습니다. 왜냐하면 그것들 가운데 두 마리가 (보통 넬슨과 콜럼버스가) 싸움이 붙고, 그들의 날개로 서로 치고 덤비기 시작할 때, 다른 열 마리의 펭귄들이 모두 싸움을 구경하고 격려하는 말을 하려고 주위로 모여들기 때문이었습니다. 이는 정말 흥미로운 작은 장면을 만들었습니다.

파퍼 씨는 또 지하 저장고 바닥의 일부분을 물에 잠기게 해 아이스 링크로 만들었고, 여기에서 펭귄들은 종종 일종의 소규모 군대처럼, 얼음을 돌아다니며 환상적인 행진 동작과 행렬하는 것을 연습했습니다. 펭귄 루이자는 이 행진하는 연습을 이끄는 것을 특히 좋아하는 듯했습니다. 파퍼 씨가 루이자에게 그녀가 자랑스럽게 엄숙한 행진을 이끄는 동안에 그녀의 부리로 작은 미국 국기를 들고 있도록 훈련을 시키자는 생각을 한 후에, 그것들을 보는 것은 꽤나 볼만했습니다.

제이니와 빌은 종종 자신들과 함께 그들의 어린 친구들을 학교에서 집으로 데리고 왔고, 그들을 모두 아래로 내려가서 몇 시간이고 펭귄들을 보았습니다.

밤에는, 그가 예전에 그랬듯이, 거실에 앉아서 책을 보고 그의 담배 파이프를 피우는 대신에, 파퍼 씨는 자신의 오버코트를 걸치고 그의 물건들을 챙겨서 아래층으로 갔습니다. 그곳에서 그는 자신의 장갑을 낀 채, 앉아서 읽으면서, 때때로 자신의 애완동물들이 무엇을 하는지 고개를 들어 보았습니다. 그는 자주 작은 생물들이 정말로 있어야 할 곳인 춥고, 먼 지방에 대해 생각했습니다.

또한, 자주 그는 펭귄들이 와서 그가 바쁘게 지내기 전에 그의 삶이 얼마나 달랐었는지에 대해서도 생각했습니다. 이제 1월이었고, 벌써 그는 봄이 와서, 그가 그들을 하루 종일 내버려 두고 다시 집을 칠하러 가야 할 때를 생각하니 몹시 걱정이 되었습니다.

13장 돈 걱정

그러나 밤이 되자, 파퍼 부인이, 아이들을 잠자리에 들게 하고 나서, 지하 저장고로 내려가려던 파퍼 씨를 멈춰 세웠습니다.

"애들 아빠." 그녀가 말했습니다. "나 당신에게 할 말이 있어요. 와서 앉아 봐요."

"알았어요, 여보." 파퍼 씨가 말했습니다. "지금 무슨 생각하고 있어요?"

"애들 아빠." 파퍼 부인이 말했습니다. "난 당신이 이토록 좋은 휴가를 보내는 걸 보게 되어 기뻐요. 그리고 나는 정말이지 당신이 언제나 지하실에 내려가 있으니까, 집을 깔끔하게 유지하는 것이 평소보다 더 쉽다는 걸 인정할 수밖에 없네요. 하지만, 애들 아빠, 우리 돈을 어떻게 해요?"

"문제가 뭐예요?" 파퍼 씨가 물었습니다.

"뭐, 물론, 펭귄들은 먹어야 하고요, 그런데 당신은 그 모든 살아 있는 물고기들에 대한 청구서가 얼마인지 알고 있어요? 나는 우리가 어떻게 그것들을 갚을지 모르겠다는 것은 분명히 알겠어요. 그리고 지하실에 냉동 시설을 놓아준 기술자가 계속 초인종을 울리면서 자신의 돈을 달라고 하고 있다고요."

"우리의 돈을 전부 다 써 버렸어요?" 파퍼 씨가 조용히 물었습니다.

"사실상 거의 다요. 물론 전부 다 써 버리게 되면, 아마도 우리는 한동안은

162

12마리의 펭귄을 먹고 살 수는 있겠지요."

"오 안 돼요, 애들 엄마." 파퍼 씨가 말했습니다. "당신, 진심은 아니겠지요."

"글쎄, 난 내가 정말로 그것들을 먹는 것을 즐길 수 있을 거라고 생각하진 않아요. 특히 그레타와 이자벨라는 말이에요." 파퍼 부인이 말했습니다.

"그건 역시 아이들의 마음을 아프게 할 거예요." 파퍼 씨가 말했습니다. 그는 한참 동안 생각에 잠겨 그곳에 앉아 있었습니다.

"나에게 좋은 생각이 있어요, 애들 엄마." 그가 마침내 말했습니다.

"어쩌면 우리는 그것들을 누군가에게 팔 수 있어요, 그렇다면 우리는 살아갈 약간의 돈을 얻게 될 거예요." 파퍼 부인이 말했습니다.

"안 돼요." 파퍼 씨가 말했습니다. "나에게 더 좋은 생각이 있어요. 우리는 펭귄도 계속 가질 수 있어요. 애들 엄마, 당신은 극장에서 공연하는, 훈련받은 물개에 대해 들어본 적 있어요?"

"물론 나는 훈련받은 물개에 대해 들어본 적이 있지요." 파퍼 부인이 대답했습니다. "나는 심지어 몇 마리를 한 번 본 적도 있는 걸요. 그것들이 자신의 코 끝 위에 공을 놓고 균형을 잡았었어요."

"그렇다면 아주 좋아요." 파퍼 씨가 말했습니다. "훈련받은 개와 훈련받은 물개가 있을 수 있다면, 훈련받은 펭귄은 왜 있을 수 없겠어요?"

"아마도 당신 말이 맞는 것 같아요, 애들 아빠."

"물론 내 말이 맞지요. 그리고 당신은 내가 펭귄들을 훈련시키는 것을 도와야 해요."

다음 날 그들은 피아노를 지하실 아이스 링크의 한쪽 끝으로 내려 보냈습니다. 파퍼 부인은 그녀가 파퍼 씨와 결혼한 이후에 피아노를 쳐본 적이 없었지만, 약간 연습하자 그녀는 곧 그녀가 잊어버렸던 몇 가지 곡을 기억해 냈습니다.

"이 펭귄들이 가장 하기 좋아하는 것은." 파퍼 씨가 말했습니다. "군대처럼 연습하고, 넬슨과 콜럼버스가 서로 싸우는 것을 구경하고, 계단으로 올라가서 터보건 썰매를 타듯 미끄러져 내려오는 것이에요. 그러니 우리는 우리 쇼의 파트를 그 장난들에 맞춰서 짜면 될 거예요."

"그것들은 어쨌거나, 의상이 필요하지 않겠네요." 파퍼 부인이 말하면서, 우스꽝스러운 작은 모습들을 보았습니다. "그것들은 이미 의상이 있거든요."

그래서 파퍼 부인은 각각 다른 쇼의 파트마다 하나씩, 지하실에 있는 피아노로 연주할 세 개의 다른 곡을 골랐습니다. 곧 펭귄들은, 음악을 듣는 것만으로도, 그들이 바로 무엇을 해야 하는지를 알았습니다.

그들이 많은 수의 군인처럼 행진해야 할 때, 파퍼 부인이 슈베르트(Schubert)의 "군대 행진곡(Military March)"를 연주했습니다.

넬슨과 콜럼버스가 서로 자신들이 날개를 갖고 싸워야 할 때, 파퍼 부인은 "메리 위도우 왈츠(Merry Widow Waltz)"를 연주했습니다.

펭귄들이 올라가서 터보건 썰매를 타듯 미끄러져 내려가야 할 때, 제이니와 빌은 얼음의 가운데로 파퍼 씨가 집을 도배할 때 사용했던 두 개의 휴대용 발판사다리와 판자 하나를 끌고 나왔습니다. 그러면 파퍼 부인이 "개울가에서(By the Brook)"라고 불리는 아름답고, 서정적인 곡을 연주했습니다.

당연하게도, 지하 저장고는 추웠기 때문에 파퍼 부인은 그녀의 장갑을 낀 채 피아노를 연주하는 것을 배워야만 했습니다.

1월 말이 되었을 때, 파퍼 씨는 펭귄들이 나라에 있는 어느 극장에 나가도 될 준비가 되었다고 확신했습니다.

14장 그린바움 씨

"여기 봐요." 어느 날 아침에 파퍼 씨가 아침 식사를 하다가 말했습니다. "여기 아침 신문에 쓰여 있기로는 팔라스 극장의 주인, 그린바움 씨(Mr. Greenbaum)가 마을에 온다고 하네요. 그는 전국 곳곳에 많은 극장들이 있어요: 그러니 나는 우리가 가서 그를 보는 것이 좋을 것 같네요."

그날 저녁—그날은 토요일, 1월 29일이었는데—파퍼 씨네 가족과 그들의 훈련받은 펭귄 12마리는, 그들 가운데 두 마리가 자신들의 부리로 국기를 들고서, 팔라스 극장을 찾아 집을 나섰습니다.

펭귄들은 이제 너무 잘 훈련되어서 파퍼 씨는 그들을 줄에 묶는 것이 필요하지 않다고 결정했습니다. 정말로, 그들은 버스를 기다리는 줄까지 다음과 같은 행군 진열로 매우 잘 걸어갔습니다: —

파퍼 씨, 그레타와 캡틴 쿡, 콜럼버스와 빅토리아, 파퍼 부인, 넬슨과 제니, 마젤란과 아델리나, 빌 파퍼와 제이니 파퍼, 스콧과 이사벨라, 퍼디난드와 루이자

버스가 모퉁이에서 멈췄고, 깜짝 놀란 버스 운전사가 항의하기도 전에, 그들은 모두 올라탔고 버스는 그대로 출발했습니다.

"제가 새들에 대해 요금을 반만 내면 되나요, 아니면 그들은 무료인가요?" 파퍼 씨가 물었습니다.

"제이니는 요금을 반만 내지만, 저는 10살이에요." 빌이 말했습니다.

"쉿, 조용히 해." 파퍼 부인이 말하면서 그녀와 아이들은 자신들의 자리를 찾았습니다. 펭귄들도 질서정연하게 안으로 따라갔습니다.

"글쎄요, 선생님." 운전사가 말했습니다. "당신은 저 전시품들을 가지고 어디로 갈 생각인 건가요?"

"시내로요." 파퍼 씨가 말했습니다. "여기 있어요, 50센트라고 치고, 그냥

그렇게 두죠."

"솔직히 말해서, 나는 그것들이 나를 지나갈 때 수를 세다 잊어버렸어요." 운전사가 말했습니다.

"그건 훈련받은 펭귄 공연이에요." 파퍼 씨가 설명했습니다.

"그것들은 정말로 새인가요?" 운전사가 물었습니다.

"오 그럼요." 파퍼 씨가 말했습니다. "저는 그저 그것들을 팔라스로 데려가서 큰 극장 주인인 그린바움 씨와 인터뷰하려는 거예요."

"뭐, 만약 제가 어떤 불평이라도 듣게 되면, 그것들은 다음 번 모퉁이에서 내려야 할 거예요." 운전사가 말했습니다.

"좋아요." 그럴 경우를 위해 환승권을 요청하고 싶었지만, 현 상태에 만족하기로 한, 파퍼 씨가 말했습니다.

펭귄들은 매우 잘 행동하고 있었습니다. 그것들은 두 명씩 자리에 조용히 앉아있었는데, 다른 승객들은 구경했습니다.

"죄송합니다." 파퍼 씨가 말하며, 버스 안에 있는 모든 사람에게 말을 걸었습니다. "하지만 저는 모든 창문을 열어야만 할 것 같네요. 이것들은 남극 펭귄들이고 그것들은 이보다 훨씬 더 춥게 지내는 것에 익숙해져 있어요."

파퍼 씨가 굳게 닫혀 있는, 창문을 여는 데 한참 걸렸습니다. 그가 다 열었을 때, 다른 승객들에게서 많은 말들이 있었습니다. 그들 가운데 많은 사람들이 운전사에게 불평하기 시작했고, 운전사는 파퍼 씨에게 그의 새들을 데리고 버스에서 내리라고 말했습니다. 그는 이 말을 여러 번 반복해야만 했습니다. 마침내 그는 파퍼 씨가 내리기 전에는 버스를 더 움직이는 것을 거부했습니다. 이때쯤에는, 하지만, 버스가 시내에 어느 정도 가까이 와 있어서 그들 가운데 누구도 거리로 나가는 것에 신경 쓰지 않았습니다.

그들에게서 단지 한 블록 앞에서 팔라스 극장의 불빛이 반짝였습니다.

"안녕하세요." 극장 관리자가 말했을 때, 파퍼 씨의 가족과 펭귄들이 그의 옆으로 무리를 지어 걸어갔습니다. "물론, 그린바움 씨가 여기 제 사무실 안에 있습니다. 있잖아요, 난 당신의 이 새들에 대한 이야기를 들었었지만, 난 그걸 정말로 믿지는 않았지요. 그린바움 씨, 파퍼 펭귄들을 만나보세요. 전 당신에게 맡겨 두겠어요. 전 무대 뒤에 가 봐야 하거든요."

펭귄들은, 이제 6마리씩 두 줄로 예의 바르게 서서, 그린바움 씨를 신기하다는 듯이 보고 있었습니다. 그들의 24개의 하얀-원형의 눈은 몹시 진지했습니다.

"문 주위에 모여든 당신들 모두, 제자리로 돌아가요." 그린바움 씨가 말했습니다. "이건 비공개 회의란 말이에요." 그러더니 그가 일어나서 문을 닫았습니다.

파퍼 씨네 가족이 앉아 있는 동안에 그린바움 씨는 두 줄로 선 펭귄들의 이

쪽저쪽으로 걸어 다니면서, 그들을 살펴보았습니다.

"그건 공연처럼 보이기는 하네요." 그가 말했습니다.

"오, 그건 공연이에요, 분명히." 파퍼 씨가 말했습니다. "그건 남극에서 바로 온, 어느 무대에서든지 처음으로 선보이는, 파퍼 씨네 재주부리는 펭귄들입니다." 그와 파퍼 부인은 공연을 위해서 이 이름을 생각해두었습니다.

"우리가 그것들을 파퍼 씨의 분홍색 발가락을 가진 펭귄들이라고 부르면 안 되겠어요?" 그린바움 씨가 물었습니다.

파퍼 씨가 잠시 생각했습니다. "안 돼요." 그가 말했습니다. "저는 우리가 그럴 수 없을 것 같네요. 그건 너무 마치 소녀 합창단이나 발레 무용단처럼 들리고, 이 새들은 꽤 진지하답니다. 저는 그것들이 그 이름을 좋아할 것 같지 않아요."

"좋습니다." 그린바움 씨가 말했습니다. "내게 그 공연을 보여 줘요."

"거기에는 음악도 있어요." 제이니가 말했습니다. "엄마가 피아노를 연주해요."

"그게 사실입니까, 부인?" 그린바움 씨가 물었습니다.

"네, 선생님." 파퍼 부인이 대답했습니다.

"뭐, 당신 뒤에 피아노가 있어요." 그린바움 씨가 말했습니다. "당신이 시작해도 좋아요, 부인. 전 이 공연을 보고 싶군요. 그것이 조금이라도 좋다면, 당

신들은 제대로 찾아온 거예요. 전 전국 방방곡곡에 극장들을 갖고 있지요. 하지만 먼저 당신의 펭귄들이 연기하는 것을 봅시다. 준비되셨나요, 부인?"

"우리는 먼저 가구들을 옮기는 게 좋겠어요." 빌이 말했습니다.

15장 파퍼 씨네 재주부리는 펭귄들

바로 그때 그들은 신음소리를 내며 들어오는 관리자에 의해 방해를 받았습니다.

"무슨 일인가?" 그린바움 씨가 물었습니다.

"신기한 마르코스(The Marvelous Marcos)가 공연의 마지막 순서였는데 나타나지 않았고, 관객들이 그들의 돈을 돌려달라고 요구하고 있어요."

"자네는 어쩔 셈이지?" 그린바움 씨가 물었습니다.

"그들에게 돈을 돌려줘야겠죠, 제가 생각하기에는 말이에요. 그리고 오늘은 토요일 밤으로, 일주일 가운데 가장 수익이 많은 밤이잖아요. 저는 그 돈을 다 잃는다고 생각하니 정말 속상하네요."

"제게 생각이 있어요." 파퍼 부인이 말했습니다. "아마도 당신들은 그 돈을 잃지 않게 될 수도 있어요. 그게 공연의 마지막 순서라면, 우리가 그냥 진짜 무대 위에서 펭귄들이 연습하게 하면 어떨까요? 우리는 더 넓은 공간을 쓸 수 있고, 전 관객들도 그것을 즐거워할 것 같아요."

166

"좋아요." 관리자가 말했습니다. "그렇게 해 봅시다."

그렇게 펭귄들은 진짜 무대 위에서 그들의 첫 번째 예행연습을 하게 되었습니다.

관리자가 무대 위로 나갔습니다. "신사 숙녀 여러분." 그가 자신의 손을 들어 올리며, 말했습니다. "여러분이 친절하게 관용을 베풀어 주신다면 저희는 오늘 밤 작은 새로운 공연을 선보이려고 합니다. 예상치 못한 상황으로 인해, 신기한 마르코스가 등장하지 못하게 되었습니다. 저희는 대신에, 여러분에게 파퍼 씨네 재주부리는 펭귄들의 예행연습을 보여 드리겠습니다. 감사합니다."

위엄 있는 모습으로 파퍼 씨의 가족들과 펭귄들이 무대 위로 걸어 나갔고, 파퍼 부인이 피아노 앞에 앉았습니다.

"당신은 피아노를 치려면 당신의 장갑을 벗어야 하지 않겠어요?" 관리자가 물었습니다.

"오, 아니에요." 파퍼 부인이 말했습니다. "저는 그것들을 낀 상태로 연주하는 것에 너무 익숙해져서 당신만 괜찮다면, 그것들을 계속 끼고 있을 거예요."

그러더니 그녀가 슈베르트의 "군대 행진곡"을 연주하기 시작했습니다. 펭귄들은 매우 잘 연습하기 시작하면서, 파퍼 부인이 그 곡의 중간에서 연주를 멈출 때까지, 선회하고 뛰어난 정확성으로 그들의 대형을 바꾸었습니다.

관객들은 열정적으로 박수를 쳤습니다.

"공연이 좀 더 남아있어요." 파퍼 부인이 반은 관리자에게 그리고 반은 관객에게 설명했습니다. "그것들이 가운데가 비어 있는 사각형을 만들어서 그 대형으로 행진하는 것이지요. 너무 늦어서 우리는 오늘 밤 그것을 넘어가고 두 번째 막으로 건너뛸 거예요."

"당신은 정말로 당신의 장갑을 벗지 않기를 원하나요, 부인?" 관리자가 물었습니다.

파퍼 부인이 미소를 짓듯이 자신의 고개를 저었고 "메리 위도우 왈츠"를 연주하기 시작했습니다.

펭귄들 가운데 열 마리가 이제 반원으로 서자 넬슨과 콜럼버스가 그들의 가운데에 서서 격렬한 싸움 시합을 벌였습니다. 그들의 둥글고 검은 머리가 뒤로 멀리 젖혀져서 그것들이 자신들의 둥글고 하얀 두 눈으로 서로를 볼 수 있게 했습니다.

"꾸엑." 넬슨이 말하며, 자신의 오른쪽 날개로 콜럼버스의 배를 때렸고, 그러고 나서 그의 왼쪽 날개로 그를 밀려고 했습니다.

"꾹." 콜럼버스가 말하며, 부둥켜안으려고 하면서 그의 머리를 넬슨의 어깨 너머에 걸치며 그는 넬슨의 등을 때리려고 했습니다.

"이봐! 정정당당하지 못하잖아!" 관리자가 말했습니다. 콜럼버스와 넬슨이 서로 풀어주는 동안에 다른 열 마리의 펭귄들은, 구경하면서, 자신들의 날개로 박수를 쳤습니다.

콜럼버스는 이제 예의 바르게 넬슨과 치고 박다가 결국 넬슨이 그의 눈을 때렸고, 그 때문에 콜럼버스는 큰 소리로 "오크"라고 말하면서 뒤로 물러났습니다. 다른 펭귄들이 손뼉을 치기 시작했고, 관객들도 그들의 행동에 동참했습니다. 파퍼 부인이 왈츠 연주를 끝내자, 넬슨과 콜럼버스 둘 다 싸우는 것을 멈췄고, 그들의 날개를 내리고 가만히 서서, 서로를 마주 보았습니다.

"어느 새가 이긴 거야? 누가 앞섰냐고?" 관객들이 외쳤습니다.

"꾹!" 반원으로 서 있던 모든 열 마리의 펭귄들이 말했습니다.

이것은 넬슨에게 "여기 봐!"라고 말하는 것이 분명했는데 넬슨이 그들을 보려고 돌아섰고, 콜럼버스가 즉시 날개 하나로 그의 배를 치고 다른 하나로 그를 쓰러뜨렸습니다. 넬슨은 자신의 눈을 감은 채, 거기에 누워 있었습니다. 콜럼버스는 그러자 엎드린 넬슨의 위에서 열을 세웠고, 다시 다른 열 마리의 펭귄들이 박수를 쳤습니다.

"저건 공연의 일부예요." 제이니가 설명했습니다. "다른 펭귄들은 모두 콜럼버스가 이기기를 원해요, 그래서 그들은 모두 마지막에 '꾹!'이라고 말하지요. 그건 언제나 넬슨이 다른 곳을 보게 하거든요. 그럼 콜럼버스가 그를 제대로 때릴 수 있어요."

넬슨은 이제 일어났고 모든 펭귄들이 줄을 서서, 관리자에게 허리를 굽혀 인사했다.

"고맙구나." 관리자가 말하면서, 허리를 굽혀 인사하며 답했다.

"이제 세 번째 파트예요." 파퍼 씨가 말했습니다.

"오, 애들 아빠." 파퍼 부인이 말했습니다. "당신은 페인트칠하는 발판 사다리 두 개와 판자를 가져오는 것을 잊어버렸어요!"

"그건 괜찮아요." 관리자가 말했습니다. "제가 무대 담당자에게 가져오라고 하지요."

순식간에 사다리 한 쌍과 판자가 가져와졌고 파퍼 씨와 아이들은 그들에게 판자가 위에 얹어지면서 어떻게 사다리가 세워져야 하는지 보여 주었습니다. 그리고는 파퍼 부인이 꽤 서정적인 곡인 "개울가에서"를 연주하기 시작했습니다.

공연의 이 시점에서 펭귄들은 항상 그들의 규율을 잊고 굉장히 흥분했습니다. 그들은 모두 누가 먼저 사다리에 올라가는지 보려는 듯이 즉시 서로를 밀치기 시작했습니다. 하지만, 아이들은 항상 파퍼 씨에게 이 밀치고 서로 다투는 모든 행동 때문에 공연이 오히려 더 재미있다고 말해왔고, 파퍼 씨는 그럴거라고 생각했습니다.

그래서 이제 큰 소리로 꽥꽥 울면서 펭귄들은 싸우고 사다리를 올라가고 완전한 혼란 속에서, 종종 서로를 아래 바닥으로 완전히 떨어뜨리기도 하면서, 판자를 가로지르며 달려갔고, 그다음엔 서둘러서 터보건 썰매를 타듯 미끄러져 다른 사다리를 내려갔고 그곳으로 올라가려고 하는 다른 펭귄들을 쳐서 떨어뜨렸습니다.

공연의 이 부분은 파퍼 부인의 섬세한 음악에도 불구하고 몹시 정신없고 시끄러웠습니다. 관리자와 관객들은 모두 그들의 배를 쥐고, 웃음을 터뜨렸습니다.

마침내 파퍼 부인이 음악의 끝부분에 다다랐고 그녀의 장갑을 벗었습니다.

"당신은 그 사다리들을 무대에서 치워야 할 거예요, 안 그러면 난 저 새들을 절대 통제하지 못할 거예요." 파퍼 씨가 말했습니다. "커튼이 이 시점에서 내려와야겠네요."

그래서 관리자는 커튼이 내려오도록 신호를 보냈고, 관객들은 일어나서 환호했습니다.

사다리가 치워졌을 때, 관리자는 펭귄들을 위해 아이스크림콘을 가져오게 했습니다. 그러자 제이니와 빌이 울려고 했고, 관리자는 몇 개 더 주문해서, 모두 하나씩 먹게 되었습니다.

그린바움 씨는 파퍼 씨네 가족을 가장 먼저 축하해 주었습니다.

"정말이지, 파퍼 씨, 난 당신이 저 새들을 가지고 완전히 독특한 무언가를 만들어냈다고 생각해요. 당신의 공연은 돌풍을 불러일으킬 거예요. 그리고 당신이 내 친구인, 여기에 있는, 관리자를 도와준 방법은 당신이 진정으로 믿음직한 사람이라는 것을 보여주고 있어요—우리가 이 연예계에서 필요로 하는 바로 그런 종류의 사람이지요. 난 당신의 펭귄들이 오리건 주에서 메인 주까지 전국에 걸쳐서 가장 큰 극장들을 사람들로 가득 채울 것이라고 장담하고 싶군요."

"그리고 이제 계약 조건에 대한 것을 말하자면, 파퍼 씨." 그가 계속 말했습니다. "한 주에 5천 달러씩, 10주간 계약을 하면 어떨까요?"

"그거면 괜찮겠어요, 애들 엄마?" 파퍼 씨가 물었습니다.

"네, 그건 몹시 만족스럽네요." 파퍼 부인이 대답했습니다.

"그렇다면, 좋아요." 그린바움 씨가 말했습니다. "그냥 이 서류에 서명하세요. 그리고 시애틀에서 다음 주 목요일부터 공연을 시작할 준비를 하세요."

"다시 한 번 고맙습니다." 관리자가 말했습니다. "잠시만 다시 장갑을 껴 주시면 안 될까요, 파퍼 부인? 저는 당신이 다시 '군대 행진곡'을 연주하기 시작해서 펭귄들이 잠깐 행진하게 했으면 좋겠어요. 저는 제 좌석 안내원들을 여기로 데려와서 저 새들을 한 번 보게 하고 싶군요. 그들에게 교훈이 될 거예요."

16장 순회공연에 나서다

다음 날에 프라우드풋 에비뉴 432번지에서는 해야 할 일이 많았습니다. 그들 모두를 위해 사야 할 새 옷이 있었고, 낡은 옷은 좀약에 싸서 챙겨 두었습니다. 그리고는 파퍼 부인은 모든 곳을 솔로 문질러 닦고 윤을 내고 정리정돈을 해야만 했는데, 왜냐하면 파퍼 씨네 가족이 떠나있는 동안에 모든 것을 뒤죽박죽으로 두기에는 그녀가 너무나 훌륭한 살림꾼이었기 때문입니다.

그린바움 씨는 그들에게 미리 그들의 첫 번째 주에 대한 보수를 보냈습니다. 그들이 가장 먼저 한 일은 지하실에 냉동 시설을 설치했던 남자에게 돈을 지불하는 것이었습니다. 그는 자신의 돈에 대해서 꽤나 불안해하고 있었고; 무엇보다도, 그가 없었더라면 그들은 결코 펭귄들을 훈련시키지 못했을 것입니다. 그다음 그들은 저 멀리 해안에서부터 신선한 물고기를 운송해 주었던 회사에 수표를 보냈습니다.

마침내 모든 일이 끝났고, 파퍼 씨는 아담한 집의 문을 열쇠로 돌려 잠갔습니다.

그들은 교통경찰과의 말다툼 때문에 기차역에 조금 늦게 도착했습니다. 그 말다툼은 두 택시 운전사에게 일어난 사고 때문이었습니다.

여덟 개의 여행 가방들과 펭귄들이 점심으로 먹을 살아 있는 생선이 든 물양동이는 말할 것도 없을 뿐더러, 파퍼 씨네 가족 네 명과 펭귄 열두 마리로 인해, 파퍼 씨는 그들이 한 대의 택시에 모두 다 타지 못하리란 걸 알았고; 그래서 그는 두 번째 택시를 불러야만 했습니다.

각각의 택시 운전사는 자신이 먼저 역에 도착해서 자기 택시의 문을 열어 여섯 마리의 펭귄을 내리게 해 그곳에 있는 사람들을 깜짝 놀라게 하기를 간절히 원했습니다. 그래서 그들은 가는 내내 서로 경쟁했고, 마지막 블록에서 그들은 서로를 앞지르려고 했고, 바퀴 덮개 중 하나가 뜯어지고 말았습니다.

교통경찰은 당연히 매우 짜증이 났습니다.

그들은 기차가 막 역에서 떠나려고 할 때 도착했습니다. 심지어 택시 운전사 둘 다 그들이 문을 지나 놋쇠 레일을 넘어서 차량 뒤편 전망대로 올라가도록 도와주고 나서야, 그들은 가까스로 탈 수 있었습니다. 펭귄들은 숨도 제대로 쉬지 못했습니다.

파퍼 씨가 펭귄들과 함께 화물칸에 타서 그들이 불안해하지 않게 하는 동안, 파퍼 부인과 아이들은 침대칸에서 기차를 타고 가기로 되어 있었습니다. 기차 끝에 있는 전망차에서 탔기 때문에, 파퍼 씨는 새들을 데리고 기차의 전체 칸을 지나가야만 했습니다.

그것들이 식당 칸을 지나가게 하는 것은 심지어 생선이 담긴 양동이를 들고 있었지만, 충분히 쉬웠습니다. 침대칸에서는, 하지만, 승무원이 이미 일부 침상들을 마련하고 있어서, 문제가 생겼습니다.

승무원들의 사다리는 펭귄들에게 너무나 큰 유혹을 던졌습니다.

열두 마리의 기뻐하는 펭귄의 부리에서 오크 하고 열두 번의 행복해하는 소리가 났습니다. 파퍼 씨네 재주부리는 펭귄들은, 완전히 그들의 규율을 잊고서, 사다리를 올라가서 위층 침상으로 가려고 싸웠습니다.

불쌍한 파퍼 씨! 한 노부인은 기차가 시간당 90마일을 가든지 말든지, 기차에서 내릴 거라고 소리를 질렀습니다. 성직자의 옷깃을 단 신사는 창문을 열어서, 펭귄들이 뛰어 내릴 수 있게 하자고 제안했습니다. 두 승무원들은 침상에서 새들을 쫓아내려고 했습니다. 마침내 차장과 제동수가 손전등을 가지고, 구해주러 왔습니다.

파퍼 씨가 그의 애완동물들을 안전하게 화물칸으로 데려가기 전까지는 한참 걸렸습니다.

파퍼 부인이 처음에는, 그들이 순회 공연을 하는 동안에 제이니와 빌이 학교를 10주나 빠진다는 생각에, 비록 아이들은 전혀 신경 쓰지 않는 것 같았지만, 약간 걱정스러워했습니다.

"그리고 당신은 반드시 기억해야 돼요, 여보." 멀리 있는 나라들에 대한 그의 동경에도 불구하고, 결코 스틸워터 밖으로 나갔던 적이 없던, 파퍼 씨가 말했습니다. "여행은 정말 견문을 넓혀 준다는 것을 말이에요."

시작부터 펭귄들은 매우 유쾌한 성공을 거뒀습니다. 심지어 시애틀에서 있었던 그들의 첫 공연도 아무 문제없이 진행되었는데—아마도 그들이 이미 진짜 무대에서 예행연습을 해 봤기 때문일 것입니다.

바로 이곳에서 펭귄들은 프로그램에 그들 자신만의 작고 신선한 공연을 더했습니다. 그들은 극장 프로그램에 가장 먼저 등장했습니다. 그들이 자신들의 평소 연극을 마쳤을 때, 관객들은 야단법석을 떨었습니다. 그들은 박수를 쳤고 발을 굴렀고 파퍼 씨네 재주부리는 펭귄들의 공연을 더 보여 달라고 크게 소리쳤습니다.

제이니와 빌은 그들의 아빠를 도와서 펭귄들을 무대 밖으로 몰아서, 다음 공연이 진행될 수 있게 했습니다.

이 다음 공연은 듀발 씨(Monsieur Duval)라는 이름의, 줄타기 곡예사의 것이었습니다. 문제는 그들이 그래야 했던 것처럼, 무대 옆에서 그를 보는 대신에, 펭귄들이 흥미가 생겨서 다시 무대 위로 걸어 나가 그를 더 자세히 보려고 했다는 것이었습니다.

불행하게도 이때 듀발 씨는 하늘 높이 달린 줄 위에서 매우 어려운 춤을 추고 있었습니다.

관객들은, 당연히, 펭귄들의 공연이 다 끝났다고 생각했었고, 그들이 다시 돌아와서 관객들을 등지고 나란히 서서 듀발 씨가, 그들 위로 높이 있는 줄 위에서 정말 조심스럽게 춤을 추고 있는 것을 올려다보고 있는 것을 보자 무척이나 즐거웠습니다.

이는 모든 사람을 정말 크게 웃게 해서 듀발 씨는 그의 균형을 잃고 말았습니다.

"오크!" 펭귄들이 말하며 그가 떨어

질 때 그의 밑에 깔리지 않으려고, 황급히 뒤뚱거리며 물러났습니다.

재치 있게 자기 몸의 균형을 되찾고서, 듀발 씨는 자신의 팔꿈치 안쪽으로 줄을 붙잡았고 자신의 목숨을 구했습니다. 그가 파퍼 씨의 재주부리는 펭귄들이 마치 그들이 그를 비웃기라고 하는 것처럼, 자신들의 열두 개의 붉은 부리들을 크게 벌리고 있는 것을 보자 그는 매우 화가 났습니다.

"저리 꺼져, 이 바보 같은 것들아." 그가 그것들에게 프랑스어로 말했습니다.

"오크?" 펭귄들이 알아듣지 못한 척하며, 말했고, 서로에게 펭귄의 언어로 듀발 씨에 대해 말을 했습니다.

그리고 그들이 나타날 때마다, 그들이 극장 프로그램에 있는 다른 공연들을 더 방해할수록 관객들은 그들을 더 좋아했습니다.

17장 명성

그 새들은 곧 정말 유명해져서 파퍼 씨네 재주부리는 펭귄들이 어느 극장에 등장한다는 것이 알려질 때마다, 관객들은 표를 사기 위해 자기 차례를 기다리느라, 길을 따라서 반 마일이나 줄을 서 있었습니다.

하지만, 프로그램에 등장하는 다른 공연하는 사람들이 항상 그렇게 기뻐한 것은 아니었습니다. 한번은, 미니애폴리스에서, 파퍼 씨네 펭귄들이 같은 극장의 프로그램에 오를 거라는 사실

을 그녀가 들었을 때 유명한 여자 오페라 가수가 정말 짜증을 냈습니다. 사실은, 그녀는 펭귄들이 치워지지 않는 한 무대에 오르는 것을 거부했습니다. 그래서 무대 담당자들이 파퍼 씨와 파퍼 부인과 아이들이 새들을 무대에서 나가서 무대 아래에 있는 지하실로 가는 아래층으로 가게 하는 것을 도와주는 동안에, 관리자는 펭귄들이 지나갈 수 없도록 무대 입구를 지켰습니다.

아래에 있는 지하실에서, 새들은 곧 위로 올라가는 다른 작은 계단을 발견했고; 잠시 후에 관객들은 폭소를 터뜨리며 소리를 질러댔는데, 펭귄들의 머리가 갑자기, 하나씩, 연주자들이 연주를 하는 곳인 오케스트라 피트에 나타났기 때문이었습니다.

연주자들은 계속 연주했고, 무대 위에 있는 여자는, 그녀가 펭귄을 보았을 때, 오히려 더 크게 노래를 불러서 그녀가 얼마나 화가 났는지 보여 주려고 했습니다. 관객들은 정말 크게 웃고 있어서 아무도 그녀의 노래 가사를 알아들을 수가 없었습니다.

파퍼 씨는, 펭귄을 따라서 계단을 올라왔는데, 그가 계단이 오케스트라 피트로 이어지는 것을 보았을 때 멈췄습니다.

"난 내가 연주자들과 같이 저기에 가면 안 될 것 같아요." 그가 파퍼 부인에게 말했습니다.

"펭귄들은 갔잖아요." 파퍼 부인이 말했습니다.

"아빠, 아빠는 녀석들이 바이올린의 줄감개나 현을 물어뜯으려고 하기 전에 그들을 떼어 놓는 것이 좋을 거예요." 빌이 말했습니다.

"오 이런, 난 어떻게 해야 할지 모르겠구나." 파퍼 씨가 말하며, 무력하게 계단 꼭대기에 앉았습니다.

"그렇다면 내가 펭귄들을 잡아 올게요." 파퍼 부인이 말하면서, 그를 지나치며 올라갔고, 제이니와 빌이 따라갔습니다.

파퍼 부인이 그들을 따라온 것을 보았을 때, 펭귄들은 몹시 죄책감을 느꼈습니다. 왜냐하면 녀석들은 자신들이 그곳에 있으면 안 된다는 것을 알았기 때문입니다. 그래서 녀석들은 무대 위로 뛰어 올랐고, 무대의 각광을 넘어 달려가서, 노래하는 여자의 푸른 치마 밑에 숨었습니다.

그게 악보에 적혀 있지 않았던 높고, 날카로운 음 하나를 제외하고서 노래하는 것을 완전히 멈추게 했습니다.

새들은 극장의 밝은 조명과 수많은, 웃는 관객들, 그리고 그 모든 여행을 정말 좋아했습니다. 언제나 새로운 볼거리가 있었거든요.

스틸워터에서 나와 태평양 연안으로 그들은 여행했습니다. 이제는 파퍼 씨네 가족이 그들이 가진 돈으로 봄까지 버틸 수 있을지 걱정해야만 했던 곳인, 프라우드풋 에비뉴 432번지에 있는 아담한 집까지는 멀리 떨어져 있었습니다.

그리고 매주 그들은 5천 달러짜리 수표를 받았습니다.

그들이 실제로 극장에서 공연하고 있지 않거나, 도시 사이를 기차로 여행하고 있지 않을 때, 그들의 생활은 더 큰 호텔에서 이루어졌습니다.

간혹 깜짝 놀란 호텔 경영자가 새들을 그곳에 묵게 하는 데 반대하곤 했습니다.

"아니, 우리는 심지어 이 호텔에 작은 애완용 개가 들어오는 것도 허락하지 않습니다." 그는 이렇게 말하고는 했지요.

"그래요, 하지만 당신은 펭귄에 대한 어떤 규칙이 있나요?" 파퍼 씨는 이렇게 물었고요.

그러면 호텔 경영자는 펭귄에 대한 규칙이 전혀 없다는 것을 인정해야만 했습니다. 그리고 물론, 얼마나 펭귄들이 단정한지, 그리고 다른 손님들이 그것들을 볼지도 모른다는 기대에 자신의 호텔을 찾는다는 것을 그가 보게 되자, 그는 매우 기쁘게 그들을 맞았습니다. 여러분은 커다란 호텔에 있는 것이 많은 펭귄들에게 장난을 칠 수많은 기회를 줄 거라고 생각할지도 모르지만, 녀석들은 전반적으로, 매우 잘 행동하며, 너무 자주 엘리베이터를 타고 오르내리고, 가끔씩 몇몇 벨보이의 유니폼에 달린 놋쇠 단추를 물어뜯는 것보다 더 심한 행동은 절대 하지 않았습니다.

일주일에 5천 달러라는 돈은 큰 액수

의 돈처럼 들리지만, 파퍼 씨네 가족은 부유함과는 거리가 멀었습니다. 웅장한 호텔에서 살고 택시를 타고 도시를 돌아다니는 것을 꽤 비쌌습니다. 파퍼 씨는 자주 펭귄들이 그냥 호텔과 극장 사이를 걸어서 오고 가는 것이 제일 낫겠다고 생각했었지만, 녀석들이 걸어가는 것은 전부 다 꼭 행진하는 것처럼 보여서 항상 교통을 마비시켰습니다. 그래서 절대로 누군가에게 폐를 끼치는 사람이 되는 것을 싫어하는 파퍼 씨는, 언제나 대신 택시를 탔습니다.

펭귄들을 시원하게 해주려고, 그들의 호텔 방으로 커다란 얼음 덩어리들을 가져오는 것도 비쌌습니다. 파퍼 씨네 가족이 흔히 그들의 식사를 하는 좋은 식당의 계산서도 종종 굉장히 액수가 컸습니다. 그렇지만, 다행히도, 펭귄들의 먹이는 그들에게 돈이 들지 않게 되었습니다. 순회공연을 하면서, 그들은 살아 있는 생선이 담긴 수조차가 자신들에게로 보내지는 것을 포기해야만 했는데, 정확한 시간에 배달을 받는 것이 정말 어려웠기 때문입니다. 그래서 그들은 새들에게 다시 새우 통조림을 먹였습니다.

이것은 그들에게 전혀 돈이 들지 않았는데, 파퍼 씨가 이런 추천서를 썼기 때문입니다: "파퍼 씨네 재주부리는 펭귄들은 오웬즈의 바다 새우를 즐겨 먹습니다."

이 말은, 열두 마리의 펭귄 사진과 함께, 모든 가장 중요한 잡지들에 인쇄되었고 오웬즈 바다 새우 회사는 파퍼 씨에게 전국에 있는 어떤 식료품 가게에서도 공짜로 새우 통조림을 살 수 있는 주문서를 주었습니다.

그레이트 웨스턴 시금치 재배업자 협회와 에너제틱 브렉퍼스트 귀리 회사와 같은, 몇몇 다른 회사들도 또한, 그가 자신들의 상품을 추천해주기를 원했고, 그에게 많은 액수의 현금을 주겠다고 했습니다. 하지만 펭귄들은 시금치나 귀리를 먹는 것을 그냥 거부했고, 비록 그 돈이 도움이 되리란 것을 알았지만, 파퍼 씨는 녀석들이 먹는다고 말하기에는 지나치게 솔직했습니다.

태평양 연안에서부터 그들은 다시 동쪽으로 향해, 대륙을 가로지르려고 했습니다. 그들은 이 짧은 순회공연에서, 단지 좀 더 큰 도시들을 들릴 만큼의 시간만 있었습니다. 미니애폴리스 다음에, 그들은 밀워키, 시카고, 디트로이트, 클리블랜드, 그리고 필라델피아에서 공연했습니다.

그들이 가는 곳마다, 그들의 명성이 그들을 앞지르고는 했습니다. 4월 초에, 그들이 보스턴에 도착했을 때, 거대한 수의 군중이 기차역에서 그들을 기다렸습니다.

이제까지는, 펭귄들을 편안하게 해주는 것이 그다지 어렵지 않았습니다. 하지만 따뜻한 봄바람이 보스턴 코먼 (Boston Common) 공원을 가로지르며 불고 있었고, 호텔에서 파퍼 씨는 그의 방들로 천 파운드나 되는 덩어리의 얼음을 가져와야만 했습니다. 그는 10주의 계약이 거의 끝나가서 다행스러웠고, 그의 새들이 뉴욕에서 출연할 바로 다음 주가 마지막 주였습니다.

이미 그린바움 씨는 새 계약서를 작성하고 있었습니다. 그렇지만, 파퍼 씨는 생각하기 시작했습니다. 펭귄들이 점차 짜증을 내고 있기도 하고, 그가 스틸워터로 돌아가는 편이 더 좋을 것 같다고 말이지요.

18장 4월의 바람

만약에 보스턴이 계절에 맞지 않게 따뜻했다면, 뉴욕은 실제로 더웠습니다. 센트럴 파크(Central Park)를 내려다보는, 좋은 타워 호텔에 있는 그들의 방에서도, 펭귄들은 심하게 그 열기를 느끼고 있었습니다.

파퍼 씨는 그들을 옥상 정원으로 데리고 올라가서 불고 있을지도 모를 그어떤 시원한 바람이라도 쐬려고 했습니다. 펭귄들은 아래에 있는 도시의 반짝거리는 불빛과 혼잡함에 마음을 빼앗겼습니다. 더 어린 새들은 옥상의 가장자리로 몰려들어 그들 아래에 있는 거대한 협곡을 내려다보기 시작했습니다. 마치 언제라도 그들이 한 녀석을 밀어서 떨어뜨리는 데 성공할 것처럼, 그들이 서로를 밀치는 것을 보자 파퍼 씨는 매우 불안해졌습니다. 그는 어떻게 남극 펭귄들이 아래에 무슨 위험이 있는지 확인하려고 언제나 이런 행동을

한다는 것을 기억했습니다.

옥상은 그들에게는 안전한 장소가 아니었습니다. 파퍼 씨는 그레타가 오기 전에, 캡틴 쿡이 정말 아팠었을 때 얼마나 몹시 자신이 두려워했었는지 절대 잊어버리지 않았습니다. 그는 이제 그의 펭귄들 가운데 한 마리라도 잃는 위험을 감수할 수 없었습니다.

펭귄들에 관련된 일에 대해서는, 아무것도 그에게는 너무 귀찮은 적이 없었습니다. 그는 그들을 다시 아래층으로 데려갔고 욕실에서 그들을 차가운 물줄기 밑에서 목욕시켰습니다. 이 일은 밤의 오랜 시간 동안 그를 계속 바쁘게 했습니다.

이 모든 수면 부족으로 인해, 그는 다음 날 아침에 그가 극장에 가기 위해 택시들을 불러야 했을 때 다소 졸려 했습니다. 게다가, 파퍼 씨는 항상 약간 멍한 사람이었습니다. 그렇게 해서 그가 첫 번째 택시 운전사에게 말을 했을 때 그의 큰 실수를 하게 되었던 것입니다:—

"레갈 극장(Regal Theater)이요."

"네, 선생님." 운전사가 말하면서, 아이들과 펭귄들 모두를 대단히 흥미롭게 한, 브로드웨이(Broadway)의 차량들 사이를 들락날락거리며 누비듯이 나아갔습니다.

그들이 거의 극장에 도착했을 때, 운전사가 갑자기 돌아보았습니다. "저기." 그가 말했습니다. "당신은 그 펭귄들이 스웬슨(Swenson)의 물개들과 같은 극장 프로그램에 나간다는 뜻은 아니겠

지요, 그렇죠?"

"나는 다른 어떤 것이 극장의 프로그램에 올라가는지 몰라요." 파퍼 씨가 말하면서, 그에게 돈을 냈습니다. "어쨌든, 여기가 레갈 극장이군요." 그리고 그들은 우르르 쏟아져 나왔고 무대 입구로 줄지어 들어갔습니다.

무대 옆에는 크고, 우람하고, 얼굴이 붉게 상기된 남자가 서 있었습니다. "그래서 이것들이 파퍼 씨네 재주부리는 펭귄들이란 말이지, 응?" 그가 말했습니다. "뭐, 내가 말해두겠는데, 파퍼 씨, 내가 스웬 스웬슨(Swen Swenson)이고, 저기 무대 위에 지금 올라가 있는 것들은 내 물개들이요, 그리고 만약에 당신의 새들이 어떤 웃긴 짓거리라도 하는 경우에는, 그것들에게 엄청 나쁜 일이 생길 거요. 내 물개들은 거칠다고, 알겠소? 그것들은 각각 두세 마리 펭귄을 먹는 일은 아무것도 아니라고 생각할거라고."

무대에서 공연을 하고 있는 물개들이 내는 쉰 목소리로 짖는 소리가 들려왔습니다.

"애들 아빠." 파퍼 부인이 말했습니다. "펭귄들은 프로그램의 마지막 순서예요. 당신이 빨리 다시 달려가서 그 택시들을 붙잡아요, 그리고 그들의 공연 시간이 될 때까지 우리가 펭귄들이 한동안 차를 타고 돌아다니게 하는 거예요."

파퍼 씨는 서둘러 밖으로 나가서 운전사들을 붙잡았습니다.

그가 돌아갔을 때는, 너무 늦고 말았습니다. 파퍼 씨네 재주부리는 펭귄들은 이미 스웬슨 물개들을 발견했습니다.

"아빠, 전 못 보겠어요!" 아이들이 울부짖었습니다.

끔찍한 혼란이 무대 위에서 벌어지는 소리가 들렸고, 관객들은 소란을 일으켰고, 커튼이 빠르게 내려왔습니다.

파퍼 씨네 가족들이 서둘러 무대 위로 달려왔을 때, 펭귄들과 물개들 모두 스웬슨의 분장실로 향하는 계단을 찾았고 위층으로 나아가고 있었습니다.

"난 저 위에서 무슨 일이 일어나고 있는지 상상할 수조차 없어." 파퍼 씨가 몸서리치며, 말했습니다.

스웬슨 씨는 그저 웃기만 했습니다. "당신의 새들이 보험에 들어있다면 좋겠어요, 파퍼." 그가 말했습니다. "그것들은 얼만큼의 값어치가 나가지? 뭐, 어서 올라가서 확인해 봅시다."

"당신이 올라가 봐요, 애들 아빠." 파퍼 부인이 말했습니다. "빌, 너는 극장 밖으로 달려 나가서 경찰을 불러와서 우리의 펭귄들 중 몇 마리라도 살려달라고 하렴."

"전 가서 소방서에서 사람을 데려올게요." 제이니가 말했습니다.

소방관들이, 요란하게 철거덕거리는 소리를 내며, 왔고 그들이 스웬슨씨의 분장실에 난 창문으로 들어갈 수 있게 자신들의 사다리를 세웠을 때, 그들은 전혀 불이 나지 않았다는 것에 약간 짜증이 났습니다. 하지만, 여섯 마리의 검은 콧수염을 단 물개들이, 방의 가운데에서 짖으면서 앉아 있고, 이와 함께 열두 마리의 펭귄들이 그들의 주위에서 사각형의 모양으로 명랑하게 행진하고 있는 것을 발견했을 때, 그들은 기분이 좋아졌습니다.

그때 경찰들이 자신들의 순찰대와 왔고, 소방관들이 건물에 기댄 채 두고 온 사다리를 타고 올라갔습니다. 그들도 역시 창문 사이로 들어왔을 때쯤에는, 그들은 자신들의 눈을 거의 믿을 수가 없었습니다. 소방관들이 소방관 헬멧을 펭귄에게 씌웠고, 이는 그 즐거워하는 새들을 매우 우스꽝스럽고 여자아이 같아 보이게 했던 것입니다.

소방관들이 펭귄들과 정말 다정하게 구는 것을 보고, 경찰들은 자연스럽게 물개들의 편을 들었고 경찰 모자를 그들에게 씌웠습니다. 물개들은 그 아래에 있는 그들의 길고 검은 콧수염과 검은 얼굴로 인해, 아주 험악하게 보였습니다.

그들의 소방관 헬멧을 쓴 펭귄들이 경찰들 앞에서 행진하고 있고, 반면에 물개들은, 경찰 모자를 쓰고서, 소방관에게 짖고 있었을 때, 파퍼 씨와 스웬슨 씨가 마침내 문을 열었습니다.

파퍼 씨는 주저앉았습니다. 그의 안도감은 정말 커서 한동안 그는 말을 할 수 없었습니다.

"당신네 경찰들은 당장 내 물개들한테서 당신들의 모자를 벗기는 게 좋을 거요." 스웬슨 씨가 말했습니다. "난 무

대 위로 내려가서 이제 공연을 끝내야겠어요." 그러더니 그와 그의 여섯 마리 물개들은 몇 번 작별 인사로 짖는 소리를 내며, 방에서 슬며시 나갔습니다.

"뭐, 잘 가렴, 오리들아." 소방관들이 말하면서, 서운해 하는 듯이 그들의 헬멧을 펭귄들에게서 벗겨 자기 머리 위에 썼습니다. 그리고는 그들은 사다리를 타고 내려가 사라졌습니다. 펭귄들은, 물론, 따라가고 싶어 했지만, 파퍼 씨가 그들을 붙잡았습니다.

바로 그때 문이 벌컥 열렸고, 극장 관리자가 방 안으로 불쑥 들어왔습니다.

"저 남자를 잡아요." 그가 경찰들에게 소리치며, 파퍼 씨를 손가락으로 가리켰습니다. "나에게는 그의 체포에 대한 근거가 있어요."

"누구, 나 말이에요?" 파퍼 씨가 어리벙벙해하며, 말했습니다. "내가 무슨 짓을 했는데요?"

"당신이 내 극장에 불법 침입해서 이곳을 난장판으로 만들었잖아, 그게 바로 당신이 한 짓이지. 당신은 평화를 깨뜨리는 놈이야."

"하지만 제가 파퍼이고, 이것들이 전국적으로 유명한, 제 재주부리는 펭귄들이라고요."

"난 당신이 누구인지 관심도 없고, 당신이 내 극장에 아무 일도 없다고."

"하지만 그린바움 씨가 우리에게 레갈 극장에서 일주일 동안의 공연에 5천 달러를 주기로 했는데요."

"그린바움 씨의 극장은 로열 극장

(Royal)이지, 레갈이 아니야. 당신은 잘못된 극장으로 왔어. 어쨌거나, 썩 꺼져, 당신과 당신의 재주부리는 펭귄들 모두. 범인 호송차가 밖에서 기다리고 있으니까."

19장 드레이크 제독

그렇게 파퍼 씨는, 캡틴 쿡, 그레타, 콜럼버스, 루이자, 넬슨, 제니, 마젤란, 아델리나, 스콧, 이자벨라, 퍼디난드, 그리고 빅토리아와 함께, 범인 호송차에 마구 쑤셔 넣어졌고 경찰서로 급히 떠나게 되었습니다.

그의 애원 중 아무것도 내근 경사에게 통하지 않았습니다.

"그 극장 관리자는 당신이 그의 극장에 침입한 방식에 대해 상당히 화가 나 있어요. 그래서 난 당신을 잡아둬야 해요. 난 당신 모두에게 좋고 조용한 감방을 줄게요—당신이 보석금을 내지 않는다면 말이에요. 난 당신에 대해서는 5백 달러 그리고 새들에 대해서는 한 마리마다 1백 달러의 보석금을 매기겠어요."

물론 파퍼 씨는 그에게 그만큼의 돈이 없었습니다. 그들이 호텔에 있는 파퍼 부인에게 전화를 걸었을 때 그녀에게도 돈이 없었지요. 호텔 청구서는 며칠 전에 미리 결제되었지만, 그녀에게 현금이 없었습니다. 마지막 주의 급료에 대한 수표도 그 주말까지는 지불되지 않을 예정이었습니다. 사실은, 그들

이 펭귄들을 교도소에서 빼내지 못해 로열 극장에서 그들의 공연을 무대에 올리는 데 오래 걸릴 테니, 이제 파퍼 씨네 가족들은 그 수표를 절대 보지 못할 것처럼 보였습니다.

그들이 그린바움 씨와 연락이 닿기만 한다면, 파퍼 씨가 알고 있듯이, 그 친절한 남자는 그들을 꺼내줄 것이었습니다. 하지만 그린바움 씨는 태평양 연안 위에, 할리우드(Hollywood) 어딘가에 있었고, 파퍼 씨네 가족은 어떻게 그에게 연락해야 하는지 전혀 몰랐습니다.

새들에게 교도소에 있는 것은 매우 지루했습니다. 수요일이 왔고 그린바움 씨에게서는 여전히 아무 소식이 없었습니다. 목요일이 되었고, 새들은 풀이 죽기 시작했습니다. 더위와 더불어, 운동 부족이, 그들에게는 감당하기 어려운 일이라는 것이 곧 분명해졌습니다. 묘기나 즐거운 게임이 더 이상 없었습니다. 심지어 더 어린 새들도 울적한 침묵 속에서 하루 종일 앉아 있었고, 파퍼 씨는 그들을 기분 좋게 할 수 없었습니다.

파퍼 씨는 그린바움 씨가 아마도 그 주말쯤에는 계약을 갱신하는 일을 처리하려고, 나타날 것 같다는 예감이 들었습니다. 하지만 그에 대한 어떤 소식도 없이, 금요일이 지나갔습니다.

토요일 아침 파퍼 씨는 매우 일찍 일어났고 그의 머리를 매만졌습니다. 그리고는 그는 그가 할 수 있는 한 잘 펭귄들의 몸에서 먼지를 털어냈습니다. 그린바움 씨가 나타날 경우를 대비해

178

서, 그는 모든 것이 가능하면 남 앞에 내놓을 만큼 좋아 보이기를 원했기 때문입니다.

10시쯤에 복도에서 발자국 소리가 들렸고, 잘그락거리는 열쇠 소리가 들리더니, 감방의 문이 열렸습니다.

"당신은 자유예요, 파퍼 씨. 당신의 친구가 여기에 왔어요."

파퍼 씨는 펭귄들과 함께 밝은 곳으로 나갔습니다.

"당신은 간신히 시간 맞춰 왔네요, 그린바움 씨." 그는 막 이렇게 말하려고 했습니다.

그때, 그의 눈이 빛에 익숙해졌고, 그는 다시 보았습니다.

그곳에 서 있는 사람은 그린바움 씨가 아니었습니다.

훌륭한 제복을 입은 멋지고, 수염이 난 남자였습니다. 웃으면서, 그가 파퍼 씨에게 자신의 손을 내밀었습니다.

"파퍼 씨." 그가 말했습니다. "난 드레이크 제독입니다."

"드레이크 제독이라니!" 파퍼 씨가 숨을 헉 하고 내쉬며 말했습니다. "남극에서 돌아온 것은 아니겠지요!"

"맞아요." 제독이 말했습니다. "드레이크 남극 탐험선이 어제 돌아왔어요. 당신이 뉴욕 시에서 우리에게 열어준 환영 연회를 봤었어야만 했어요. 당신은 그것에 대해 오늘 신문에서 읽을 수 있을 거예요. 하지만 나는 당신이 펭귄들로 인해 겪고 있는 어려움에 대해 읽었고, 그래서 제가 여기에 오게 된 겁니다. 나는 당신에게 말해 줄 긴 이야기가 있어요."

"우리가 호텔에 가서 그에 대해 이야기할 수 있을까요?" 파퍼 씨가 물었습니다. "제 아내는 저희를 다시 보기를 간절하게 바라고 있을 거예요."

"물론이지요." 제독이 말했습니다. 그리고 그들이 호텔에 있는 파퍼 씨네 방들에 모두 자리를 잡고, 펭귄들도 듣기 위해 주위에 모였을 때, 드레이크 제독은 말하기 시작했습니다: ―

"당연히, 내가 미국으로 돌아올 것을 알게 되었을 때, 나는 종종 내가 펭귄을 보냈었던 남자에 대해 생각했었지요. 그곳에서는, 우리가 상황에 대해 듣는 데 오랜 시간이 걸려요, 그리고 나는 자주 당신과 새가 어떻게 지내는지 궁금해했습니다. 지난 밤, 우리를 위한 시장의 만찬 행사에서, 나는 당신이 전국을 돌면서 선보이고 있는 아주 뛰어난 훈련받은 펭귄 공연에 대해 들었어요. 오늘 아침 나는 신문을 보았고, 내가 읽은 가장 첫 기사는 파퍼 씨와 그의 열두 마리 펭귄들이 여전히 교도소에 갇혀 있다는 것이었어요. 하지만 열두 마리 펭귄이라니, 파퍼 씨―도대체 어떻게―"

그러자 파퍼 씨는 어떻게 그레타가 오게 되어 캡틴 쿡이 외로워지는 것을 막아 주었는지, 그리고 어떻게 새끼 펭귄들이 자랐는지, 그리고 상황이 좋아 보이지 않았을 때, 어떻게 그 영리한 소규모의 무리가 파퍼 씨네 가족을 곤경에서 구해주었는지 말했습니다.

"정말 굉장해요." 드레이크 제독이 말했습니다. "나는 평생 많은 펭귄들을 봤었지만, 절대로 이것들처럼 잘 교육받은 녀석들을 보지 못했어요. 그건 분명히 인내심과 훈련이 무슨 결과를 낼 수 있는지를 보여 주는 거예요."

"하지만 이제 내 진짜 요점을 말할게요, 파퍼 씨. 당신은 아마 내가 남극과 마찬가지로 북극도 탐험했었다는 것을 알고 있겠지요?"

"오 그럼요." 파퍼 씨가 존경한다는 듯이 말했습니다. "나는 당신의 북극 탐험뿐만 아니라 당신의 남극 탐험에 대해서도 책을 읽었어요."

"그렇다면, 좋아요." 제독이 말했습니다. "어쩌면 당신은 왜 우리 탐험가들이 남극을 선호하는지 알까요?"

"그건 펭귄들 때문일까요, 제독님?" 매우 열심히 듣고 있었던, 제이니가 물었습니다.

드레이크 제독이 그녀의 머리를 쓰다듬었습니다. "그래, 얘야. 그 긴 극지방에서의 밤들은 너에게 같이 놀 애완동물이 없다면 꽤나 지루해진단다. 물론저 위에는 북극곰들이 있기는 하지만, 너는 그것들과는 같이 놀 수 없단다. 아무도 왜 북극에 펭귄이 한 마리도 없는지 알지 못하지. 오랫동안 미국 정부는 펭귄 품종을 정착시키려는 목적을 위해 내가 탐험대를 저 위로 이끌고 가기를 원하고 있었단다. 내가 요점을 말해야만 할 것 같네요, 파퍼 씨. 당신은

당신의 이 새들로 이렇게 뛰어난 성과를 거두었잖아요, 내가 그것들을 북극으로 데려가서 그곳에서 펭귄 품종을 번식하게 하면 어떻겠어요?"

바로 그때 그린바움 씨와 다른 신사가 자신들의 도착을 알렸습니다. 그들은 모두 돌아가며 악수를 했고 제독에게 소개되었습니다.

"글쎄, 파퍼 씨." 그린바움 씨가 말했습니다. "극장에 대한 혼동이 생겨서 참 안됐어요. 하지만 신경 쓰지 말아요. 여기는 클라인 씨(Mr. Klein)인데, 그는 거대한 영화 회사를 소유하고 있어요. 그는 당신이 많은 돈을 벌게 해줄 거예요. 당신은 더는 가난한 사람이 아닐 겁니다, 파퍼 씨."

"가난하다니!" 파퍼 씨가 말했습니다. "난 가난하지 않아요. 이 새들이 우리에게 일주일에 5천 달러나 벌어다 주었는걸요."

"오, 5천 달러라니." 클라인 씨가 말했습니다. "그게 뭡니까? 푼돈에 불과해요. 난 그 새들을 영화에 넣고 싶어요, 파퍼 씨. 우리는 벌써 극본 부서에게 그들을 위해 이야기를 쓰게 하고 있어요. 아니, 나는 그 새들 각각 한 마리씩 계약을 해서 당신과 당신의 부인이 남은 평생 풍족한 삶을 살게(on Easy Street) 해 주겠어요."

"애들 아빠." 파퍼 부인이 속삭였습니다. "난 이지 스트리트에서는(on Easy Street) 살고 싶지 않아요. 난 프라우드풋 에비뉴로 돌아가고 싶어요."

"잘 생각해 보는 것이 좋을 겁니다, 파퍼 씨." 제독이 말했습니다. "난 당신에게 저런 제안을 할 수는 없어요."

"당신이 말하기를 북극에 있는 그 사람들이 거기에 펭귄이 없어서 외로워한다고요?" 파퍼 씨가 물었습니다.

"몹시 외로워하지요." 제독이 말했습니다.

"하지만 만약에 펭귄들이 저 위에 있게 된다면, 북극곰들이 그것들을 먹지는 않을까요?"

"오, 평범한 펭귄들이라면, 그렇겠지요." 제독이 현명하게 말했습니다; "하지만 당신의 것처럼 그렇게 고도로 훈련된 새들은 그렇지 않을 거예요, 파퍼 씨. 그것들은 어떤 북극곰보다도 한 수 앞설 수 있을 거예요, 내가 생각하기에는 말입니다."

이제는 클라인 씨가 말할 차례였습니다.

"미국에 있는 모든 영화 상영관에서는 어린아이들이 파퍼의 재주부리는 펭귄들에 의해 연기되어진 이야기를 보는 즐거움을 누릴 수 있을 거예요." 그가 말했습니다.

"물론 우리가 북극에 품종을 정착시키는 데 성공한다면." 제독이 말했습니다. "이름이 약간 바뀌어야만 할 겁니다. 내가 상상하기에 지금으로부터 백 년 뒤에는 과학자들이 그것들을 파퍼 북극 펭귄이라고 부르고 있겠지요."

파퍼 씨는 잠시 침묵했습니다.

"여러분." 그가 말했습니다. "전 두분 모두에게 감사를 드리고 싶네요. 전 여러분에게 내일 제 결정을 알려주겠습니다."

20장 안녕, 파퍼 씨

그것은 내리기 어려운 결정이었습니다. 손님들이 가고 난 뒤에도 한참 동안, 파퍼 씨와 파퍼 부인은 앉아서 모두를 위해 무엇이 최선인지에 대해 논의했습니다. 파퍼 부인은 양쪽의 제안이 지닌 장점을 알 수 있었고, 그녀는 그에게 영향을 미치지 않으려고 하면서, 이것들을 지적했습니다.

"난 펭귄들이 정말로 당신의 책임이라고 믿어요." 그녀가 말했습니다. "그리고 당신은 당신의 마음을 정해야만 하고요."

다음 날 그의 결정을 발표할 준비가 된 사람은 바로 창백하고 초췌한 파퍼 씨였습니다.

"클라인 씨." 그가 말했습니다. "전 얼마나 제가 저의 새들을 영화에 넣겠다는 당신의 제안을 고맙게 생각하는지 당신이 알아주었으면 합니다. 하지만 제가 거절해야만 해서 안타깝게 생각합니다. 전 할리우드에서의 삶이 펭귄들에게 좋을 것 같지 않아요."

그리고는 그는 드레이크 제독에게로 돌아섰습니다. "드레이크 제독님, 전 당신에게 새들을 주겠어요. 이렇게 하면서, 저는 새들을 최우선으로 고려하고 있습니다. 전 그들이 저와 함께 있으면서 편안하고 행복했었다는 것을 알고 있어요. 최근에 들어서는, 하지만, 그 소동과 따뜻한 날씨로 인해, 난 그들에 대해서 염려하고 있었습니다. 새들이 저를 위해 정말 많은 것을 해주었기 때문에 저도 그들을 위해서 최선의 일을 해주어야만 해요. 어쨌든, 그들은 추운 기후에 속해있지요. 그리고 저는 시간을 보내는 것을 도와줄 펭귄도 없이, 저 위 북극에 있는 그 남자들에 대해 불쌍하게 여기지 않을 수가 없었어요."

"당신의 정부에서 고맙게 생각할 겁니다, 파퍼 씨." 제독이 대답했습니다.

"축하해요, 제독님." 클라인 씨가 말했습니다. "아마도 당신이 그 점에 관해서는 옳을 거예요, 파퍼. 할리우드는 새들에게는 너무 무리였을 수도 있어요. 그래도, 난 당신이 내가 여기 뉴욕에서 그것들에 대한 짧은 영화 한 편을 찍을 수 있게 해주었으면 좋겠네요, 그것들이 가기 전에요. 그저 그것들이 무대 위에서 하는 것들에 대한 영화예요, 알겠지요. 우리는 이것들이 드레이크 제독이 이끄는 미국 북극 펭귄 정착 탐험대에 의해 북극으로 옮겨진 유명한 파퍼 펭귄들이라는 알림 문구나, 뭐 그런 비슷한 말과 함께 모든 곳에서 영화를 보여줄 겁니다."

"전 그게 정말 마음에 드네요." 파퍼 씨가 말했습니다.

"물론, 우리는 당신에게 돈을 줄 거예요." 클라인 씨가 계속 말했습니다. "당신이 우리가 그것들과 계약하게 했다면 우리가 줄 수 있었던, 거금은 아닙니다, 하지만, 말하자면, 2만 5천 달러 정도가 되겠네요."

"우리가 그 돈을 쓸 수 있겠네요." 파퍼 부인이 말했습니다.

"프라우드풋 에비뉴 432번지는 정말 조용해지겠어요." 모든 사람이 떠났을 때, 파퍼 씨가 말했습니다.

파퍼 부인은 대답하지 않았습니다. 그녀는 자신이 할 수 있는 그 어떤 말로도 정말로 그를 위로할 수 없다는 것을 알았습니다.

"그렇지만." 파퍼 부인이 말했습니다. "이제 봄이 왔으니, 많은 사람들이 자신들의 집을 페인트칠하기를 원하고 있을 테니, 우리는 돌아가는 편이 더 좋을 것 같아요."

"어쨌든." 빌이 말했습니다. "우리는 학년이 한창 진행 중일 때 10주 통째로 방학을 얻었고, 스틸워터의 아이들 중 그래 본 적이 있는 아이는 얼마 없을 거예요."

다음 날 촬영기사들이 펭귄들이 그들의 묘기를 부리는 것을 영화로 찍으려고 도착했습니다. 파퍼 씨네 가족들이 탐험대를 배웅하기 위해 딱 그 정도의 시간 동안 뉴욕에 머무르도록 마련되었습니다.

그동안에, 항구에서는, 드레이크 제독의 대형 범선이 북쪽으로 가는 그 긴 여정에 대한 준비를 갖추고 있었습니다. 매일 온갖 종류의 물품들이 담긴 커다란 상자들이 급히 배 위에 실렸

182

습니다. 배에 있는 가장 편안한 방들은 그 여정의 목적인 펭귄들에게 넘겨졌습니다.

캡틴 쿡은 이미 그 배에 상당히 익숙해졌는데, 그것은 드레이크 제독이 남극으로 타고 갔었던 것과 같은 배이고, 남극에서 캡틴 쿡은 그 배를 자주 봤었기 때문입니다. 그레타도 또한, 그런 종류의 선박들을 본 적이 있었습니다. 그들 둘은 넬슨, 콜럼버스, 루이자, 제니, 스콧, 마젤란, 아델리나, 이자벨라, 퍼디난드, 그리고 빅토리아에게 모든 것을 보여 주고 설명하느라 매우 바쁘게 지냈습니다.

선원들은 모두 그 호기심 많은 작은 새들이 그들의 탐험을 하는 것을 보는 데 가장 큰 기쁨을 느꼈습니다.

"마치 이것이 꽤나 활발한 여행이 될 것처럼 보이네요." 그들은 이렇게 말하곤 했습니다. "이 파퍼 펭귄들은 확실히 그들의 명성에 부응하네요."

하지만 결국에 모든 것이 준비되었고, 파퍼 씨네 가족이 내려가서 작별 인사를 해야 할 날이 왔습니다. 빌과 제이니는 배 안의 모든 곳을 뛰어다녔고, 배의 건널 판자를 끌어당길 시간이 되었을 때에도 떠나기 싫어했습니다. 제독은 아이들과 파퍼 부인과 악수를 했고, 과학에 진정한 기여를 하게 될 그 뛰어난 펭귄들을 훈련시키는 데 도움을 준 것에 대해 그들에게 고마워했습니다.

파퍼 씨는 아래로 내려가서 그의 새들에게 개인적으로 작별 인사를 했습니다. 그가 완전히 감정을 주체하지 못하고 무너지지 않게 해주는 것은 단지 그가 그것들을 위해서 최선의 일을 하고 있다는 사실이었습니다. 먼저 그는 모든 더 어린 펭귄들에게 작별 인사를 했습니다. 그다음은 캡틴 쿡을 살려주었던, 그레타에게 했습니다. 다음에는, 가장 마지막으로, 그는 몸을 숙여서 파퍼 씨에게 와서 삶을 정말 달라지게 해주었던, 캡틴 쿡에게 특별한 작별 인사를 했습니다.

그러더니 그는 자신의 눈을 닦았고, 그의 등을 꼿꼿하게 세웠고, 드레이크 제독에서 작별 인사를 하려고 갑판으로 올라갔습니다.

"안녕히 가세요, 드레이크 제독님." 그가 말했습니다.

"안녕히 가세요?" 제독이 따라서 말했습니다. "아니, 그게 무슨 뜻이에요? 당신은 우리랑 같이 가지 않을 건가요?"

"제가—당신과 함께 북극에 간다고요?"

"아니, 물론이지요, 파퍼 씨."

"하지만 제가 어떻게 당신과 함께 가나요? 전 탐험가도 아니고 과학자도 아니잖아요. 전 단지 주택 도장공일 뿐인데요."

"당신은 펭귄들의 사육사이잖아요, 그렇지 않나요?" 제독이 큰소리로 말했습니다. "맙소사, 그 펭귄들이 이 전체 탐험의 이유가 아닌가요? 그리고 당신이 함께 가지 않는다면 누가 그들이 잘 있고 행복한지 알겠어요? 가서 우리 나머지처럼, 그 털로 된 옷을 입어요. 우리는 곧 닻을 올릴 거예요."

"애들 엄마." 파퍼 씨가 이미 건널 판자를 건너간, 파퍼 부인에게 외쳤습니다. "나도 갈 거예요! 나도 가게 되었다고요! 드레이크 제독님이 말하기를 그가 내가 필요하대요. 애들 엄마, 내가 일 이년 정도 집에 오지 않아도 괜찮겠어요?"

"오, 그것에 대한 거라면." 파퍼 부인이 말했습니다. "난 당신을 무척 그리워할 거예요, 여보. 하지만 우리는 몇 년 동안 먹고 살 돈이 있어요. 그리고 겨울에는 하루 종일 앉아 있기만 하는 남자가 없는 것이 집을 깔끔하게 유지하기가 훨씬 더 쉽지요. 나는 스틸워터로 돌아갈 거예요. 내일은 교회 여성 단체의 모임이 있는 날이에요, 그리고 난 시간을 딱 맞추게 되겠네요. 그러니 잘 가요, 여보, 그리고 행운을 빌어요."

"안녕히 가세요, 그리고 행운을 빌어요!" 아이들이 그대로 따라서 말했습니다.

그리고 펭귄들은, 그들의 목소리를 듣고서는, 갑판으로 허둥지둥 걸어 올라왔고 그곳에 제독과 파퍼 씨 옆에 섰습니다. 그리고는 대형 범선이 천천히 강을 따라서 바다로 향해 움직이는 동안에 그들은 엄숙하게 자신들의 날개를 들어 올려 흔들었습니다.

184